W9-CUJ-711

Censorship

Communication and Society,
edited by George Gerbner and Marsha Siefert

IMAGE ETHICS: *The Moral Rights of Subjects in Photographs,
Film, and Television,*
edited by Larry Gross, John Stuart Katz, and Jay Ruby

CENSORSHIP: *The Knot That Binds Power and Knowledge,*
by Sue Curry Jansen

SPLIT SIGNALS: *Television and Politics in the Soviet Union,*
by Ellen Mickiewicz

TELEVISION AND AMERICA'S CHILDREN:
A Crisis of Neglect,
by Edward L. Palmer

Censorship
The Knot That Binds
Power and Knowledge

SUE CURRY JANSEN

NEW YORK   OXFORD
OXFORD UNIVERSITY PRESS
1988

Oxford University Press

Oxford   New York   Toronto
Delhi   Bombay   Calcutta   Madras   Karachi
Petaling Jaya   Singapore   Hong Kong   Tokyo
Nairobi   Dar es Salaam   Cape Town
Melbourne   Auckland
and associated companies in
Berlin   Ibadan

Copyright © 1988 by Oxford University Press, Inc.

Published by Oxford University Press, Inc.,
200 Madison Avenue, New York, New York 10016

Oxford is a registered trademark of Oxford University Press

Library of Congress Cataloging-in-Publication Data
Jansen, Sue Curry.
Censorship : the knot that binds power and knowledge / Sue Curry Jansen.
p.   cm. Bibliography: p.   Includes index.
ISBN 0-19-505325-7   1. Censorship   I. Title.
Z657.J3 1988 025.2'13—dc19
88–4202 CIP

Printing (last digit): 9 8 7 6 5 4 3 2 1

Printed in the United States of America
on acid-free paper.

Contents

Part I: Parables of Persecution

One   Introduction, 3
Two   The Censor's New Clothes, 14
Three   Socrates' Children, 26
Four   Diderot and Company, 60
Five   Marx's Critique of Bourgeois Censorship, 84
Six   Censorship in Socialist Societies, 99
Seven   Censorship in Capitalist Societies, 131

Part II: Artful Dodges

Eight   The Imprimatur of Power, 181
Nine   The Semantics of Censorship and Resistance, 192
Ten   Dialogue and Democracy, 202

Notes, 219
Bibliography, 253
Index, 271

Parables of Persecution

"Explain yourself!"
"I can't explain myself, I'm afraid sir" said Alice,
"because I'm not myself, you see."

Lewis Carroll

CHAPTER ONE

Introduction

i

The Problem of Censorship

"In the right key," George Bernard Shaw maintained, "one can say anything, in the wrong key nothing." Finding the right key to say what I have to say about freedom and control is difficult. My message goes against the grain of much conventional wisdom. It challenges established canons in philosophy, history, political theory, and literary criticism. It questions fundamental assumptions about the nature of human autonomy, political consent, power, authority, hierarchy, and knowledge. My message even violates prevailing semantic conventions.

I did not begin this inquiry with iconoclastic intentions. I am not, by nature or disposition, a rabble-rouser. I don't enjoy upsetting apple-carts, shattering illusions, or throwing salt on old wounds. But much reading and reflection on the question of censorship has convinced me that what I have to say—what I think needs to be said—cannot be said within the established vocabularies of contemporary intellectual discourse.

These vocabularies imply that there is very little left to be said about censorship. They indicate that the Western world solved "the problem of censorship" during the eighteenth century when the great heroes of the Enlightenment, Voltaire, Diderot, D'Alembert, Franklin, Jefferson, and Madison, took away the stamps of church and state censors. In short, they tell us that Liberal societies have abolished censorship.

Canons of Enlightened thought maintain that the abolition of censorship was the decisive achievement of the Enlightenment. Indeed the word, 'enlightenment,' means "the free use of reason", the exercise of reason unfettered by external constraints (*Webster's New Collegiate Dictionary*). According to the dominant wisdom, then, the Enlightenment set thought free from the distortions of church and state censorship and patronage. This wisdom maintains that Enlightenment severed the knot that had always bound knowledge to power. It removed the mind-bindings that secured knowledge to human interests. It made free inquiry, scientific progress, and objectivity possible. In sum, according to the Enlightenment's history of itself, the triumph of "The Age of Reason" marked a decisive break with a superstitious, ignorant, and tyrannical past.

Since the the deep structure of Enlightened discourse is secured by a founding premise which asserts that the evils of censorship have been exorcised, Enlightened discourse can say nothing new about censorship. When it raises the issue at all, it is in a pejorative context. Censorship is a devil term. It refers 'back to' a Dark Age in Western history. It refers 'down to' reactionary elements: un-Enlightened or foreign elements which threaten to reverse the tide of progress in Liberal societies. In short, Enlightened discourse views censorship as something others do: a regressive practice of un-Enlightened (non-Liberal) societies.

My understandings of the issues of freedom and control cannot be accommodated by—are foreign to—the conventions of Enlightened discourse. My readings and reflections on the question of censorship lead me to conclude that the deep structure of Enlightenment is secured in sand.

My historical and semantic digs convince me that censorship is an enduring feature of all human communities. They indicate that knowledge and power are still bound together in an inextricable knot. Moreover they suggest that no amount of human ingenuity, scientific rigor, or political will can sever this knot. These digs force me to reject the claim that the Enlightenment abolished censorship. They lead me to conclude that Enlightenment merely transferred the office of Censor from a civic to a private trust. So that Liberalism's "Good Lie"—its claim to have abolished censorship—merely replaced church and state censorships with market censorship. And that as a consequence the discontinuity that separates pre- and post-Enlightenment censorships is largely semantic.

My argument is not an argument for censorship. It is an argument for the development of a self-conscious and self-critical awareness of what we do. It is an argument for a new enlightenment which recognizes that reason can never free itself from the fetters of human concerns. I believe this second enlightenment is urgently needed today because the broken promises of the first Enlightenment are seriously imperiling the margin of freedom that is still possible in a complex world.

ii

Finding Words

Saying what I have to say involves more than just finding "the right key." It requires a new vocabulary and a new grammar of critical discourse. Extensive definitional exercises, historical reclamations, and epistemological mess-making are needed to empower the voice of this critical inquiry. Much rubble must be cleared away, and some words need to be retooled before the story can be told. The power to un-name and re-name must be asserted.

Confucius said that the first step toward social reform is to change the names. Players have to be able to call a spade a spade before they can write rules for a new card game. Articulations of new values and a new consciousness need a new language. The process of creating a new language for democratic discourse requires us to mobilize a broadly based semantic rescue mission. This rescue mission is necessary because the established systems of power have taken the 'good' (community-founding) words hostage and have translated them into their own codes of control. The purpose of the rescue effort is to reclaim these words, restore their critical edges, and return them to the people. So that, for example, a semantic rescue mission dedicated to reclaiming the emancipatory elements in classic Liberalism might recover the meanings that words like 'freedom,' 'equality,' and 'justice' had during the seventeenth and eighteenth centuries when they were essential terms in the language of the repressed rather than in the vocabularies of administrators, merchants, and diplomats.

Rescuing and restoring the vocabulary of democracy is ultimately the work of the people. Confined to books, it is a lifeless exercise. The powers to un-name and re-name are not powers that can be realized in isolation. The discourse of egalitarian social reform is secured by talk (dialogue), not by the monologues of scholars, encyclopedists, vanguards, and experts.

In order to help the reader to deal with burden of re-namings, I use this Introduction to present four—related—concepts which are essential cornerstones of my argument: *power-knowledge, constitutive censorship, regulatory censorship*, and *reflexive power-talk*. Other concepts in my critical vocabulary are introduced and explained within appropriate contexts throughout the body of the work.

In addition to these definitional exercises, I use the remainder of this Introduction to: (1) identify and amplify the major argument of the book; (2) explain why I have singled out Liberalism for criticism here even though historically Liberalism played an emancipatory role in advancing the causes of freedom of inquiry and freedom of the press; and (3) outline the general organization and objectives of the book.

iii

Power-knowledge

The Enlightenment claimed it separated theory (knowledge) from practice (power) and thereby made objectivity possible. In contrast, a power-knowledge thesis suggests that Enlightened discourse suffers from Faustian illusions.

This argument maintains that knowledge emerges out of human struggles, labors, interests, plans, passions, and amusements. As a result, knowledge bears the imprimatur of power. Power-relations provide the groundings of knowledge whether that knowledge is profound or frivolous, evocative or austere, emancipatory or repressive.

The powerful require knowledge to preserve, defend, and extend their advantage. For them, knowledge is power. The way the powerful say things are is the way they are, or the way they usually become because the powerful control the power to name. Susanne K. Langer described the power to name as "the vastest generative idea that ever was conceived." The powerful use this power to generate and enforce definitions of words and of social reality that enhance their sovereignty.

The powerful do not just have the first and last say. They do not just control access to podium, presidium, or press room. They also determine the rules of evidence, shape the logic of assertion, define the architecture of arguments. The powerful are not just talkers. They are makers and shakers who draw the lines in language and life which others dare not cross.

My argument describes the lines drawn by the powerful as *power-knowledge*.[1] It does not view the trajectories of these lines in simple Machiavellian terms. It does not conceive of knowledge as merely an instrument of power. To the contrary, my argument recognizes that the knot that binds power and knowledge has two loops. Power secures knowledge, but knowledge also secures power. Systems of power-knowledge contain both emancipatory and repressive elements. They do not just set limits on human freedom, they also make it possible.

The lines drawn by the powerful restrict the powerless, but they also inform and instruct them. They present the drama of power to the people. They state the official version of events, procedures, and rules. They tell the powerless what they are up against. The powerless use this knowledge of power to negotiate their own recipes for survival. These recipes may season the gaps in the official version with piety, laughter, skepticism, or contempt. But whether they recommend docile compliance or cunning defiance, folk recipes, wisdom, and lore are inherently subversive. They suggest that the official version is not the only version. They encourage the powerless to think for themselves.

iv

Constituent and Regulative Censorships

The Enlightenment claimed it substituted the rule of Reason for the rules and regulations of Censors. In contrast, I suggest that in its translation from a revolutionary covenant to a ruling strategy, the Enlightenment gave birth to new forms of constitutive censorship.

The term *constituent censorship* is used to call attention to a form of censorship which Liberal political theory ignores or denies.[2] Contra Liberalism, I maintain that in all societies the powerful invoke cen-

sorship to create, secure, and maintain their control over the power
to name. This constitutive or existential censorship is a feature of all
enduring human communities—even those communities which offer
legislative guarantees of press freedom. Because this fundamental
censorship is largely unrecognized, its influence is insidious. It casts
a shadow over all human consciousness: subverting all Promethean
aspirations and belying the most studied professions of objectivity.
Specific canons of censorship (*regulative censorships*) vary in time,
space, and severity. Magic, God, Purity, Mammon, Party, National
Security, or other warrants may provide their rationales. But constitutive or existential censorship provides their precedent and anchor. Specific indices of censorship can be identified, profiled, and
evaluated in terms of humanistic standards such as: levels of violence
required to secure and enforce control, grossness of the inequalities
and hypocrisies preserved, types of deviance produced, degrees of
tolerance for heterodox ideas permitted, or frequency and intensity
of the ritual purgations required. Regulative censorships can be
amended or revolutionized in ways that raise or lower bodycounts,
numbers of books banned or citizens ghettoed or gulaged. Rules and
conventions of censorship do change. But censorship remains a rule-
embedded phenomenon. No revolutionary compact in human history—not even the scientific revolution of the seventeenth and eighteenth centuries—has ever abolished constitutive censorship. And,
no proclamation or amendment has ever severed the knot that binds
power and knowledge.

v

Reflexive Power-talk

The Liberal Enlightment articulated principles of consensual government. It established the idea that democratic social compacts are
secured by the talk of the people, and it devised institutional frame-
works designed to keep governors responsive to the governed. This
was a heroic achievement. However, the program of the Liberal
Enlightenment was based upon inadequate understandings of the
sociological and psychological basis of human perception, language,
community, and power-knowledge. Furthermore, the principles of

Liberalism were articulated before the triumph of industrialism: before the advent of mass production, electronic media, modern advertising, public relations, consumerism, and mass education. For these reasons, Liberal societies have not been able to keep the promises which secured their political covenants. And Liberal efforts to create institutional structures which can nourish the vitality of consensual dialogues have not succeeded.

Liberal power-knowledge was secured by an intellectual vanguard, Encylopedists and Publicans, and it is sustained by socially structured silences which continue to privilege the voices and interests of some citizens at the expense of others. Socialism presented itself as an emancipatory alternative to the abuses which the market censorship of Liberal societies supports. But existing socialist societies are also top-heavy. They enforce silences of their own, abuse individual freedom, and continue to privilege the voices of some citizens at the expense of others.

Reflexive power-talk is a method for identifying and criticizing the socially structured silences which make arbitrary forms of censorship possible. It is also a strategy for democratizing dialogic opportunities and outcomes.[3] It offers a recipe for conducting legitimating discourses according to egalitarian rules: rules based upon principles of rationality, consistency, and equity. Reflexive power-talk is not anarchistic. It acknowledges the necessity of formal systems of social control in complex industrial societies, and it recognizes the importance of the roles played by managers, intellectuals, and experts in these systems. However, in contrast to the practices prevailing in contemporary Liberal and Socialist societies, the rules of reflexive power-talk take away the special epistemological privileges that intellectuals, experts, and other vanguards routinely invoke when engaging in talk about issues involving knowledge and public policy. In short, it provides the people with a set of rules for ensuring that all of their arguments receive a fair hearing. It provides them with a rationale for granting or refusing their consent, and gives them a set of dialogic rules for conducting their own un-namings and re-namings.

The parables of persecution reviewed in this book support the conclusion that reflexive power-talk is a promising idea which may permit the people to transcend the failures of the Liberal Enlightenment and realize the telos of a new enlightenment. Reflexive power-talk is not word magic. It cannot solve the problem of power-knowledge. It cannot resolve the conflicts and contradictions that have perplexed political philosophers and moralists for centuries. It cannot make citizens noble and wise or remove the tensions and conflicts inherent in all social compacts. It cannot eliminate constituent censorship or even ensure that regulative censorships will not be imprudently instituted or enforced. I believe, however, it can provide a mechanism for asserting some control over our controllers.

vi

Socrates' Children

The Enlightenment made more promises than it could keep. The Enlightenment's "Good Lie"—its claim that it abolished censorship—has silenced criticism of constitutive censorships. The Enlightenment offered objectivism as a talisman against authoritarianism. It offered the promise of impersonal, disinterested, neutral reason as an arbiter of human events. It was a good promise. A promise that advanced the cause of science. But a promise that failed to stem the tide of human violence.

Consequently a new defense against censorship must be forged if (1) the great emancipatory ideas of classic Liberalism are to be reclaimed, and (2) the repressive actions of Liberal societies are to be brought under the discipline of self-criticism and self-restraint.

My readings and reflections on censorship lead me to conclude that the infamous history of persecution in the West is power-knowledge which can provide a platform for renewing emancipatory defenses against state censorship and provide grounds for articulating a comprehensive critique of market censorship. In short, I am suggesting that the lessons we can learn from parables of persecution can provide the protection against authoritarian censorship we so desperately need.

This is not an original idea. It is a background assumption and key rhetorical element in the arguments of the founders of the French Enlightenment as well as in the polemics of their most vigorous antagonist, Karl Marx.

It is a neglected idea. The dark Manichean undersides of the founding arguments of the modern outlook have been suppressed by elaborations of the positive (reformist) plans of their authors into effective codes and technologies of legitimation and/or domination. This suppression has impoverished the critical traditions of post-Enlightenment cultures. It has undermined the claims of these critical traditions to moral authority, muted their sense of history, and constricted the range and resonances of their formats.[4]

Recovery and reassertion of this neglected idea can restrain relativism. It can serve as a defense against authoritarian censorship for two reasons. First, because it forthrightly recognizes that knowledge is secured through human struggles, labors, passions, and interests and thereby encourages systematic and sustained scrutiny of constituent censorships. Second, because it provides knowledge of power which is secured in the persuasive documents of human biography.[5]

The parochialism of my heavy dependence on Western texts is acknowledged. Today a disproportionate number of the rightful heirs of the Socratic tradition—those who are asking the most incisive questions about freedom of thought—are speaking in defense of the integrity of non-Western cultural traditions. They are the heterodox of the world system who refuse to narrow their horizons to conform to the 'Either . . . Or' alternatives insisted upon by spokespersons for the First and Second Worlds.[6] Their strategic vantage points can allow them special insight into the hypocrisy and hubris of Western ideologies. For them, progress has frequently been a bittersweet destiny. Thus they may understand, better than most Westerners the compelling irony in Wendell Phillips's aphorism: "Every step of progress the world has made has been from scaffold to scaffold and from stake to stake."

If my parochialism has any justification, it is in its rhetorical intent. My narrative is addressed primarily to citizens of Liberal societies who assume that censorship is something others do. They see themselves as lonely defenders of the ramparts of freedom in a world increasingly engulfed by authoritarian ideologies. They are repelled (as I am repelled) by the overt reliance of the Second World and parts of the Third World on arbitrary forms of state censorship. Yet, they refuse to assume a self-critical stance. They insist that no enlightened nation censors. They refuse to consider the possibility that 'the free market of ideas' has been replaced under corporate capitalism by market censorship both at home and abroad. Moreover, they ignore the fact that some of their compatriots are now defining 'freedom' in world forums as "freedom of multi-national corporations from restrictions in the proper conduct of their business" regardless of the national interests of the countries in which that business is conducted.[7] Consequently, they are genuinely mystified by the fact

that they are now perceived in many parts of the world, as well as
in many quarters within their nativelands, as emperors without
clothes.

vii

Telling the Story

My narrative has two parts. Part One presents the drama of censorship. It displays the knot of power-knowledge within historical contexts by examining censorial practices under ecclesiastic, state, and
market controls.

Part One includes this Introduction and six additional chapters.
Chapter Two continues the un-namings and re-namings begun here.
It encourages the reader to consider the link between censorship and
sense-making. It also introduces the characters and sets the stage for
what is to follow. Chapter Three outlines the epistemological warrant
that justifies the historical narratives. It secures the intent of this work
as an exercise in synthesis rather than as an act of historical discovery.
This chapter also offers a revisionary view of Greek democracy which
suggests that it is only a 'golden age' to those who look back at it
from the distance of many centuries. Finally, it examines Roman
innovations in the technology of censorship. Chapter Four chronicles
the triumphs of the outlaw empire of ink, the operations of clandestine
printers and book markets, the Encyclopédie movement, and the
emergence of Enlightened power-knowledge. Chapter Five examines
Marx's critique of censorship and critiques the censorial elements in
Marx's theory and rhetoric. Chapter Six examines the chasm separating Socialist theory from Socialist (Soviet) practice. Chapter Seven
examines the chasm separating democratic theory from capitalist
(U.S.) practice. Readers distressed by the ideological fires set in
Chapters Six and Seven may want to sneak a peak at Chapter Ten
because that is where the attempt is made to bring these fires under
control.

Part Two presents the dramaturgy of censorship. It explains the
theory behind the casting of the figures in the historical narratives.
Chapter Eight explores the epistemological implications of the theory
of power-knowledge developed in this book. It situates it in relation

to recent developments within the philosophy of science and the sociology and anthropology of knowledge. Chapter Nine develops a theory of double-meaning which tries to illuminate the nature of censorship, irony, and communication. Chapter Ten yields to the temptation to try to find a way around, but not out of, the knot that binds knowledge and power. That is, it examines the promise and limitations of reflexive power-talk.

Theorists may find their beginning in my ending. That is, they may want to read Part Two first and climb down the ladder of abstraction into the texture of the historical narratives. Most readers, however, will find the logic of the arguments clearer and their rhetoric more compelling if they make their way up the ladder in the smaller steps that ascent from the historical narratives permits. Since I seek reconciliation of theory and practice, I consider the division of this book into two parts artificial—a concession to the monologic requirements of print. However, I try to counter the costs of this concession by permitting theoretical ideas to invade, colonize, and inform the historical chapters.

CHAPTER TWO

The Censor's New Clothes

i

The Cense of Censorship

The *Oxford English Dictionary* offers two definitions of censor:

> 1). The title of two magistrates in Ancient Rome, who drew up the register or census of the citizens, etc., and had the responsibility of the supervision of public morals.
> 2). An official in some countries whose duty it is to inspect all books, journals, dramatic pieces, etc., before publication, to insure that they shall contain nothing immoral, heretical, or offensive to government.

The *OED* notes that the word, 'censor,' derives from the root *cense*: from the Latin *censure*—to estimate, rate, assess, be of opinion, judge, reckon.

In Ancient Rome the responsibilities of the census-taker and the censor were closely aligned. The census-taker counted and classified people. The censor assessed and classified the products of the people's minds: ideas and their surrogates, books. The entitlement of the *Index Librorum Prohibitorum* indicates that the offices of papal censorship were similarly conceived.

Like the census, *censorship* is a form of surveillance: a mechanism for gathering intelligence that the powerful can use to tighten control over people or ideas that threaten to disrupt established systems of order.[1]

Prior censorship controlled by state or religious authorities remains the norm in many parts of the world. Western Liberals consider such

14

surveillance regressive and label regimes that practice it totalitarian or authoritarian.

ii

Censors Without Stamps

Lawyers have assumed custody of the term, 'censorship,' in contemporary Liberal societies. Cut away from the fabric of history, the term has lost much of its resonance. Current Anglo-American usages of the term conceive of censorship narrowly as a monopoly power of the state which is exercised in Liberal societies only under extraordinary circumstances, e.g. in wartime and other temporary emergencies, to control extreme sexual lasciviousness, and to make possible prosecutions for libel and slander on behalf of private citizens. This configuration discourages inquiry into the most serious forms of censorship operating in Liberal societies today: censorships routinely undertaken by state bureaucracies in the name of 'national security' and censorships routinely sanctioned by the 'profit principle.' By reducing dialogues on censorship to litigations involving publishers' claims to profits, the Anglo-American legal community has removed a powerful emancipatory concept from the vocabulary of the people.

Liberal perspectives on censorship had their genesis in the Enlightenment. They were emancipatory, even revolutionary, within a context in which the Church and Crown held exclusive monopolies over public channels for the distribution of knowledge: pulpit, politics, press and pedagogy. Liberalism defended the rights of individuals against the encroachment of powerful institutions. But the platform that secured liberty for Diderot and Company has proven too narrow to accommodate critics of intelligence agencies and corporate conglomerates. Liberalism has now become an administrative stance. Under the cover of tolerance (pluralism), modern Liberalism protects the political and economic interests of a plurality of powerful elites. The absence of an adequate vocabulary of resistance makes it very difficult to describe effectively Cato's new clothes. It permits the corporate-state to use the language of liberty to deny liberty.

In contemporary Liberal societies, census-takers continue to wear official badges and are still entrusted to count and classify people. But their methods are remarkably archaic, even primitive, when compared with the sophisticated technology of surveillance developed by market researchers, corporate demographers, pollsters, credit investigators, bill collectors, tax assessors, and police agents. In Liberal societies, censors seldom wear badges. Yet they have developed systems for counting and classifying people's ideas that are far more comprehensive and invasive than the most Draconian measures envisioned by Roman censors or Spanish inquisitors.

Liberalism did not eliminate censorship. It forced censors underground. It eliminated the warrant for censorship but not the need for it. It secularized the mana of control from fealty to realty. The marketplace, not the priest or feudal lord, became the ultimate arbiter of Liberal power-knowledge. The immediate effect of this secularizing process was to radically democratize the criteria for classifying people and ideas. For a time, it also democratized profit-making opportunities and made it possible for industrious tradesmen of humble origins, like Ben Franklin, to accumulate sizable holdings. The transition from entrepreneurial to corporate capitalism, however, inverted the terms of the bargain once more. The emergence of the corporate state skewed the social arrangements of mass production to concentrate power and profits in the hands of a nascent industrial elite. In short, liberalism separated Church from State but sanctioned the union of state and commerce.

Under the new cosmology of the corporate state, success became, in the words of Andy Warhol, "what sells." Or, more accurately, what is sold!

In attempting to rationalize their marketing strategies, corporate decision-makers, like the censors of Rome, assume the mantle of mediators of public morals (as well as managers of private profits). Those who control the productive process determine "what is to be mass produced in the cultural area and what will not be produced."[2] These *market censors* decide what ideas will gain entry into "the marketplace of ideas" and what ideas will not. They inspect books, journals, dramatic pieces, etc., before publication, to ensure that they contain nothing that seriously challenges the basis of the existence of the corporate state. That is, *they decide what cultural products are likely to ensure a healthy profit margin.* And most of the time the products that survive the prior censorship of marketing research—the books, news, scripts, games, coupons, programmed learning modules, syllabi, styles, visuals, advertisements, party platforms, etc.—

incorporate ideology and values that celebrate the corporate state and villify its critics.[3]

iii

Socially Structured Silences of Liberalism

Those who historically have been denied full access to the privileges of Liberalism—members of the lower classes, women, blacks, radicals, homosexuals, foreigners, etc.—have provided the most compelling testaments against abuses by the corporate state. But grievances filed by the walking wounded do not project healthy sales profiles. They seldom make the papers. Even authors of the caliber of Ralph Ellison and Richard Wright could only cross the profit line that bars publication in America by addressing their narratives of black oppression to whites rather than to other blacks.

The most comprehensive critique of capitalism was, of course, put forth by Karl Marx. The confrontational style and the revolutionary program empowered by the nineteenth-century journalist's indictment of "the material censorship" of Liberalism invited both the excesses of overzealous followers and the stern repressions by authorities. Marx responded to the excesses of his followers by complaining that he was "not a Marxist!" But Marx's complaint could not contain 'Marxism' or its opposition, and the spiraling escalation of excesses resulted in marginalization of the Marxist critique in most of the West and its near eclipse in the United States. Similarly, the institutionalization of excess—including installation of state censorship by triumphant Marxist-Leninist regimes–led to the suppression of Critical Marxism within Soviet bloc nations, as well as to the legitimization of official repression of Communist Party activities in Liberal societies.[4] The sensational slogans invoked by the corporate state to justify its retreat from the principles of democratic tolerance— Labor Insurrection, Commie Plots, The Red Menace, the Yellow Peril, etc.—not only made the papers, they made the headlines!

Exiles from enemy regimes have posed a special problem for corporate Liberalism. They are news. Good news! They generate healthy sales profiles and superb ideology. They offer compelling testaments of the genuine dangers inherent in all systems of statist control.

But exiles are dissidents. They play by a different set of rules. Their emancipatory dreams carry the imprimatur of alien systems of power-knowledge. Therefore they cannot always be relied on to measure success by what sells. Aleksandr Solzhenitsyn was not the first Russian dissident outraged by the "moral bankruptcy" of Western materialism. The great nineteenth-century humanist Aleksandr Herzin abandoned his homeland in protest against Czarist censorship, but later expressed profound disillusionment with the extremely narrow limits of permission imposed on freedom of expression by market censorship in the West.

iv

Liberal Critical Traditions

The established canons of Liberal aesthetics and literary criticism do offer some modest precedents for protest against the imperatives of commercialism. These precedents, however, are frankly elitist. Embracing the nineteenth-century cult of genius, they celebrate the heroism of the lonely artist who defends the integrity of his/her work against the coarse demands of a philistine patron: industrial capitalism. But they ignore the plight of ordinary people who are cut off from the generative powers of creativity by conditions of cultural production in industrial societies.

There are two main currents within this tradition of Liberal criticism. The first is a souvenir of pre-industrial aristocratic pastoral humanism. It bears the imprimatur of the romantic rebellion against the demon-god, Progress. Baudelaire's definition of Progress expresses the angst of the Romantic reaction against the advance of industrialism: "the progressive privation of the spirit, the progressive domination of matter."[5]

The second critical precedent is a distinct artifact of the class system of Liberal societies. It posits a dichotomy between 'high culture' (authentic culture) and 'mass culture' ('schlock'). This dichotomy places the blame for the blighted condition of most of the arts in the twentieth century on consumers not producers. It rationalizes the elitism of art for the few on the grounds that the many (cum 'masses') have abysmal taste. It deflects attention away from the fact that 'mass culture' is produced for the people, not by the people. It papers over the dirty little secret that 'mass culture' is manufactured by elites to make money and to inhibit the development of authentic cultures of resistance among members of the underprivileged classes of Liberal societies. It robs language of its integrity and critical resilience by anthropomorphizing the social arrangements of production: by using the term 'mass' to refer to people rather than the conditions of production (mass production) under which they must work.

In America, complaints about the distortion of 'serious art' by commercial considerations have generally combined the elitism of the old humanism with the new hubris of cultural materialism. Melville's complaint—"Dollars damn me . . . What I feel most moved to write, that is banned, it will not pay"—typifies the convention of aesthetic classism in American literary criticism.[6]

This aesthetic classism fails to provide an effective platform for cultural criticism because it can say nothing about the epochal changes in the deep structure of power-knowledge brought about by the mass production of culture. It cannot address the profound implications of the collapse of the perennial schism in Western cognitive structures which had always separated official versions of reality from folk constructions: a dualism that prospered even under the rule of the medieval church. As Mikhail Bakhtin points out, in the Middle Ages and in the early modern period, "an immense world of forms and manifestations of laughter opposed the official and serious tone of medieval ecclesiastical and feudal culture."[7] With the transformation to mass-produced culture, however, laughter, carnival, profanity, rebellion, contact with forbidden worlds, even criticism itself became synthetic commodities mediated by corporate-controlled communication networks.

In sum, Liberal critical traditions deflect attention away from serious analysis of the new technology of power-knowledge which has brought the laughter of the powerless under the discipline of the powerful.

V

Mass Production and the Production of Knowledge in Liberal Societies

The myopia of Liberal criticism reflects a larger failure in the scope of the democratic vision that empowered the political covenants of

the Enlightenment: the fact that free speech guarantees have never
applied to the social organization of production in industrial societies. When American wage-earners enter the factory gate or close
the office door, they effectively surrender their rights to free assembly, free speech, and democratic decision-making. Although the
only form of 'prior censorship' formally legitimated by the U.S. Supreme Court applies to government employees (specifically, employees and former employees of intelligence agencies), David W.
Ewing maintains that as far as free speech is concerned "people in
government agencies fare a little better than people in tightly controlled private corporations."[8] Academe is a workplace: a major
center for the production and distribution of knowledge in industrial cultures. In *The Higher Learning in America* (1918), Thorstein Veblen documented the fact that from the beginning market
censorship has skewed the foundations of academic culture in
America.[9]

Mass production requires centralized control systems. If democracy
is to survive, citizens of industrial societies must discover, recover,
or reclaim the emancipatory vocabulary necessary to articulate and
enforce effective strategies for controlling the controllers. We must
sharpen the critical edges of terms like liberty, democracy, enlightenment, public opinion, and censorship.

vi

Changing Models of Censorship

Freud contended that it is a mark of the advance of civilization
when men are no longer burned—merely their books.[10] But many
men and women were burned before this fateful advance to civilization occurred. In *The Fear of the Word: Censorship and Sex*
(1974), Eli Oboler reconstructs a detailed picture of the clumsy
apparatus of un-Enlightened surveillance in post-Reformation
Switzerland:

> Suppose you are living in Geneva, Switzerland, in the year 1553.
> You can expect a minister and an elder to visit you and your fam-
> ily once a year, and these men will question you about the most
> intimate details of your way of living. You may not frequent tav-

erns or dance or sing 'indecent or irreligious' songs. You are cautioned against excesses in entertainment, extravagance in living, and immodesty in dress.

The law even specifies how many different items can be served at one meal, and which colors and what quality of clothing you may wear. If you are a woman and wear jewelry or lace or frilly hats, you will certainly be admonished by the ruling clergy; you know that a neighbor was put to jail for 'arranging her hair to an immoral height.' Books which are considered wrong in religious tenets or tending toward immorality are not available to you. You may not attend any theatrical performances; as a matter of fact none is to be found in Geneva at this time . . . Your children must have names to be found in the Bible. If you write books disagreeing with Calvin, you will not have to retract your opinions, but will have to throw all available copies of your writing into the fire with your own hands.

You may feel that your child is disrespectful—but you don't dare report this to authorities, even if he happens to hit you; the child next door was actually beheaded for striking his parents. If you serve more than three courses at any meal, even at a wedding or other banquet or feast occasion, watch out for the ecclesiastical police . . . If you visit a Geneva inn, you will not be permitted to sit up after nine o'clock at night, unless you are known to be a spy by profession . . . The ruler of Geneva during the mid-decades of the sixteenth century, John Calvin, is probably the epitome of all censors . . . When Calvin set up a theocracy in Geneva . . . it naturally included a very strong censorship, perhaps the strongest religiously-motivated censorship of all time, even stronger than that of the Roman Catholic Inquisition.[11]

If the Calvinist ethos cultivated the groundings for the development of mercantile capitalism, its mode of surveillance proved much too cumbersome to control the large and heterogeneous workforce necessary to keep the wheels of industrial capitalism turning. The imperatives of mechanized production required a radical reformulation of humankind's temporal rhythms. The installation of Big Ben in the center of London symbolized the new mechanized conception of time. In "Time, Work-Discipline, and Industrial Capitalism," E.P. Thompson systematically explores the ways in which early factory workers were disciplined into internalizing a vision of time which no longer relied on the categories of sun or season.[12] Thompson maintains that this discipline—this resocialization—was marked by widespread resistance and conflict which brought about massive social unrest and violent class conflict.

vii

The Science of Panoptics

Jeremy Bentham's *Panopticon* (1843) exemplified the new technology of Enlightened censorship. The Panopticon offered a model for centralized control which could circumvent open (visible) conflicts between the masses and moral agents. Architecturally the Panopticon serves equally well as a model for a prison, factory, school, or asylum. Within the Panopticon, small individual cells are arranged in a circle so that inmates, workers, students, or patients are under constant observation by moral authorities—guards, managers, teachers, or physicians. The cells isolate those enclosed within the Panopticon from one another. Moreover the lighting system combines with a series of louvered blinds to prevent inmates from seeing the observer. Several famous penitentiaries are literal copies of Bentham's plan. Richard Sennett points out that,

> This design was the purest application of the principle that the people in command should always be in a position to oversee, anticipate, and discipline the movements of those in their charge. In such a setting for moral reform, the factory foreman or prison official acquires far more power than the natural parent, and nuturance is replaced by one-sided control: the subject is influenced but cannot approach or influence those who are taking care of him or her.[13]

In his novel *Falconer*, John Cheever uses the Panopticon as a symbol of modernity. Foucault maintains that Panopticonism is the paradigm of Liberal authority.[14]

Panopticonism provides a working model for agents of subterranean censorship. It is technically superior to all previous forms of censorship because it secures its mechanisms of control within the epistemological foundations of the social order it empowers. Metaphorically, the Panopticon describes the architecture of the modern bureaucracy, corporation, spy network, system of mass marketing, and mass education. It also describes the circuitry which makes possible radio, television, computers, and global satellite systems: the Electronic Panopticon which replaces Bentham's louvered blinds with neatly concealed matrices of wires, transistors, and silicon chips. So that today nearly every citizen of an enlightened society is wired to the Tower and yet remains only marginally aware of the attachment.

Electronics revolutionized the science of Panoptics. Discipline is no longer limited to the penitentiary, factory, school, asylum, or military regiment. It now penetrates (and erodes) the privacy of the home so that even the physical arrangement of furniture in the typical American living or 'family room' comes to resemble the lay-out of Bentham's Panopticon. Chairs are no longer arranged to facilitate conversation among people in the room but rather to provide optimal viewing of the signals transmitted from the Tower to the receiver that each citizen eagerly places in his or her home. From infancy it is now possible for a citizen of the corporate state to absorb the prevailing code of domination in a painless and entertaining way.[15] From infancy many children are taught that the message from the Tower is more important than anything they might have to say by parents who routinely tell them: "Be quiet! I want to hear this!"

The Electronic Panopticon has brought about far more radical modifications in human temporal rhythms than those required by the mechanization of production. And it has done so without any significant resistance! Moreover, the Electronic Panopticon does not need to isolate physically those enclosed within its cells. It achieves the same effect by limiting opportunities for meaningful interpersonal relations: relations built upon conversation, listening, privacy, intimacy, and a shared sense of community. In short, it not only eliminates the power to resist, but also the desire to resist. For even if we turn the switch off there is nothing left to fill the void. Like characters in a Samuel Beckett play, we discover that the only thing we have to say is that we have nothing to say.

Moreover, during the early morning hours when that switch is finally turned 'off' in most American homes, other hardware in the technology of the Electronic Panopticon remains 'on': computer storage systems which contain information about the birth, death, marital status, monetary transactions, as well as the educational, work, military, and criminal records of virtually every American citizen; electronic surveillance systems which unobtrusively video-tape the movements of citizens in retail outlets, hotel lobbies, banks, airports, and border crossings; and polygraph apparatus which not only permits employers to monitor the credentials, reputations, and public assertions of prospective employees but also their thoughts. Once the wires are in place, the Electronic Panopticon works automatically. Only minimal supervision from the Tower is required. Official and quasi-official control is exercised through licensing, regulation, and broad-casting codes and standards, but the decisive controls are the controls that are built into the marketing system itself.

John Calvin's representatives made their inspections once a year. The Electronic Panopticon exerts its discipline twenty-four hours a day. And, with the installation of an international network of communications satellites, it now has the power necessary to extend its reach throughout the globe.[16]

Under Panoptic discipline no ecclesiastical police force is needed to inspect your table or measure the height of your coiffure. And no cop is needed to bust your head to get you to work on time. Ham-handed tactics can be abandoned. *This is an advance.* It is better to burn books rather than authors, and to change heads rather than break them.

But minds changed, cultivated, or colonized to facilitate the pur-poses, priorities, and plans of distant elites are not free minds. Pan-optic control systems do not satisfactorily resolve the contradictions of freedom and control. They betray the egalitarian promises of the Enlightenment and place arbitrary constraints on human autonomy. They render the controller, warden, or censor invisible and thereby permit him/her to operate outside of the rules of participatory de-mocracy. Moreover, they endow the cense of censorship with a "phantom objectivity" which makes it extremely resistant to criticism.[17]

viii

Exposing the Wiring

A state which carries out its routine operations behind closed doors is not a democracy. Enlightenment which requires the cover of dark-ness is not real enlightenment. Censors who call themselves by other names are still censors.

If censorship is ever justified in a democracy, it is only when its groundings are open to public scrutiny. Liberal critical traditions have discouraged us from asking fundamental epistemological questions about the relationship of power and knowledge.

The essential question is not, 'Is there censorship?' but rather 'What kind of censorship?' Posing this question is not an affirmation of darkness but an invitation to enlightenment. To expand the boundaries of human freedom, we must first identify them.

CHAPTER THREE

Socrates' Children

i

Epistemological Warrant

History is a form of storytelling. Napoleon described it as "the fable agreed upon." We cannot know history "as it really happened."

All historical interpretations are contingent. Memories, documents, and testaments are filtered through perceptual, linguistic, organizational, and hierarchical grids which are skewed by prevailing patterns of power-relations.

History is a linguistic phenomenon: "a speech act," "a selective use of the past tense."[1] Historical texts speak "from" as well as "to."

The epistemological claims that we can make for our interpretations of these texts are modest. Even substantive remains such as buildings or archaeological ruins are "texts" which require "reading": location within a context of verbal signification. History has no material reality outside of our interpretive belief in linguistic records. As George Steiner points out,

> Where worms, fires of London, or totalitarian regimes obliterate such records, our consciousness of past being comes on blank space. We have no total history, no history which could be defined as objectively real because it contained the literal sum of past life. To remember everything is a condition of madness. We remember culturally, as we do individually, by conventions of emphasis, foreshortening, and omission. The landscape composed by the past tense, the semantic organization of remembrance, is stylized by and differently coded by different cultures.[2]

Every reading of history is therefore a re-reading, and, in a sense, a *violation* of history "as it really happened." Hans Georg Gadamer underscores this when he asserts, "a hermeneutic that regards understanding as the reconstruction of the original would be no more than the recovery of dead meaning." History attains relevance for us only because it is viewed in terms of our own futurity (Heidegger) and our prejudices (Gadamer).[3]

We can only approach the landscape of history as plunderers. Neither methodological asceticism nor reflexive rigor can save us. A historical vision formed in an imperialistic era sees history as battle-scarred. Revisionary sequels may project gentler frames. But no coherent picture of the past can be constructed without frames: paradigms or prejudices which focus our attention. Our eyes are jaundiced. The past speaks to us, comes alive through us, only when we successfully effect a "fusion of the horizons" of past and present.[4] From the point of view of a linguistically informed historiography, there are no 'primary' historical sources. All historical texts are 'secondary sources': readings of readings of events. Claims to definitive readings of historical events are therefore power-claims.

The truth yielded by our historical readings are postulates, parables, or cautionary tales, not scientific precepts. They are *validated* by their resonances: their capacity to speak to us. But they are not amenable to *verification* by procedures appropriate for testing the propositions of mechanistic models of the universe. Hans Magnus Enzensberger makes this clear in *Der kurze Sommer der Anarchie*:

> History is an invention for which reality supplies the material. But it is not just any invention. The interest it arouses is based upon the interests of those who tell it; and it allows those who listen to recognize and determine more precisely their own interest as well as their enemies. Scientific scholarship that imagines itself to be value-free has given us a great deal; but it remains a Schlemihl, a fictional figure.[5]

Because its narratives are framed so near the edges of relativism, an approach to history which surrenders all positivistic claims requires a self-critical stance. In so far as possible—and it is never fully possible—those who regard history as simply a systematic form of storytelling must try to consciously articulate the motives behind their narratives. They must try to specify the *from* as well as the *to* of their historical incursions.

The guiding vision of my historical narrative—its *from* and its *to*—is cogently captured by Thomas Hardy's ironic aphorism from "In Tenebris":

Who holds that if way to Better there be,
It exacts a full look at the Worst.

My historicism is an exercise in victimology. I view the censored as epistemological criminals: spoilers. In the terminology suggested by Michel Foucault's "anatomy of power," I regard the censored as symbolic surrogates who represent "the inverted figure of the king."[6]

Nevertheless I acknowledge the methodological arrogance implicit in all attempts to impute and calibrate the sufferings or repressions of others. I find the burden of arrogance less encumbering than the callousness of neglect. I try to lighten this burden by recognizing the limits of my mission. I secure my theory in the documents left by lives lived within the warp of history. I do not treat this theory as an immutable code into which the documents of all lives must be translated.

Further I recognize that those who want to tell the stories of the censored face special methodological problems. Some of these problems should be identified. First, the winners in political conflicts become the authors and custodians of the accredited records of the conflict. Thus, for example, Boris Pasternak and other non-conformists writers ceased to exist in the annals of Soviet literature after 1928. Second, attempts by later scholars to vindicate the position of the losers are often conceived in the heat of anger and delivered in the dialectically sterile language of ideology. We can, for example, see this in some recent rewritings of the history of the Vietnam War which vindicate U.S. involvement. Third, accounts of infamous cases involving prominent figures like Galileo crowd the historical record while the parts played by ordinary people are not usually recorded. In the past decade the "new history" and feminist scholarship have underscored the distortion of the historical record that this elitism creates, and have committed themselves to recovering the "lost lives" of ordinary people.

All histories of censorship are histories of elites.[7] That is, they are histories of celebrated or notorious individuals. This elitism is unavoidable because freedom of opinion, unlike regulation of property, industry, mobility, or sexuality, affects only a small minority in any society: those who advocate unconventional, heretical, or revolutionary ideas.

Rethinking the history of censorship requires revisiting and remapping benchmarks established by others. For this reason my account follows Liberal precedent and reviews infamous cases. But it also challenges Liberal interpretations of these cases and calls attention to the socially structured silences they sustain. As a result, the coverage of my narrative is vast. This chapter alone examines the history of censorship in the Western world from Ancient Greece to the dawn of Enlightenment. Selection of the cases—the parables of persecution—included in these pages is guided by the following criteria: the significance of these cases as precedent for Liberal ideas on free speech and censorship; their usefulness as critical resources for developing new theories and practices of resistance; their rhetorical power; and their intrinsic interest.

ii

Omissions

Few of the holes in my narrative can be directly attributed to worms or fires of London. Personal fallibility and ignorance are the primary sources of my culpable silences. But one major gap in this narrative requires explanation: the failure to provide a detailed examination of censorship under National Socialism.

This omission is not an oversight. It is a studied decision which continues to give birth to second thoughts. The original outline for this book included a chapter on National Socialism; however, development of the power-knowledge thesis moved my narrative in directions I did not fully anticipate.

As I pondered twentieth-century censorships, it became increasingly apparent to me that since 1945 ideological discourse in both Soviet and capitalist spheres have used the Nazi precedent as a cathartic sponge to both deny and excuse their own crimes. Hangman's justice allowed them to view Nazism as different "in kind" from other systems of power-knowledge. For those of us whose historical memories were formed after 1945, the Nazis have become the 'bogeyman' of history. In American popular culture, portrayals of Nazi racism have been almost completely non-reflexive. They have deflected our attention away from reflections on American racism. They encouraged us (members of a racially separated society) to see ourselves as the 'good guys,' and to see the Nazis as the 'bad guys.' A similar mythos permitted the Soviets to see themselves as liberators of the

repressed peoples of the world without reflecting on their own domestic repressions.

The cartoon version of Nazism provided both the U.S. and the
U.S.S.R. with the most potent weapon in the arsenal of power-knowledge: the excuse of an evil enemy. Moreover, the simplistic storyline
it projected allowed for an easy recasting of characters after World
War II. Soviets simply replaced the fascist devil with the capitalist
devil, and Americans replaced it with the communist devil. Political
demonology thereby became a routine part of the exercise of power
in the postwar period.

The Nazis were indeed 'bad guys!' Nazism was an evil, racist
dogma. I am in no sense suggesting that Nazism can be vindicated.
The winners wrote the history of World War II, but, in my judgment,
they wrote that part with accuracy. What I am suggesting is that the
winners have also used this history as power-knowledge to vindicate
their own violence. If we consider bodycounts, the costs of Hitler's
atrocities were indeed high (20 million), but so were the costs of
establishing the Soviet state (22 million) or Mao's "Great Leap For-
ward" (10 million).[8] However, the costs of securing capitalist interests
throughout the world have also been enormous. The tolls taken by
centuries of colonialism and neo-colonialism, and wars in defense of
these exploitive economic and political arrangements, exceed the
combined costs of Hitlerism, Stalinism, and Maoism. This simple
arithmetic of repression puts the Nazi outrage in a somewhat different
perspective. Bodycounts are, of course, vulgar industrial measures
of the calculus of human suffering. But in the twentieth century's
progress from scaffold to scaffold, bodycounts have increased geo-
metrically. Industrialism has perfected the technology of terror.
Auschwitz and Hiroshima are artifacts of this progress. Even the
cartoon histories of Nazi horrors created by mass media confront us
with the bankruptcy of the Faustian dream.

The Nazi story must be told and retold if we are to exorcise its
evil: if those who come after Auschwitz are to become, in Emil
Fackenheim's words, "once again human." The testament of survivors continues to provide us with resonant power-knowledge for use
in resisting totalitarian statism. I defer to the emancipatory power-
knowledge provided by those witnesses.[9]

For the purpose of this narrative, the Nazi parable is treated as a
background assumption and founding premise. To force it into my
storyline would be to risk collaboration with those who reduce Nazism
to the formulaic scenarios of popular culture. To dismiss Hitler and

his accomplices as a band of 'gangsters,' 'monsters,' or 'madmen' is to fail to learn the lessons of our discourses on power-knowledge. It is comforting perhaps? It allows us to believe that it can't happen again, or that it can't happen here. But it is just such denials, such refusals to see, which create the conditions that could permit it to happen again.

Nazism was not a historical anomaly or aberration. The government of Adolf Hitler was, for a time, the legitimately constituted government of Germany. Some of the men who served in the Third Reich were graduates of the best universities in the world. They had theories and hopes, not just fanaticism and gas chambers. Most of these men probably believed they were serving a just, or at least necessary, cause.

Hannah Arendt's reflections on the trial of Adolf Eichmann are invaluable precisely because they force us to confront these facts. They require us to consider the possibility that the men who operated Auschwitz were ordinary men. Her reflections reveal the banality of evil.[10]

It is easy to exorcise aberrations. The vengeance of the hangman takes care of that. But it is far more difficult to discover ways to restructure social systems and human institutions so that they do not encourage ordinary men to behave like monsters. This is the essential dilemma that we who come after the Holocaust must ponder.

Until we resolve this dilemma we cannot seriously entertain the illusion that it cannot happen again. The power-knowledge which legitimates the two dominant world-systems today, Soviet socialism and American political capitalism, does not differ "in kind" from the power-knowledge that secured National Socialism. To be sure, these two systems were secured by more laudable (humane) ideational foundations than Nazism. These ideals have, at times, acted to constrain the violence of authorities within each system. But these ideals (freedom, equality, justice) have also been routinely invoked to legitimate violence. In sum, the threat is still with us. We have not exorcised the banality of evil.

Cartoonists are not the only ones who have posited links between fascism and capitalism and fascism and communism. Some critics of capitalism see fascism as a logical extension of capitalism. Franco's Spain provides their case in point.[11] Others suggest that there is no necessary relation between the two systems, but warn that capitalism is in no sense a prophylaxis against fascism. I believe that recent structural changes in American capitalism make it more vulnerable to fascist temptations than ever before. However, I do not believe that America must necessarily yield to those temptations.

Critics of socialism contend that it necessarily leads to totalitarianism. These critics take the Soviet experience as paradigmatic and ignore the possibility of a democratic socialism. I believe that democratic socialism remains a utopian ideal which still awaits articulation of workable institutional supports. I do not preclude the possibility that these supports may one day be secured within the Soviet sphere of influence, but I am not optimistic.

In sum, in the pages that follow, I devote much of my narrative to trying to uncover parables of hope—triumphs of the human spirit—which might encourage ordinary men and women to engage in dialogues on the possibilities of creating human institutions and systems of power-knowledge which do not encourage ordinary people to act like monsters.

The remainder of this chapter will examine the place of books and print in securing the dialectic of repression and illumination prior to the Enlightenment. More specifically, it will review: (1) the history of Greek censorship and the role classicism played in the struggle against religious orthodoxy in the medieval and early modern period; (2) Socrates' special place in the annals of Western censorship and his influence on Liberalism; (3) the development of methods for bureaucratic administration of censorship by the Romans; (4) the constituents of sacred and secular systems of power-knowledge; (5) *The Index Librorum Prohibitorum* and the Inquisition as artifacts of the typological revolution; (6) print as an instrument of power-knowledge; (7) the Reformation and "the witch craze"; and (8) censorship as an affirmation of the power of books.

iii

Inventing Greeks

The stories medieval and early modern scholars told themselves about the Greeks were allegorical. The images they projected of a democratic and heterodox past were subversive images. Moreover, these images were packed into a scenario of loss and redemption that res-

onated with Christian cosmology. Only a change of signs from sacred
to secular was required to translate the contrast into critique, protest,
and plan. But this change of signs had radical political implications:
the Christian heaven was a promise that was to be kept in an afterlife,
the heaven of the Greeks was history—a promise that had been made
and kept by men in this life. Accounts of the Greeks disturbed the
peace of medieval churchmen. They empowered humanistic ideals
which suggested that justice, tolerance, and honor could be achieved
within human communities. They provided word-pictures of a past
that could be conceived as a possible future. For this reason the
Greeks, or more precisely Greek lore, played a decisive role in struggles for intellectual and political freedom which led to the Renaissance
and Enlightenment.

Scripture begins with Genesis: with the parable of the Fall of Man.
History begins with the Greeks: with a second parable of corruption—
the Fall of Man from Periclean democracy. In *The Greeks and the
Irrational*, E.R. Dodds suggests that if the Greeks had not existed
we would have had to invent them.[12] Gadamer would, of course,
point out that this is exactly what we have done.

The Greeks we have invented, or more precisely the Greeks we
have inherited from four centuries of historical scholarship, were
invented as protest against censorship and apology for free speech.
They were invented by sixteenth-century Venetian translators and
printers in a struggle to wrench some margin of autonomy for their
craft and commerce under conditions of hegemonic Church control.
They were re-invented by nineteenth-century opponents of Gothic
revivalism.[13]

These Greeks, or at least the conceptual frames through which we
see them, are four, not twenty-four, centuries old. Elizabeth Eisenstein underscores the importance of this textual time-warp in her
outstanding reconceptualization of early modern history, *The Printing
Press As an Agent of Change: Communications and Cultural Transformation in Early Europe*:

> The automatic adoption of modern conventions often masks earlier
> conditions, and this seems to be particularly true when we try to trace
> textual traditions that were shaped in the age of scribes. Before the
> advent of printing, for example, the order in which texts were composed
> was by no means the same as that in which they became available to
> Latin-reading scholars within Western Christendom. Any history of
> Western philosophy must make some allowance for the migration of

manuscripts (must place the works of Aristotle after those of Augustine, and certain dialogues of Plato after both, for instance) when
accounting for the views of medieval schoolmen.[14]

Thus, for example, the chronology of texts, not the chronology of
events, is decisive in accounting for the way medieval scholars viewed
intellectual freedom and censorship. They came 'from' *The City of
God* 'to' Socrates.

The founders of the humanist revival were survivors not innocents.
They were the most heterodox faction within one of the least tolerant
cultural milieus the world has ever known. For them, discovering
(recovering) the Greeks was a radicalizing experience. Against the
background of a Dark Age, Ionia, Athens, even Imperial Rome could
only have been perceived through golden frames. These frames suggested that liberation from the mind-bindings of Christian orthodoxy
could offer deliverance: that it could provide humankind with the
power-knowledge required to create heaven on earth.

Secular scholars, printers, importers, and booksellers had a vested
interest in gilding these frames. Expanding heterodoxy meant the
rebirth of humanism, it also meant the birth of capitalism. Early
printers were businessmen as well as classical scholars. The cities in
which early capitalism took root were cities with flourishing printing
houses. According to Eisenstein, "As pioneers in new manufacturing
and marketing techniques, early printers shared something in common with other urban entrepreneurs; but as pioneers in advertising
and publicity, in agitation, propaganda, and bibliography, they must
be placed in a class [sic] by themselves."[15] The vision of Greek humanism these propagandists invented—as exemplar and subversive
agent—was that of a near-perfect democracy secured by free expression and heterodoxy.

In his *History of Freedom of Thought*, J.B. Bury points out that,
"From the sixteenth century to the French Revolution nearly all
important historical events bore in some way on the struggle for
freedom of thought."[16] Within this context, celebrations of the
Golden Age of Greek antiquity were heady stuff. The humanist 'recovery' of the classic texts should not be read as merely reconstruction
or exegesis of a dead culture. It should be read as protest against an
existing culture (medieval Christendom) and apologia for a new one.
Plato's *Apology for Socrates* was "news," not archive, when it was
introduced to Europe for the first time in the fifteenth century by
Leonardo Bruni.

The veneration of the Greeks did not end with the French Revolution. Bury himself perpetuated it with the enthusiasm of pre-World War I positivistic innocence. He believed that the classic revival had returned the West to its rightful course, secured the triumph of rationality over religious superstitions, and ensured the march of scientific and civic Progress. The Petrarchean revival in late nineteenth-century European scholarship also articulated its vision of freedom within the vocabulary of Greek humanism. The neo-Romantic movement led by Stefan George continued the veneration of the Greeks. Even distinctly modernist and pessimistic twentieth-century philosophies like existentialism are not free of the cycle of loss and redemption imposed upon parables of Greek humanism by medieval and Renaissance scholars.

Yet other interpretations of the classic texts are plausible. Indeed a compelling, but much less salutary, alternative crowds the margins and footnotes of Bury's text as well as the texts of other champions of Graeco-Roman humanism. The view that struggles for articulation in these notes suggests quite simply that *persecution of heterodox ideas has been a fact of life in the Occident from the very beginning*. I find evidence supporting this view far more persuasive than the evidence securing the propaganda of the early Italian printers.

In *Persecution and the Art of Writing*, Leo Strauss embraces a similar revisionary interpretation. Contrary to the Golden Age mythos, Strauss maintains that even the Greeks forced the heterodox to write-between-the-lines (or more precisely to speak out of both sides of their mouths since dialogue, not print, was the primary pedagogical method of Greek culture). Citing documentation from the hermeneutic scholarship of Lessing, Strauss shows that "all ancient philosophers" distinguished between their *exoteric* and *esoteric* teachings: teachings intended for all interested citizens (and censors), and teachings intended to be deciphered only by a carefully screened audience of sympathizers.[17] If there was an exception to the Lessing-Strauss thesis it was Socrates, who conversed with anyone who would listen to him and taught the same lesson to street sweepers and scholars.

Compared with medieval Europe, classical Greece was a Golden Age. The arts flourished. There was a polytheism of gods. Some of the population enjoyed the advantages of participatory democracy. The pleasures of the flesh had not yet been soured by the Christian concept of sin. Heterodox ideas could be found in public forums, in drama, epic tales, and in accounts of the adventures of warring gods.

But there was censorship. Greek democracy was supported by

slavery. Women, regardless of class, enjoyed no more civil rights than slaves. The heterodox were frequently persecuted for their ideas, especially if these ideas could be construed as blasphemous. Thus, for example, only Pericles' personal intervention on behalf of a friend saved Anaxagoras from execution. The philosopher was banished to Lampsacus for teaching that the gods are only abstractions and the sun merely a mass of flaming matter.

Socrates heads every list of martyrs who gave their lives in defense of free speech. But his persecution is less of a paradox than Plato leads us to believe. Careful rereading of the subtext (background comments) of Plato's *Apology for Socrates* indicates that by the time Socrates was brought to trial, Athenian censorship was so extensive that a hierarchy of sanctions ranging from prohibition of public speech (banning) through denial of civil rights, exile, imprisonment, and execution was routinely invoked to suppress dangerous ideas. It also indicates that Athenian concepts of justice allowed the rich to buy their freedom even in capital cases.

Even Bury acknowledges that the Greeks may have been the first book burners. The Sophist Protagoras wrote a book, *On the Gods*, in which he sought to prove that the existence of the gods could not be demonstrated by formal reasoning. The opening passage was, "Concerning the gods, I cannot say that they exist nor yet that they do not exist."[18] A charge of blasphemy was placed against him and he fled Athens to avoid persecution. However, copies of the work of Protagoras were collected and burned. This was especially remarkable because written texts were still rare, esoteric forms. But Bury insists the Greeks did not censor because they did not censor systematically (e.g. copies of Anaxagoras' work remained available in Athenian bookstalls even after he was exiled). Further, he contends that since the prosecution of the heterodox was frequently only a cover for political motives, it should not be regarded as an authentic expression of a censorial mentality! A curious piece of rationalist alchemy since Bury does not hesitate to describe politically motivated acts of censorship by the Roman Catholic Church as expressions of a malevolent mentality!

Bury maintains that more direct advocacy of censorship can be found among the philosophers than among Greek officials. Certainly Plato's *Republic* provides the most dramatic case in point. Plato proposed to ban the arts and eliminate all freedom of discussion from the ideal State. Moreover, he would require compulsory adherence (sanctioned if necessary by imprisonment or death) to a set of religious beliefs ("the Good Lie") which were to be formulated entirely on pragmatic grounds as mechanisms of social control.

If Greek officials did not advocate censorship, they did practice it. Moreover this practice was not confined to the purgation of eccentrics like Socrates. It was also directed against mainstream figures like Aristotle, who was forced into exile to escape a blasphemy charge, and Euripides, who was prosecuted for impiety.

iv

Using Socrates

It was Socrates, the disreputable eccentric, who gave us the first—and, in my view, most compelling—testament for freedom of conscience and free speech. He gave it to us ironically: through the script of Plato, one of the most outspoken advocates of censorship the Western world has known.

In *Paideia: The Ideals of Greek Culture*, Werner Jaeger observes, "To write a history of Socrates' influence would be a gigantic task."[19] I would suggest that it is an impossible task. We cannot recover Socrates through historical exegesis: the texts are too slim and the context too far removed. But we can *use* Socrates as an *exemplar*. We can emulate him. We can practice what he preached by restoring the unity of theory and practice.[20]

No facet of Greek lore disturbed the peace of medieval and early modern ecclesiastics more than the *Apology*, Plato's defense of Socrates. Citizens of Bayle's outlaw "Republic of Letters" venerated "Saint Socrates." So did the fathers of Enlightenment: Jefferson considered it a "blasphemy" that we know Socrates through the text of the authoritarian Plato. Diderot regarded Socrates as the patron saint of the Encyclopedists, and viewed his own battles against censorship and for press freedom as extensions of the Socratic legacy.

Bury cites two passages from Plato's *Apology* as essential cornerstones of Western Liberalism:

> (1) "If you propose to acquit me," he says, "on condition that I abandon my research for truth, I will say: I thank you, O Athenians, but I will obey God, who, I believe, set me this task, rather than you, and

so long as I have breath and strength I will never cease from my occupation with philosophy. I will continue the practice of accosting whomever I meet and saying to him, "Are you not ashamed of setting your heart on wealth and honours while you have no care for wisdom and truth and making your soul better?" I know not what death is— it may be a good thing and I am not afraid of it. But I do know that it is a bad thing to desert one's post and I prefer what may be good to what I know is bad."
(2) "In me you have a stimulating critic, persistently urging you with persuasions and reproaches, persistently testing your opinions and trying to show you that you are really ignorant of what you suppose you know. Daily discussion of the matters about which you hear me conversing is the highest good for man. Life that is not tested by such discussion is not worth living."[21]

The first passage affirms the sovereignty of conscience against arbitrary authority. The second establishes the social importance of discussion and criticism. To the extent that it has incorporated these principles into its practice, Liberalism has advanced the cause of emancipatory communication. But Liberalism's *use* of Socrates has often been a marriage-of-convenience: a matter of coattails which provided the pizzazz of Continental tailoring to a basically Utilitarian wardrobe.

A friendly use of Socrates would accost advocates of the practices of mature Liberalism with interrogations about their faithfulness to the passages Bury cites. It would also accost them with an additional passage from the *Apology for Socrates*: a passage that Bury does not cite. This passage is an essential tenet of Socrates' thinking, but it did not become a founding premise of Liberalism:

But I have been always the same in all my actions, public as well as private, and never have I yielded any base compliance to those who are slanderously termed my disciples, or to any other. For the truth is that I have no regular disciples: but if any one likes to come and hear me while I am pursuing my mission, whether he be young or old, he may freely come. Nor do I converse with those who pay only, and not with those who do not pay; but any one, whether he be rich or poor, may ask and answer me and listen to my words; and whether he turns out to be a bad man or a good one, that cannot be justly laid to my charge, as I never taught him anything. And if any one says that he has ever learned or heard anything from me in private which all the world has not heard, I should like you to know that he is speaking an untruth.[22]

Consistency in public and private—no scandalizing or awe-inspiring secrets, no double-dealings—a simple principle! Yet Socrates acknowledges that during the Golden Age of Greek democracy, no man in public life could live by it. This is why he did not enter public life, and why those who did found it necessary sooner or later to cover their tracks: to censor in the name of God, decency, or the survival of democracy. Inconsistencies between public professions of morality and private practices still require public figures to cover their tracks. Such cover-ups blunt the emancipatory thrust of contemporary Liberalism.

In contrast a double-reading of the history of Liberalism suggests that the public/private schism which undermines the resonance of modern Liberalism actually served to advance the cause of intellectual freedom in the seventeenth and eighteenth centuries. It suggests that the dualism in Western thought which rightfully distresses twentieth-century moralists, philosophers, and critical theorists of all ideological persuasions actually provided the opening—the dialectical opportunity—which made possible modern concepts of intellectual autonomy, objectivity, justice, equality, and consistency. That is, my reading suggests that mature Liberalism bears the scars of its genesis in the repressive political and religious climates of late medieval and early modern Europe.

The dualism, which Socrates and his disciples lament, permitted the founders of the Enlightenment to compartmentalize public and private behaviors and to separate theory from practice. These ruptures secured epistemologies which empowered canons of instrumental reason and prepared the way for development of "the double-standard" which has eroded the moral authority of mature Liberalism. Conservative and radical critics of Liberalism have correctly identified the resulting moral inversion as the Achilles' heel of Liberal thought.

The grammar of motives of contemporary critical discourse is far removed from the grammar of motives of seventeenth- and eighteenth-century emancipatory discourse. The fathers of Enlightenment were not moral truants, crude opportunists, or hypocrites as some strains of revisionary criticism seem to imply. Indeed, measured against prevailing public and private standards of priestly and princely behaviors, their conduct was remarkably pristine. Their crimes against propriety were petty crimes.

For them, separation of theory and practice was a strategic move in their heroic struggle to free Reason from the mind-bindings of monarchical and ecclesiastical control. This move advanced the cause of free inquiry and provided the auspices for the scientific revolutions of the seventeenth and eighteenth centuries.

It was a *necessary* move because prior to the Enlightenment, the only legitimate theory was theory secured in Dogma. And the only acceptable concept of causation was causation secured by a First Cause, Divine Authority.

The work of the laboratory and the print shop could only be separated from the work of the chancery and monarchy if these fundamental cosmological connections could be severed. Practitioners— empiricists, utilitarians, encyclopedists and philosophes—could only get on with the business of Enlightenment if they could keep the theorists—priests, kingsmen, censors, and inquisitors—off their backs. They did this by carefully covering their tracks: by writing freedom between the lines of obscure, arcane, or superficially pious texts. To escape the inquisitors, they praised the Lord but then passed the ammunition of free thought. Thus, for example, David Hume's assertion that theories cannot be derived from facts was much more than an esoteric technical argument within the philosophy of science. It was also a pragmatic attempt to secure some latitude for fact-finders.

Unless we consider the 'context' of the texts of Enlightenment— the repressive religious and political climates—which cultivated the dialectical ground in which Liberalism took root, we cannot fully understand or fairly assess the conundrums in mature Liberalism. We can only explain in sinister terms Liberalism's failure to emulate Socrates' third principle. Our dialogue is stillborn. We cannot dream the dream of a new Socratic enlightenment. We cannot emulate Socrates.

v

Correcting Romans

Tacitus was mistaken when he asserted that Augustus was the first censor, the first ruler to punish words unaccompanied by action. He was also mistaken when he claimed that Augustus was the first book-burner.

As we have seen, in censorship as in most civilized customs, the Greeks were more advanced than the Romans. But the Greeks did not invent censorship either.

All societies have exercised controls over words, symbols, and ideas. Durkheim traces the origins of these controls to the interdictions that surround the categories of totem and taboo in pre-literate languages.[23] Childe maintains that censorship of written symbols was present in early Sumerian and Egyptian civilizations.[24] Rigid social controls were built into the structure of Chinese ideography from its inception.[25] And in the Old Testament we are told that the Hebrews burned the prophecy of Jeremiah (36:23) because the vision of the future it projected caused despair.

While Romans did not invent censorship, they did bring their administrative genius to bear upon the task. The Romans established their censorial bureaucracy and commissioned their first censors in 443 B.C. This censorship was not conceived in the interest of regulating literature or the arts. Rather, two Censors were appointed for five-year terms and entrusted with the responsibility of conducting the official census of Roman citizens. The census rolls were used for political, military, and taxation purposes. In order to count citizens, the Censors had to establish standards for citizenship. These standards included moral standards. The Censors could deprive any man of his citizenship if they disapproved of his public or private behavior. The decisions of the Censors were absolute. They could even remove a Senator from office if they deemed his behavior immoral or dishonorable. Cato the Elder (235–149) was the most famous of the Roman Censors. Unlike many Censors, he was considered to be scrupulously honest and fair. But, as the following caricature from Plutarch's *Lives* indicates, he was also feared and hated:

Porcius, who snarls at all in every place,
With his grey eyes, and with his fiery face,
Even after death will scarce admitted be
Into the infernal realms by Hecate.[26]

Even though Augustus was not the first censor, he was the first ruler in the Western world to codify a law proscribing libelous or scandalous writings (*libelli famosi*). This law legitimated public book-burnings. The texts of Labienus provided the first tinder.

Tiberius strengthened regulations against oratorical and literary intemperance. In matters of religion, he was tolerant. He dismissed those who pleaded for censorship of blasphemy by asserting, "If the gods are insulted, let them see to it themselves." However, in matters of state Tiberius was more vigilant. Under his reign Cremutius Cordus was deprived of his livelihood, and all of his books were burned by order of the Aedile because he had described Gaius Cassius as "the last Roman." In his *History*, Tacitus notes the paradoxical effect of Nero's censorship: "So long as the possession of these writings was attended by danger, they were eagerly sought and read: when there was no longer any difficulty in securing them, they fell into oblivion."[27] Tacitus' point has not eluded modern advertisers or modern censors. The have cynically used the *Tacitean principle*, the lure of forbidden fruit, in their marketing strategies and security plans.

The Emperor Domitian added a new twist to Roman literary censorship. He ordered the historian Hermogenes crucified on the grounds that his writings libeled the Emperor. Domitian then cut off distribution of the offensive writings by extending the death sentence to any bookdealer caught selling Hermogenes' text. Later inquisitors, censors, and marketeers perfected the *Domitian strategy*. They realized effective censorship and information management requires control over networks for the distribution of ideas.

But the most comprehensive persecution in polytheist Rome was, paradoxically, directed against alien religious groups: Christians and, to a lesser extent, Jews. Under the reign of Tiberius (who said the gods should take care of their own business), Jesus Christ was crucified by order of the procurator Pontius Pilate. Before his death, Jesus urged his followers to scatter throughout the world and seek converts in his name. He concluded a parable by admonishing his disciples, "Compel them to come in." By Nero's time many Christian proselytes were active in Rome. Tacitus called the capital of the period "the common asylum which receives and protects whatever is impure, whatever is atrocious."[28] But even in "the common asylum," the ways of the Christians were so alien that the followers of Jesus stood out as extremists for their "hatred of humankind" (Tacitus).

When the great fires of Rome gutted ten of its fourteen quarters, suspicion fell upon the head of the mad Emperor. Rumors circulated that he had burned his own capital as an amusement. In order to divert criticism, Gibbon tells us, Nero found it necessary to invent some fictitious criminals. He seized upon the Christians as ideal scapegoats and persecuted them unmercifully. According to Tacitus:

> They died in torments, and their torments were embittered by insult and derision. Some were nailed on crosses; others sewn up in the skins of wild beasts and exposed to the fury of dogs; others again, smeared over with combustible materials, were used as torches to illuminate the darkness of night.[29]

After Nero's orgy of blood-letting, the Christians of Rome were apparently left to pursue their curious ways in relative peace. As Gibbon notes, "it is evident that the effect, as well as the cause, of Nero's persecution, were confined to the walls of Rome; that the religious tenets of the Galilaeans, or Christians, were never made a subject of punishment, or even of inquiry; and that, as the idea of their suffering was, for a long time, connected with the idea of cruelty and injustice, the moderation of succeeding princes inclined them to spare a sect oppressed by a tyrant whose rage had been usually directed against virtue and innocence."[30]

During the period from Nero to Domitian, the population of Christians multiplied rapidly. So much so that Domitian took measures against proselyzation of Roman citizens because he objected to what he perceived as the exclusiveness and intolerance of the alien beliefs of Christians. Trajan declared the profession of Christian beliefs a capital offense. The Roman authorities apparently hoped these prohibitions would be a sufficient deterrent because they were very casual about enforcing their terms. Thus, for example, the accused could avoid punishment by recanting, lying, or leisurely vacating the jurisdiction. But Christians proved intractable.

Nevertheless full-scale persecutions were not undertaken until the closing years of the reign of Diocletian (284–313). Gibbon describes Diocletian as "averse to the effusion of blood": a reluctant inquisitor who assumed the role only as a result of the insistent urgings of Galerius, "the first and principle author of the persecution."[31] He maintains that initial Roman tolerance of Christians contributed to the severity of the Diocletian persecutions. For unlike the texts of Labienus, Cremutius Cordus, Verjinto, and Hermogenes, "The copies as well as the versions of Scripture were already multiplied in the empire, that the most severe inquisition could no longer be attended with any fatal consequences; and even the sacrifice of these volumes which, in every congregation, were preserved for public use, required the consent of some treacherous and unworthy Christians."[32] Therefore Christians and churches were burned instead of books.

Both J.D. Bury and Max Weber embrace the metaphor of "a polytheism of gods" as a talisman against intellectual intolerance. If they are correct, how can this terrible incongruity in the behaviors of practicing polytheists be explained?

To my knowledge, Weber did not directly answer the question. Bury borrowed his answer from Edward Gibbon, who locates the genesis of the polytheists' intolerance in the Gordian Knot that all thoughtful defenders of freedom of expression must sooner or later confront: *Tolerance is achieved through intolerance of the intolerant. Or to put the paradox in different terms: 'Free speech' is achieved by censoring the censors.* In Gibbon's words:

> A reason has been assigned for the conduct of the emperors toward the primitive Christians, which may appear the more specious and probable as it is drawn from the acknowledged genius of Polytheism. It has already been observed that the religious concord of the world was principally supported by the implicit assent and reverence which the nations of antiquity expressed for their respective traditions and ceremonies. It might therefore be expected that they would unite with indignation against any sect or people which should separate itself from the communion of mankind, and, claiming the exclusive possession of divine knowledge, should distain every form of worship except its own as impious and idolatrous. The rights of tolerance were held by mutual indulgence: they were justly forfeited by a refusal of the accustomed tribute.[33]

Gibbon maintains that the polytheists reluctantly tolerated Jews in spite of their exclusiveness because the Jews were members of a 'nation' persevering in the sacred traditions of their ancestors. But this tolerance was not extended to members of the Christian 'sect' because, "They [Christians] dissolved the sacred ties of custom and education, and presumptuously despised whatever their fathers had believed as true or had reverenced as sacred."[34]

Gibbon, of course, also points out that later accounts of the persecutions are greatly exaggerated. Relying on testaments of Diocletian's contemporaries, he calculates that during the ten years of actual persecutions fewer than two thousand Christians were martyred. He maintains that, "it must still be acknowledged that the Christians, in the course of their own internecine dissensions, have inflicted far greater severities on each other than they had experienced from the

zeal of infidels." If Grotius is to be believed, the number of Protestants executed in a single province and a single reign (100,000 in
the Netherlands under Charles V) far exceeded the toll of three
centuries of Roman animosity toward Christians.[35]

vi

Sacred and Secular Record Keepers

Gibbon defends the authority of his revision of Church history by
pointing out that, "The sectaries of a persecuted religion, depressed
by fear, animated with resentment, and perhaps heated by enthusiasm, are seldom in a proper temper of mind calmly to investigate,
or candidly to appreciate, the motives of their enemies, which often
escape the impartial and discerning view even of those who are placed
at a secure distance from the flames of persecution."[36] Gibbon accurately describes the motives of the 'sectaries' of Christian history.
Indeed the Church of Rome forthrightly admitted that the texts placed
under its *imprimatur* consisted of Apologetics and Propaganda. It
drew lines clearly. The books of its enemies were forbidden: proscribed as heretical, immoral, pernicious.

The Roman Church did not always keep complete field notes. It
did not always file accurate reports of the numbers of souls prema-
turely dispatched to the next world through inquisition, crusade, or
conquest. But it did keep extraordinarily complete bibliographic records. These records facilitated supervision of the faithful. They also
indirectly advanced the dialectic of protest. In 1627 the anti-papist
Thomas James described the *Index* as an indispensable guide to the
medieval literature of protest. In *A Treatise on the Corruption of
Scripture, Councils, and Fathers by the Prelates, Pastors, and Pillars
of the Church of Rome, for the Maintenance of Poetry and Irreligion*,
he wrote:

> *Indices Expurgatorii* invaluable as records of the literature of the doc-
> trines and opinions obnoxious to Rome . . . Their *Indices Expurgatorii*
> are very good commonplace books and repertories (for that use we
> make of them) by help of which we may presently find what any author
> by them censured has uttered against the vulnerable parts of the Cath-
> olic system. In these *Indices* we are directed to the book, the chapter,

and line where anything is spoken against any superstition or error of
Rome; so that he who has the *Indices* cannot want testimonies against
Rome.[37]

James's *Treatise* was addressed to the curators of the Bodleian Library
(where Gibbon did much of his research a century and a half later).
It was intended as a reader's guide to works acquired and preserved
in their unexpurgated editions. True to *the Tacitean principle*, the
Indices served to keep alive a number of important works (as well
as a substantial amount of trivia) which would have otherwise van-
ished from the historical record without a trace.

The censorship system of the Roman Church was harsh and authoritarian. But its parameters were crystal clear. There were no
attempts to disguise its interests. No claims of 'impartiality.' The
Decameron was condemned because it contained offensive references
to ecclesiastics. When the sexual adventurers in Boccaccio's stories
were changed from nuns to noble ladies, from monks to conjurers,
and from abbesses to countesses, the book was passed and published
in authorized editions. There is nothing mysterious about the 'from'
and the 'to' of Christian purifications of texts.

But Gibbon's work also has a 'from' and a 'to.' Flames of persecution also cast an afterglow on its pages. Gibbon's 'from' is an
attempt to revive Renaissance humanism. It is a protest against
orthodoxy, against the Roman Church's violent suppression of all
winds of diversity in Western culture whether Polytheist, Pagan,
Gnostic, Agnostic, Humanist, or Protestant. This 'from' can be
deciphered through Gibbon's heavy irony ('praise that blames'
and 'blame that praises'); and more directly by virtue of the fact
that *The Decline and Fall of the Roman Empire* was placed on
the *Index* in 1783 and was never removed. The 'to' of Gibbon's
work was Enlightenment.

vii

The Golden Age of Censorship: The Index Librorum Prohibitorum

The Golden Age of Censorship was born when the followers of the
Christian sect "erected the triumphant banner of the cross on the

ruins of the [Roman] Capital."[38] When Christian zeal for proselytizing combined with Roman genius for administration and record keeping, the responsibilities of the offices of censors increased enormously. Where Cato and the other early Roman Censors merely counted and credentialled citizens for participation in the public forum, ecclesiastical censorship also undertook supervision and surveillance of private thoughts and extended its authority beyond the grave.

The radical separation of clergy and laity in the early Christian Church had no precedent among the Greeks and Romans. Indeed the polytheists often treated their gods more casually than Christians were allowed to treat their priests. Latter-day evangelical Christians would see the Roman hierarchical structure as a betrayal of Jesus' intent. But if historical precedent counts, it suggests that Jesus Himself was the author of the hierarchical authority of the Church. As an heir of the House of David, Jesus was a carrier of the traditions of Moses, the lawgiver. He established the priestly class of the new church by selectively recruiting Apostles who were required to forsake all earthly commitments and swear absolute allegiance to His cause. Moreover Jesus set the terms of Christian exclusiveness through the sacrament of Baptism.

The apostle Paul provided Christianity with a Scriptural warrant for censorship. In Acts (19:19), for example, Paul endorsed book-burning as an act of faith. He praised the converts at Ephesus because they surrendered books worth fifty thousand pieces of silver to be burnt in the purifying fires of orthodoxy. In renouncing false gods and the magical arts, the Ephesians affirmed their faith *and* enhanced the authority of the clergy.

Books, particularly unauthenticated versions of the Gospels, severely challenged the consolidation of Church authority in early Christendom. The first official act of Church censorship is reported to have taken place in 150 A.D. at Ephesus, where *Acti Pauli* was condemned and prohibited. George Putnam, author of the authoritative two-volume work, *The Censorship of the Church of Rome and Its Influence upon the Production and Distribution of Literature* (1906), contended that *Acti Pauli*, a history of the life of Paul, was suppressed because it was inauthentic.[39] However, Joseph McCabe, a vehement critic of the Church (and of Putnam), maintained in his *The History and Meaning of the Catholic Index of Forbidden Books* (1931) that the motive of this first censorship, like so many subsequent Church censorships, was to consolidate and reinforce ecclesiastic authority. McCabe maintains,

The treatise itself, let me say, is not at all erotic, but it does represent the virgin Thecla as holding a very prominent position in the early Church, and that is why the bishops attempted to suppress it. The first authentic act of censorship was in the interest of the masculine monopoly of offices in the growing Church.[40]

Book-burnings and proscriptions were also used to suppress the Gnostic 'schism.' The Gnostics were learned Neo-Platonists, authors of hundreds of texts, including the *Gospel of Thomas*, the *Apocryphon* (Secret Book) *of John, The Gospel of Philip, The Gospel of Mary*, and others. The Gnostics revered Jesus Christ but traced a path to salvation through scholarship and self-knowledge, *gnosis* or insight. Like *Acti Pauli*, but unlike orthodox Judaism and Christianity, much Gnostic scholarship empowered a female principle in the Godhead. The systematic purge of the Gnostics was well under way by 180 A.D. when Bishop Irenaeus of Lyons wrote a five-volume treatise, *The Destruction and Overthrow of Falsely So-called Knowledge*. Irenaeus condemned Gnosticism as "an abyss of madness and of blasphemy against Christ." In 220, Hippolytus also condemned Gnosticism as a "wicked blasphemy of the heretics." With Emperor Constantine's conversion in the fourth century, possession of the books of the Gnostics became a crime as well as a heresy.[41]

The early Church's response to Gnosticism exemplifies the dual edge of the *imprimatur* of power. *Ephesian motives* can be sincerely grounded in the desire to preserve the integrity of the epistemological warrant of a system of authority, in this case the authorized Gospels. Indeed sincere motives are the most efficient engines of power. Viewed as an expression of the duality of *Ephesian motives*, the facts of early Christian censorship appear less sinister. Suppressions of the texts of the Gnostics, Porphyry's paganism, and Origen's heterodoxy were attempts to both preserve the doctrinal purity of Jesus' monotheism *and* consolidate the authority of the priestly class. Suppressions of the texts on Thecla and *The Gospel of Mary* were attempts to both preserve the integrity of Jesus' teachings on the secondary role of women in the Temple *and* consolidate the authority of the priestly class. Suppressions of the texts of the Ephesians and the Roman mathematician Eunomius were attempts to both preserve the singularity of Jesus' miracles by distancing them from the performances of magicians and astrologers *and* measures to consolidate the authority of the priestly class. It is not a matter of relativism, but rather of the necessity for all power to be secured by a canon of knowledge (and for all canons of knowledge to be secured by power). The fires at Ephesus and the purges of the Gnostics demonstrate that Christianity was both a triumph of knowledge (monotheistic orthodoxy) *and* a deadly blow to knowledge (polytheistic heterodoxy).

A single text, the Bible, contained the canon of knowledge securing early Christendom. This was not a triumph for literacy. Under other circumstances it might have been. But in a context in which clergy and laity were so clearly stratified in both the eyes of God and man, it was perhaps inevitable that ecclesiastics would monopolize access to the sacred text.

I am not suggesting that literacy was the norm in the ancient world. It was the norm for only a small minority of elites: inhabitants of cities favored by the hereditary qualifications necessary for citizenship. At least among the early proselytizers, qualifications of birth were dissolved. Christianity embraced the masses and the masses were illiterate. Thus the hierarchy not only established a monopoly over access to the sacred text, it also secured a near-monopoly over all texts. The literate could follow texts of the Mass in church but even this learned elite was required to swear fealty to ecclesiastical interpretations of these texts. Thus, Putnam notes, until the invention of print:

> For the space of fifteen centuries, the education of the people had remained almost exclusively under the direction of the Church. The faithful believers (and unbelievers were but few) had accepted their entire intellectual sustenance at the hands of the priests. The instruction given at the parish school instituted by the Church was almost entirely oral, although some use was made of written alphabet tables and of written psalters with musical notations.
>
> The instruction for those who took up higher branches of study, students who were for the greater part destined for the Church, was naturally, during the manuscript period, carried on by the priests, not only because few others possessed anything that could be called scholarship, but also because it was in the collections of the monasteries (the *armaria*) that the requisite manuscripts could be found... The association of education and intellectual training with the Church is in fact fairly indicated by the use of the term "cleric."[42]

The oral tradition of the Roman Church had little in common with the oral tradition of Socratic dialogues. If it has an analogy in Athenian history, it is in Plato's Ideal State where all knowledge is organized around a central model of social control. The Christian oral tradition emanated from one source: one supreme authority, a written text carefully guarded and interpreted by a clerical elite.

Consequently the first lists of forbidden books issued by Innocent I (405) and Galasius (496) were not apolitical (as Putnam claims). These foreunners of the *Index* are almost entirely concerned with 'authenticity': with suppressing errant gospels. Similarly the papal documents issued at periodic intervals throughout the Middle Ages proscribing unauthorized gospels, lives of saints, and theoretical ideas or liturgical practices are not apolitical (as Burke claims).[43] But neither are these censures *only political* (as McCabe claims). For they are *constitutive as well as regulatory*: articles of faith as well as articles of condemnation. They define the limits, mark the boundaries, identify the heretics, and tell the faithful who they are and what they must do.

viii

Print: Challenge to the Oral Traditions of Catholic Authority

Print destroyed the Church's monopoly over texts. Books permitted lay access to the totem of sacred words; and reading, without priestly supervision, empowered heterodox interpretations of the Scriptures.

The Inquisition was the Church's response to this profound challenge to its system of power-knowledge. But neither faith nor fire could contain the "winged words" made possible by Gutenberg's press. The Inquisition gave birth to a dangerous but highly profitable clandestine book trade which reaffirmed the salience of the Tacitean principle: the appeal of forbidden fruit.

The Inquisition failed to contain the power of the press, but it almost succeeded in destroying the Church. The suppression of all seeds of heterodoxy within the Church led to internecine battles and corruption on a scale that even the most vehement enemy could not have anticipated. In 1453, Aeneas Sylvius described the moral rot of Christendom:

> Whether I look upon the deeds of princes or of prelates I find that all have sunk, all are worthless. There is not one who does right, in no one is there pity or truth. There is no recognition of God upon earth; you are Christians in name, but you do the work of heathens. Excretion and falsehood and slaughter and theft and adultery are spread among

you, and you add blood to blood. . . . you are either swollen with pride, or rapacious with avarice, or cruel in wrath, or livid with envy, or incestuous in lust, or unsparing in cruelty. There is no shame in crime, for you sin so openly and shamelessly that you seem to take delight in it.[44]

Sylvius was a worldly adventurer, not an ascetic. Moreover, as Henry Lea reports, this kind of testimony is too prevalent in the historical archives and too uniform to be dismissed on the assumption that it only represents the disenchantment of puritanism.[45]

The harm done by censuring and burning books pales—is trivialized—by the far greater evil the Inquisition perpetrated upon the people of Europe. But that is the thread our narrative traces on the assumption that book-burnings are not only surrogates but also preludes to persecutions.

When the institutionalization of the Inquisition began in the twelfth century, books and readers were scarce. But prohibitions were not. Literacy spread as the Inquisition progressed "from scaffold to scaffold." The Inquisitors saw themselves as guardians of authenticity: defenders of the Truth of the Sacred Text. Their official trust was eradication of error: elimination of false testaments, oral or written. It was therefore predictable that the Inquisitors would seek and secure considerable control over the "flying leaves" that were capable of compounding error on a scale previously unknown.

The documents of ecclesiastical censorship issued during the Inquisition retained the harshness of the Domitian strategy. It punished distributors as well as producers. However, the Inquisition extended and refined methods for surveillance and control over distribution networks. The following selection represents the escalation of the battle against books:

1231:   *Decree of Gregory IX*: Condemns Aristotle's *Libri Naturales* until expurgated.

1239:   *Degree of Gregory IX*: Orders all copies of the *Talmud* burned.

1325:   *Bull of John XXII*: Orders all writings on conjuring and exorcism destroyed.

1467:   *Decree of Innocent VII*: Orders all books submitted to local Church authorities for inspection before release for general reading. A license to publish *(Imprimatur)* followed by the name of the local Ordinary (usually the bishop) must be printed in each book.

1479:   *Decree of Sextus V*: The Rector of the University of Cologne is ordered to impose the penalties of the Church upon all who print, sell, or read heretical works.

1486:   *Edict of Berthold, Archbishop of Mayence*: No translations from Greek, Latin, or any other books in the vernacular, may be printed without prior approval.

1487:   *Bull of Innocent VII*: Books are recognized as constituting a grave danger to society. Alliances are to be formed between Church and political authorities to suppress unbelief arising from natural science, philosophy, and Protestantism.

1516:   *Decree of the Lateran Council*: Censorship strictures of Innocent VII are to be universally applied.

1521:   *Edict of Worms*: Political and Church authority in Germany unite to impose imperial censorship to suppress heresy, reformation, and treason.

1543:   *Edict of the Inquisitors-General*: All heretical literature is to be suppressed. All book-dealers in Italy are prohibited under penalty of excommunication, fine, or other punishments, to sell or possess any books tainted by heresy. All stocks, present and future, must be inspected and approved before they can be sold. Similar prohibitions apply to printers. The Inquisitor of Ferrara and Bologna is to inspect all printing-offices, book-shops, libraries, churches, convents, and private homes, and destroy all heretical books. The name of anyone who refuses to cooperate is to be reported.

1545:   *Index of the Inquisition of Rome*: Published first list of prohibited books and authors.

1545:   *Council of Trent*: Began eighteen years of deliberations to produce a comprehensive plan for the control of literature.

1550:   *Bull of Pope Julius III*: All permissions and dispensations given to scholarly ecclesiastics are withdrawn.

1555:   *The Inquisition of Rome*: Orders the confiscation of copies of the Talmudic books from the houses of Jews, and subsequently orders all copies burned.

1564:   *Trintine Index*: Comprehensive list of prohibited books issued under Papal authority. Becomes the model for all future indexes.

1596: *Decree of the Roman Inquisition*: The cargoes of all incoming ships are to be inspected for heretical works.

Multiply these strictures by several thousand. Add to the equation the fact that parish priests, bishops, cardinals, inquisitors, the Vatican and its councils, as well as secular authorities in every jurisdiction, were each entitled to issue independent orders of censure. Only then does the awesome machinery of censorship that held all Europe in its grip at the eve of the Reformation become visible.

Nevertheless, the collapse of the hegemony of the Roman Church did not bring an end to the terror produced by ecclesiastical censure. In his history of the *Index, Der Index der Verbotenen*, Joseph Hilger (a Jesuit) claims that the birth of Lutheranism (like the birth of the Holy Roman Church) was celebrated with massive book-burnings. This time texts bearing the *imprimatur* of Rome made up the tinder.[47] (Hilger's tale may be apocryphal?) But the same Martin Luther who vehemently defended the right of individual inquiry also shared the Papal conviction that the authority of Scriptures must be protected from heresy. As early as 1525 he invoked the assistance of censorship regulations in Saxony and Brandenberg to suppress the "pernicious doctrines" of the Anabaptists and Zwinglians; and sought the co-operation of the Protestant princes in instituting censorial machineries in all the Protestant states. Melanchthon, Calvin, and Zwingli subsequently enforced censorial controls that were far more restrictive than any instituted by Rome or by Luther. Anabaptists, Mennonites, Schwenckfeldians, Weigelians, and Socinians immediately joined the fierce competition for protesting souls and for the censorial power to contain their protest.

ix

Malleus Maleficarum: The Encyclopedia of Witch-Hunters

The invention of the printing press, which facilitated the scientific revolution of Copernicus, Galileo, Kepler, and Newton, also had a dark side. Print made possible rapid communication of diabolical ideas as well as progressive ideas. Publication of *Malleus Maleficarum*

(The Hammer of Witches), written in 1486 by the Dominican inquisitors Heinrich Kramer and Jacob Sprenger, was responsible for the widespread dissemination of 'the witch craze' of late medieval Europe. Trevor-Roper affirms:

> Whatever allowance we may make for the mere multiplication of evidence after the discovery of printing, there can be no doubt that the witch craze grew, and grew terribly, after the Renaissance. Credulity in high places increased, its engines of expression were made more terrible, more victims were sacrificed to it. The years 1550–1600 were worse than the years 1500–1550, and the years 1600–1650 were worse still. Nor was the craze entirely separable from the intellectual and spiritual life of those years. It was forwarded by the cultivated popes of the Renaissance, by the great Protestant Reformers, by the saints of the Counter-Reformation, by the scholars, lawyers, and churchmen of the age of Scaliger and Lipsius, Bacon and Grotius, Berulle and Pascal.[48]

In Europe, persecution of witches antedates Christendom. Anthropologists see European witchcraft as analogous to witchcraft in contemporary pre-literate societies. However, historians point out that by the time of the European witch-craze, the political organization, family structure, and educational traditions of Europe were significantly different from those in other parts of the world.[49] In pre-literate (tribal) societies, persecution of witches is, by definition, a local phenomenon: a communal rite of exorcism. As such, interdictions surrounding witchcraft are embedded in the unique historicity of the tribe: in its own myths, values, and temporal rhythms. In contrast, the de-contextualization of print-grounded medieval European witch-hunting in abstract principle—in the power-knowledge of a system of theoretical discourse. Witch-trials in sixteenth- and seventeenth-century Europe were bureaucratically ordered procedures based upon empirical rules of evidence. Thus Kors and Peters maintain, contra anthropological arguments, that "the problem of European witchcraft demands less the study of magic as pure folklore than the study of the intellectual, perceptual and legal processes by which 'folklore' was transformed into systematic demonology, systematic persecution, and, as both contributing cause and resultant effect, to widespread, absolute, undeviating horror."[50]

Malleus Maleficarum is learned discourse. Arguments are developed logically. Scholarly conventions of evidence are observed, and citations from the relevant literature are invoked. References are drawn not merely from Exodus, Ecclesiastes, Proverbs, Matthew,

Aquinas, St. John Chrysostom, St. Jerome, and Canon Law, but also from case histories of witchery, historical precedents in Greece, Rome, Syria, and Hungary, as well as the testaments of Cato, Seneca, Terence, Cicero, Boethius *and* Socrates. *Malleus Maleficarum* relies upon Aristotelian concepts of teleology, since the Aristotelian worldview is more hospitable to diabolical explanations than Neo-Platonism. Neo-Platonists did not insist on a linear chain of causal events to explain natural phenomenon. They were tolerant of mystery, awe, and wonder.[51] Paradoxically, it was the rigorous naturalism of Aristotelianism—its attempt to purge the world of mystery—that left it vulnerable to diabolicalism. Kieckhefer notes,

> Neo-Platonists might readily accommodate in their worldview the idea of various kinds of mysterious powers, both individual spirits and non-individuated forces, susceptible of human manipulation. But the Aristotelian conception was more parsimonious. It recognized matter and distinguishable spirits, but nothing further that was not a property of a material substance or a spirit. It could not acknowledge the efficacy of preternatural, magical forces except by postulating that they were in the control of spiritual beings, whether angels or devils.[52]

Learned discourses on diabolicalism were put forth by many Aristotelians including the Christian humanist, Thomas Aquinas. Even the deliberations of the Royal Society and the epistemological assumptions of Francis Bacon's scientific methodology were influenced by dogma on diabolicalism.[53]

Malleus Maleficarum is undoubtedly the most malignantly misogynist document ever to attain statutory recognition in Western legal conventions. Yet, the beliefs and practices it formalized are not, as Rossell Hope Robbins contends, merely a fabrication or fiction devised to further the ambitions of theologians and inquisitors.[54] Kieckhefer persuasively demonstrates that while learned knowledge about witches focused and legitimated medieval public perceptions of witches, this learned knowledge incorporated prevailing male folk-wisdom regarding the carnal nature of women.[55] In *Malleus Maleficarum*, the evidences of Scripture and Philosophy were synthesized to *prove* that, "All wickedness is but little to the wickedness of a women."[56] This learned proof exorcised fears of castration, impotence, nocturnal emissions, menses, female orgasm, abortion, midwives, thunderstorms, and natural disasters. Everything that terrified, puzzled, or confounded men—all of the anomalies of nature and society—were imputed to the powers of diabolical women. As the

devil's consorts, witches unambiguously symbolized the inverted figure of the Godhead. Purgation of witches provided the elect of the
cosmological order of scholasticism (males, especially celibate priests)
with congregation through segregation. It legitimated aggression
against "imperfect animals" who resist submission to the Divinely
Ordered authority of men: "And blessed be the Highest Who has so
far preserved the male sex from so great a crime: for since He was
willing to be born and to suffer for us, therefore He has granted to
men this privilege."[57]

Inquisitions of witches differed from trials for heresy in several
respects: (i) after an initial investigation of the charge, inquisitors
usually turned witches over to civil authorities for trial; (ii) the identity
of the accuser was never made known because the witch had supra-
human powers of retaliation; (iii) torture was considered the only
way of eliciting a confession from witches since they were, by nature,
deceptive; (iv) authorities could, in good conscience, use false promises of leniency to encourage a confession because the crime was so
grave; (v) even the repentant were frequently burned because witches
were regarded as evil by nature: the offspring of semen implanted in
their mothers' wombs by Beelzebub.[58]

Because witchcraft was a civil crime, *Malleus Maleficarum* was more
resonant than other sectarian documents. It was regarded as the
authoritative source, the encyclopedia, for the inquisition of witches.
Protestants were as vigilant as Catholics in their enforcements of the
Biblical imperative: "Thou shalt not suffer a witch to live" (Exodus
22:18). Luther affirmed, "I should have no compassion on these
witches; I would burn all of them."[59] John Wesley maintained that
belief in witches is a requisite of belief in the Bible.

Malleus Maleficarum silenced (pre-censored) all opposition to persecution of witches by equating doubts regarding the existence of
witches with heresy. Nevertheless, a few heroic individuals, like John
of Salisbury in the twelfth century, and Fray Lope de Barrientos in
the sixteenth, did raise voices in opposition. But belief in witches
survived well into the 'Age of Reason.' Witches were legally burned
in Europe as late as the 1780s. The number of witches burned at the
stake or hanged between the fourteenth and seventeenth centuries is
a matter of controversy. But historians today generally agree that the
figure is much higher than popularly assumed. Conservative estimates
range between 50,000 and 300,000. Radical feminist scholarship has
produced the astounding figure of nine million.[60]

Even one thousand would have been a horrible toll to exact by ink. *Malleus Maleficarum* is a sobering reminder that the power of early print did not always advance progressive causes. This document is an artifact of a discredited genre of rationalism, not of irrationalism. It displays *in extremis* the double-edge of the *imprimatur* of power. *Malleus Maleficarum* and Galileo's *Dialogo* each express the world-view of medieval scholasticism. They are two faces of the Janus-headed monster which sees by not seeing. Diabolicalism is the dark underside of the paradigm of knowledge (Aristotelian naturalism) which made possible the Galilean enlightenment.

The capacity of *Malleus Maleficarum* to incite the emotions of this writer even after five hundred years is an awesome testament to the power of the pen. And to the relative lack of progress in civilizing relations between the sexes! The fantasies of *Malleus Maleficarum* closely parallel the fantasies conquered by Freudian analysis. They recur in all of their medieval malevolence in contemporary "hard-core" sado-masochistic pornography. The victimization of women in the 'snuff' film, and the purgation of witches, tap a common canker in the heart of medieval and modern sexuality.

X

The Totem of the Text

Ecclesiastical surveillance of texts began in an attempt to establish and secure the paradigm of the Christian faith (the recognized gospels). It culminated in an effort to control all texts, all literacy, all thought, through Inquisition. It ended in pathos: in the moribund attempt to protect twentieth-century readers from the dangerous thoughts of Gibbon, Erasmus, Descartes, Hobbes, Hume, Newton, Voltaire, Heine, Taine, Rousseau, Flaubert, Hugo, Stendhal, Sterne, Acton, Goldsmith, Ranke, Bentham, Milton, Montesquieu, Montaigne, Darwin, Bacon, Locke, Berkeley, Bergson, Kant, Spinoza, Defoe, Pascal, Diderot, Sand, Dumas, Marx, Comte, Spencer, Durkheim, Freud, Gide, and Sartre—thoughts (texts) still proscribed by the *Index* when its administration was suspended by the Second Ecumenical Council in 1967.

The verdict of history, or at least the verdicts of those historians who maintain that church censorship was never successful, can be disputed. They are the new 'clerics,' and their judgments are apologies for the power-knowledge of modernity. If they could be heard, the polytheists, Porphyry, Eunomius, the Gnostics, rustic women, witches, and Albigensians, the Jansenists, anon. and thousands of other nameless martyrs of truth would probably render a different verdict.

As apology, the Roman Church's literary policy was universally successful in the Western world for fifteen centuries, and it still resonates in many quarters throughout the world today. The knowledge of power that this policy provided skeptics and heretics also continues to resonate in Enlightened systems of power-knowledge. The contradictions and corruptions of the medieval Roman Catholic Church provided the groundings for both the Copernican and Protestant revolutions. It shaped the 'prejudices' (re: Gadamer), the portals of openness to new experience, through which critique could resonate.

In our Enlightened age, the Roman Church is often disparaged as anti-intellectual, contemptuous of knowledge. But Redmond Burke's apology—"The Catholic Church always had great respect for books"—cannot be dismissed by anyone seriously interested in the anatomy of power.[61] The authority of the parish priest was secured within oral traditions. But the Roman Church itself was *built upon a book*. Its hierarchical scaffolding came to rest upon limiting access to that Book. Throughout the history of the Church's ascendancy, attempts were made to restrict or prohibit lay-readings of Scriptures. Vernacular Bibles were forbidden. Moreover when members of the laity began to master Latin, the Latinate Bible was proscribed. In pre-literate societies, acts of daring and bravery or accidents of birth secured power. The power of primitive Christianity was secured in words: "In the beginning was The Word." Exegesis was the source, the *mana*, of its power. As the ecclesiastical monopoly ravaged itself with the corruption and hubris of unrestrained power, even the Book upon which the Church's authority was founded became dangerous, accusatory, ironic. The Bible itself secured the protest that empowered the Reformation. With the public houses of Rome crowded with celibate clergy, indulgences for sale on the steps of every church and magnificent treasures of mammon locked within them, all texts became dangerous. As Henry Lea notes, "The *prima facies* was against all books; their innocence had to be proven before their circulation could be allowed and even after this they were still liable at any time to adverse judgment."[62]

What dangers censors and inquisitors must have apprehended in the newly discovered gospel of Socrates which preached consistency between public and private behavior, affirmed the primacy of individual conscience, and celebrated the moral efficacy of public criticism! Greek texts were, by definition, suspect wherever they were not in fact illegal. In some places it was believed that the Greek language was actually an Aesopean invention of subversive scribes: an ingenious form of writing-between-the-lines. Heresbach reported hearing the following admonition in a sermon in Paris in 1540: "A new language has been discovered which they call Greek. Against this you must be carefully on your guard for it is the infant tongue of all heresies."[63] A popular slogan among the intellectual vanguard of the period was, "The Greeks really existed." Whether the Greeks were invention, allegory, heresy, or archive, the censors knew they were dangerous.

Father Burke is right. The Church always had great respect for books. At the height of the Inquisition, the Church undoubtedly had far greater respect for the power of books then does our own age, which has grown weary of the burden of paper. For the hierarchy's monopoly over the power of the Text was the canon of knowledge that secured its fortune. This fortune was threatened by dispersion of exegetical powers. Within this context, book-burnings were not renunciations of the power of words, but affirmations. They were symbolic rites analogous to the transubstantiation of the Eucharist in the Consecration of the Mass. They expelled the pollutions of contaminated ideas and celebrated the purity of the Word. These rites affirmed the totem of texts and the taboo against lay access. Thus while votaries were burning the texts of the Greeks, the best collections of Greek books in Europe were safely sealed behind monastery walls. But in the catacombs of the nascent empire of ink, power, and profit were being illicitly secured through a canon of knowledge that required dispersion of the totem of texts.

CHAPTER FOUR

Diderot and Company

i

The Literary Underground Before the Reformation

Protestantism did not begin when Luther nailed his ninety-five theses to the church door at Wittenberg in 1517. It did not begin when John Wycliffe's bones were exhumed and burned by order of the Council of Constance in 1429. Archives of persecution indicate it began before the cross was permanently secured upon the ruins of the Roman capital. Protest against the absolutism of early Church leaders began with the humanistic ideas and reforms ('heresies') proposed by the Gnostics and the Anti-Nicene fathers. Archives of mercantilism indicate that Protest prospered as illicit trade in the black-market commerce of outlaw *scriptorems*, woodcutters, importers, stationers, bookdealers, and early typographers.

Luther's initiative was dramatic. But it was the quiet engineering genius of the faithful Gutenberg, not Protestant daring, which provided the medium that permitted Luther's theses to fracture the foundations of Christendom. Even Luther professed astonishment at the resonance the "flying leaves" of Wittenberg gave his words.

The underground communications network, which quickly but selectively carried Luther's message to the most receptive souls of Europe, had been carefully laid long before the dawn of the Reformation. The genesis of this network can be traced to the failure of an early innovation in book production, the *pecia* system, and the resulting enfranchisement of secular *scriptorems.*[1]

The secular *scriptorem*, like the early print shop, proved a fertile breeding ground for clandestine activity. The *cartolai* (early stationers) who financed these *scriptorems* recruited the services of an intellectual vanguard: literate lay people not sufficiently enticed by the powers of the Church to enter its service; former (by definition, dissident) monks, notaries, itinerate scholars, men of science who could faithfully render astronomical tables; illuminators, enumerators who could accurately serve tradesmen—and perhaps surreptitiously employed Jews and other non-Christians who preserved a heritage of heterodox scholarship. In short, the *scriptorems* were staffed by the early architects of Pierre Bayle's "Republic of Letters": Protestants, Capitalists, Scientists, and Freethinkers.

Where there is censorship, there is usually clandestine activity. From the time of the suppression of the manuscripts of Protagoras, disgruntled or enterprising scribes copied and preserved censored texts. But this was an individual enterprise in which much was lost, and much of what was preserved was corrupted. However, the establishment of secular *scriptorems* created opportunities for organizing collaborative efforts to subvert censorship. It made available for the first time reliable networks for the production and distribution of suppressed texts.

Little is known about the day-to-day operations of these networks, but there is sufficient evidence available to indicate that in some districts respectable *cartolai* ran two businesses: one serving legitimate institutional needs, the other serving the illegal but steady demand for proscribed works. In some instances the *cartolai*'s illicit trade was barely concealed: ignored by local censors as a result of indifference, tacit consent, bribery, or ignorance. Contemporary accounts suggest that these networks were fairly widespread since proscribed titles were available at competitive prices. These accounts also indicate that the clandestine networks were highly profitable, and that the presence of illicit profits may have been the decisive factor in determining which *scriptorems* would have the capital necessary for conversion to print.

ii

The Typological Revolution: The New Groundings of Knowledge and Censorship

In *Novum Organum*, Francis Bacon observed, printing "changed the appearance and state of the whole world."[2] Print severed the groundings of oral and scribal cultures and secured the guy-wires which continue to support the "typographical culture" today.[3]

The revolutionary significance of this transformation in communication is still not adequately appreciated by historians. Not only did printing advance the cause of Reformation, it also facilitated the dissemination of the ideas of the Renaissance.[4] It changed the very conditions of knowledge. Print provided an unprecedented spur to creativity and synthesis. For the first time the contradictions in existing systems of knowledge as well as the puzzles posed by divergent traditions became readily apparent. Moreover, print made it possible for a scholar to see more books in a few months than earlier scholars had been able to examine in a lifetime of travel. Michael Clapham puts the issue of quantity in dramatic terms: "A man born in 1453, the year of the fall of Constantinople, could look back from his fiftieth year on a lifetime in which about eight million books had been printed, more perhaps than all the scribes of Europe had produced since Constantine founded his city in A.D. 330."[5] In the time it had taken even a careless scribe to produce hastily a few corrupted copies of a manuscript, a printer produced two hundred uniform copies.

Whether or not Gutenberg's backer, Doctor Fust, was the actual prototype of Goethe's Doctor Faust, there is little doubt that the contemporaries of the printer of Mainz perceived his invention as a miraculous knowledge-machine. In 1459, Felix Fabri, prior of the Dominican monastery in Ulm, wrote in his *Historia Suevorum*: "no art that the world has known can be considered so useful, so much to be esteemed, indeed so divine as that which has now, through the Grace of God, been discovered in Mayence."[6] The Vatican was among the earliest purchasers of a mechanical press. The Abbot of Sponheim, Johannes Trithemius, who lavishly sang the praises of the scribal life as the discipline best suited for the organization of monastic life, took his own writings (including the text of *De Laude Scriptorem*) to the press-works of Peter von Freidberg so frequently that one commentator suggests it could have been called the "Sponheim Abbey Press."[7]

Before the middle of the fifteenth century, printers' workshops were unknown anywhere in Europe. By 1500 they could be found in every significant municipal center. As showplaces for the new mechanical technology as well as gathering places for scholars from every discipline, the printers' workshops surpassed the university as a center of learning. The enthusiasm generated by print was contagious. Literacy rates among ordinary people increased rapidly.

The press, which introduced the principle of interchangeable parts centuries before its full industrial portent would be realized, produced a general thrust toward standardization, codification, and rationalization of the various branches of knowledge. Dictionaries, encyclopedias, morphological systems for classifying flora and fauna, uniform weights and measures, systematic accounting procedures, mapping conventions, standardized spellings, and grammatical rules were among the earliest products of this movement. The revolutionary character of these advances can perhaps only be appreciated (especially by members of a generation which is seeing them rendered obsolete by computer retrieval systems) when it is realized that before Gutenberg even scholars frequently did not know the ordinal arrangement of the letters of the alphabet: it was esoteric knowledge with few practical applications in a scribal culture.[8]

Typography modified and rationalized the format of the book. Title pages inscribed with the printer's colophon, standardized margins, and pagination in Arabic numerals were among the most obvious innovations. Titles made indexing possible; enormous increases in output made it necessary.

The card-file and the *Index Librorum Prohibitorum* were both responses to this imperative. The card-file brought order to the chaos of newly burdened libraries. The *Index* was an attempt to impose order upon the newly 'burdened' minds of the faithful (and the not so faithful); an attempt to extend an archaic system of ecclesiastical domination, grounded in the scarcity of the Word, to a new, reified order in which words could literally be produced faster than *any thing*.

To the printer, words are things: arrangements of type. B. Franklin, printer, makes this clear in his *Apology for Printers* (1730):

> ... hence arises the peculiar Unhappiness of that Business, which other callings are no way liable to; they who follow Printing being scarce able to do any thing in their way of getting a Living, which shall not probably give Offence to some, and perhaps to many; whereas the

> Smith, the Shoemaker, the Carpenter, or the Man of any other Trade, may work indifferently for People of all Persuasions, without offending any of them; and the Merchand may buy and sell with Jews, Turks, Hereticks, and Infidels of all sorts, and get Money by every one of them, without giving Offence to the most orthodox, of any sort; or suffering the least Censure or Ill-will on the Account from any Man whatever . . . Printers . . . cheerfully serve all contending Writers that pay them well, without regarding on which side they are of the Question in Dispute . . . Being continually employed in serving all Parties, Printers naturally acquire a vast Unconcernedness as to the right or wrong of Opinions contained in what they print; regarding it only as the Matter of their daily labour . . . [9]

As indulgences had become a commodity in trade for corrupt priest-profiteers, words (including the Word) became a commodity in trade to printers. Gutenberg's first book was a Bible. And the age of incunabula produced more Bibles than any other text. This piety may have served the interests of God. It unquestionably served the interests of the printers! For it irrevocably dispersed the *mana* of the ecclesiastical monopoly of power-knowledge. The immediate beneficiaries of this dispersion were, of course, printers who could count the blessings of the new freedom in cash receivables.

The card catalogue was in perfect harmony with the imperatives of the new, reified order with its "vast Unconcernedness as to the right or wrong Opinions contained." The card catalogue organized things—titles—according to the ordinal arrangement of type in the printer's drawer. As innovative technology of a new system of power-knowledge, it fostered revolutionary advances in science, business, and humanistic scholarship, both directly and serendipitously, for five centuries. In the process, it also helped secure the groundings of social control for the new, reified order of the typographical culture. . . . Could the card catalogue have been the literal prototype of Bentham's Panopticon?

The *Index Librorum Prohibitorum* was, of course, inherently unsuited to the new format. Its *raison d'être* was *concernedness* with the right or wrong of Opinions contained in print. Yet, like the card-file, it also proved to be an enormous incentive to scholarship. But the impact of the *Index* on the emerging system of power-knowledge was circuitous, dialectical. In attempting to force its *imprimatur* upon the new order, the *Index* helped consolidate forces in opposition. It united the outlaw empire of ink: sharpened the cutting edge of its protest, and cleared the way for its ultimate succession to power.

iii

Clandestine Book-Trade after the Appearance of the Index

The provisions of the Lateran Council mandating universal censorship were articulated a year before Luther's revolt. Thus the machinery of enforcement was mobilized under conditions of civil war within the Church, and it assumed a martial character. Similarly, clandestine book trade took on many of the features of later genres of war-profiteering.

The prolonged deliberations at Trent delayed the appearance of the first *Index* until 1564. By then, it was already too late to arrest the Faustian spirit unleashed at Mainz. Putnam affirms:

> ... the authority of the Church was exerted to repress or at least to restrict the operations of the printing-press and to bring printers and publishers under a close ecclesiastical supervision and censorship. It was, however, already too late to stand between the printing-press and the people. Large portions of the community had become accustomed to a general circulation of books and to the use without restriction of such reading matter as might be brought within their reach, and this privilege they were no longer willing to forgo ... Even in Italy, however, the critical spirit was found to be too strong to be crushed out, and from Venice, which became the most important of the Italian publishing centres (because it was the freest from papal control) it proved possible to secure for the productions of the printing press a circulation that was practically independent of the censorship of Rome.[10]

Having lost control over the source of the Word, the Church relied upon Domitian strategy. It sought control over the distribution of words through licensing (*Imprimatur*), prohibition (*Index*), and persecution (*Inquisition*). But this trinity of terror could not extinguish the critical spirit. The *Index* became a reader's guide to the essential literature of Protest: it "provided Protestant firms with a list of profit making titles and free advertising while alerting potential Catholic purchasers to the existence of forbidden fruit."[11] Indeed in 1589 the Church found it necessary to outlaw lay possession of copies of the *Index Librorum Haereticorem* (a catalogue of proscribed titles prepared annually) because booksellers were using it to locate the titles which would be in greatest demand on the illegal market in the coming year. Eventually Protestant publishers took full advantage of the exploitive possibilities by listing the *Index*'s prohibition on the title page below the printer's colophon—the location of the *imprimatur* on Catholic publications.

There were some 'safe' cities like Venice in Catholic states. But generally trade in proscribed titles involved border violations in which printers in the northern Lutheran states made handsome profits from black-market trade in France, Italy, and to a lesser extent Spain and Portugal. But most black-marketeers were not motivated by profit alone. The work was very dangerous. Even in an open city like Venice, dealing in illicit texts was a capital crime. Pietro Longo, a Protestant partisan, was drowned by the Venetian Inquisition in 1588 for importing books from "distant lands." Syndicates organized around family connections (and extended through marriage liaisons) were common, especially in Italy. Sons carried on the work of their fathers. Or, in the absence of heirs, widows continued the tradition. Other cabals were organized around allegiance to secret societies like the Family of Love, the Palatinate, Free Masonry, and Rosicrucians.[12]

The market for forbidden books included nobles, commoners, scholars, and clerics. Titles most in demand in Venice in the sixteenth century included: (1) Bibles, which made up more than half of the trade in illicit literature (presumably the clergy were among the best customers); (2) occult works, especially those of Agrippa; (3) the work of northern humanists like Erasmus and of well-known Italian authors like Machiavelli and Arentino; (4) scientific works; (5) commentaries on the Bible and on Protestant doctrinal works, the most dangerous and most effectively quarantined literature.[13] Although banned titles—save for the texts of Luther, Calvin, et al.,—were plentiful in Venice, Church censorship did slow the presses and lead to excessive reliance on reprints which did not require an *imprimatur*.

In France, censorship of the presses was far more effective. Free thought was kept alive in France during two centuries of police and ecclesiastical control of publication by reverting back to the traditions of clandestine manuscript trade. Even Voltaire's *Épître à Uranie* circulated in handwritten copies for sixteen years before it could be published. Eventually exile presses were established in Protestant states and, until the end of the eighteenth century, France's most prominent writers published abroad.

German printers established presses in Spain as early as 1474. Christopher Columbus was, in fact, a bookdealer by trade. But the

Inquisition virtually destroyed the book trade in both Spain and Portugal. Lea contends that in these countries "the diffusion of intelligence was reduced to a minimum."[14] Even clandestine operations were apparently too dangerous to be profitable. Putnam notes the crippling effect:

> The books that were published during the 16th century, and indeed for a century later, bore everywhere marks of the subjection to which the press and those who wrote for the press were alike reduced. From the abject titlepages and dedications of the authors themselves through the series of certificates collected from their friends to establish the orthodoxy of works that were often as little connected with religion as fairy tales, down to the colophon supplicating pardon for any unconscious neglect of the authority of the Church or for any too free use of classical mythology, we are continually impressed with painful proofs, not only how completely the human mind was enslaved in Spain, but how grievously it had become cramped and crippled by what it had so long borne.[15]

There was, then, nothing approaching uniform enforcement of the provisions of the *Index* or of the terms of Inquisition in Catholic states. And, conversely, not all Protestant states were outposts of free thought. Before the Diet of Worms, publishing prospered in German cities like Frankfurt and Ulm. After Worms, the empire of ink established a stronghold in Holland, where Louis Elsevier's publishing house made available the books of 'outlaws' like Galileo, Scaliger, Hobbes, Pascal, Descartes, and More. But Protestant cities like Zurich and Geneva had censorial regimes as repressive as any Catholic state. Similarly, civil authorities in Protestant states frequently tightened their grip on the presses as soon as Church authorities relaxed theirs. The most famous document of free speech produced during the pre-Enlightenment era, John Milton's *Areopagitica* (1644), was produced in Protestant England; but as protest, not apology.

iv

Irony and Intellect in Exile

Although the critical spirit was kept alive by exile presses and black-market book-trade, it was effectively forced underground in most of

Catholic Europe for two centuries. Universities offered no refuge as they were under tight ecclesiastical control and subject to frequent Inquisitions. To be sure, an occasional Church-affiliated scholar received a dispensation that allowed him access to a limited number of titles in order to pursue his research, but such licenses were very rare. Under the rigid censorship of Inquisition, the public life of the mind atrophied. The esteemed nineteenth-century Oxford scholar and essayist Mark Pattison describes the effect upon humanistic studies:

> If we ask why Italy did not continue to be the centre of the Humanist movement which she had so brilliantly encouraged, the answer is that the intelligence was crushed by the reviviscence of ecclesiastical ideas. Learning is the result of research, and research must be free and cannot co-exist with the claim of the Catholic religion to be superior to enquiry. The French school, it will be observed, was wholly, in fact or in intention, Protestant. As soon as it was decided (as it was before 1600) that France was to be a Catholic country and the University of Paris a Catholic University, learning was extinguished in France. France saw without regret and without repentance the expatriation of her unrivalled scholars. With Scalinger and Saumaise, the seat of learning was transferred from France to Holland.[16]

Scientific ideas were stillborn. Copernicus's death shortly after the first printing of *De Revolutionibus* in 1543 spared him persecution. His work was indexed as heretical and erroneous. In 1615 a general prohibition was issued against all writings relating to Copernican theory or presenting similar ideas. This prohibition was directed primarily against Galileo, who agreed to correct his errors. Publication of Galileo's *Dialogo* was permitted in 1632 on the condition that a Preface be added which described the Copernican theory as a mere play of imagination and not a challenge to Ptolemaic doctrine. *Dialogo* reached a large and receptive audience which had no trouble reading between the lines of the disclaimer. Pope Urban VIII claimed the book made the Church look ridiculous and turned Galileo over to the Inquisitors. The Inquisition found the arguments of *Dialogo*, "foolish, absurd, false in theology, and heretical, because expressly contrary to Holy Scripture." Over a period of sixteen years Galileo was under the direct control of the Roman Inquisition, frequently imprisoned and constantly harassed. In 1633 he was forced to make the following public recantation: "I, Galileo, being in my seventieth year, being a prisoner and on my knees, and before your Eminence, having before my eyes the true Holy Gospel, which I touch with my hands, adjure, curse, and detest the error and heresy of the movement of the earth."[17] The *Index* had also condemned Kepler's *Epitome Astromia Copernicae*. After Galileo's disavowal of "the heresy of the movement of the earth," learned theologians produced Scriptural refutations of Copernican theory as well, which were given wide circulation throughout the Catholic states. In Rome the sun did not stop revolving around the earth until 1822, when the Inquisition granted permission for printing of texts consistent with the principles of modern astronomy. Rome did not suspend the condemnation of Galileo until 1982.

The irony between the lines of Galileo's recantation is characteristic of the dissimulation censored writers of the period used to keep the critical spirit alive. Erasmus had announced a conspiracy of Enlightened thinkers in 1517 when he asserted:

> All over the world, as if on a given signal, splendid talents are stirring and conspiring together to revive the best learning. For what else is this but a conspiracy when all these great scholars from different lands share out work among themselves.[18]

The metaphoric conspiracy described by Erasmus turned into a very real conspiracy shortly after his words were written. The provisions of Trent made all heterodox thinkers 'outlaws' and created a literary underground that stretched across Europe. Conspiracy was required to buy a book or share a scientific idea. Pierre Bayle described the outlaws who engaged in this conspiracy as citizens of the "Republic of Letters." Censors and Inquisitors elected citizens of the new republic. They were pious men, bookish men, occultists, scientists, pornographers, fabulists, exorcists, revolutionaries, rogues, and profiteers—epistemological criminals and cosmological mess-makers united by the ink of heresy.

The language of Aesop became the *lingua franca* of the new republic. Anon. published far more than ever before, as did citizens with eccentric names like Juan Philadelpho of Venice (Jean Crispin of Geneva) and exotic addresses like Utopia, Cosmopolis, and Jericho. Swift, Montesquieu, Montaigne, and Voltaire would join Erasmus and Bayle as laureates of the outlaw language before the end of the republic's exile. And even scientists, like Newton, would express a preference for writing in "a cryptic and complicated manner to discourage ignorant quibblers."[19] The *Eirons* of the exiled empire played a deadly serious game. They used the slippery edges of language to comply with the letter of the law of Inquisition, while boldly defying its spirit. Thus Erasmus, who professed the canon of "Sancte Socrates," praised Folly and packed radical social criticism between the lines of that praise: "I have prais'd Folly, but not altogether foolishly."[20] Censors read Erasmus's praise of folly as frivolous nonsense. However, citizens of the "Republic of Letters," disciples of Aesop and Socrates, easily grasped the sense in the nonsense.

Print shops came to serve as a kind of underground railroad for the exiled republic:

> In the age of religious wars, such print shops represented miniature 'international houses.' They provided wandering scholars with a meeting place, message center, sanctuary and cultural center all in one.[21]

In these international houses, Jews, Turks, Hereticks, and Infidels shared the bread and fish of Katholicks and Fallen-Away Katholicks. And Pietists and Pornographers shared the same bed. Lives were risked, and sometimes lost, for books. Printers become co-conspirators in the criminal plans of their authors. Elsevier assisted Galileo in smuggling *Discourses on Two New Sciences* to Leiden for publication two years after the famous recantation.

Old morals failed. The outlaws had to devise novel codes of conduct to fill awkward silences. Oliver Goldsmith (whose fame, like the fame of Erasmus, Copernicus, Galileo, Kepler, Bayle, Montesquieu, Montaigne, Swift, and Voltaire, was secured in the *Index*) wrote a series of literary letters entitled *Citizens of the World* in which he romanticized exile and cosmopolitan ideals.

The new cosmopolitan ethos fitted the interests of printers. As men of learning, they found it edifying. As businessmen, they found it profitable: a means of expanding markets. In the words of B. Franklin, ambassador, statesman, author, scientist, and printer, they found it "pay(s) them well, without regarding on which side they are of the Question in Dispute."

Cosmopolitanism opened new worlds. It de-sacralized the imperatives of the *ancien régime*. It provided the exiled citizens of the "Republic of Letters" with emancipatory knowledge. It not only facilitated recovery of the Greeks (as anti-Papist power-knowledge), it also encouraged cosmological musings: the world-building of constitutionalism, utopianism, ideologizing. In an age of discovery, tales of strange and exotic lands were eagerly sought, but frequently proscribed by princes and popes. Swift, Goldsmith, Montesquieu, Voltaire, and others brought the language of Aesop to bear upon the travel narrative and thereby translated it into a genre of critique and protest. Cosmopolitanism stimulated markets for the atlases, dictionaries, encyclopedias, and almanacs that print had made possible. B. Franklin, almanacist and revolutionary, D. Diderot, encyclopedist and revolutionary, and F. Voltaire, dictionarist and revolutionary, secured their cosmopolitan systems of power-knowledge in these markets. Cosmopolitanism, like movable type, supports the de-contextualization of communication. It breaks up traditional combinations, and suggests new arrangements. Cosmopolitanism is a present- and future-oriented canon of knowledge: pragmatic and empirical. It makes science possible, desirable, and profitable. This point did not escape B. Franklin, scientist, or D. Diderot, Enlightened tinkerer. Cosmopolitanism makes international monetary exchanges possible, desirable, and profitable. This point did not escape entrepreneurs like Dr. Fust, P. Longo, C. Panckoucke or apologists of capitalism like B. Franklin and A. Smith. Cosmopolitanism also makes daily newspapers possible, desirable, and profitable. This point did not escape the bankers who founded the first newspapers; or B. Franklin, publisher of *The Pennsylvania Gazette*, utilitarian and revolutionary; or K. Marx, editor of the *Rheinische Zeitung*, London correspondent of the *New York Daily Tribune*, materialist, and revolutionary.

V

The Interests of the Areopagites

The interests of the *citizen of the world* are different from the interests of the *City of God*. One of the earliest and most eloquent apologists of the new canon of power-knowledge, John Milton, saw it as anointing a new order of men: Areopagites.

Ares was the Greek god of war. Areopagus is a hill situated at an elevation above Athens. In the ancient city of learning, Areopagus was the site of the meetings of the supreme Tribunal. In Milton's Protestant Utopia, the most gifted citizens—"men of rare abilities and more than common industry"—are chosen by God "not only to look back and revise what hath been taught heretofore, but to gain further and go on some new enlightened steps to the discovery of truth." Milton maintains that these carriers of the Truth must be free of the "iron molds" of censorship which have "bejesuited" free inquiry and suppressed truth: "if it come to prohibiting, there is not aught more likely to be prohibited than truth itself, whose first appearance, to our eyes bleared and dimmed with prejudice and custom, is more unsightly and unplausible than many errors. . . . "[22] In Milton's view, no censors, no licensers, can ever be found who will be qualified to judge their superiors, the Aeropagites. Thus he professes opposition to all prior censorship: all licensing of wordcraft:

> Truth and understanding are not such wares as to be monopolized and traded in by tickets and statutes and standards. We must not think to make a staple commodity of all knowledge in the land, to mark and license it like our broadcloth and our woolpacks.[23]

The blind poet, well-born son of privilege, sees writing as a Promethean communion with Truth (God)—not as a technological advance made possible with movable type; not as a commodity or ware sold only to those who pay well.

On the surface the seventeenth-century aristocrat's defense of Areopagitica appears to celebrate a more 'interest-free' conception of knowledge than that protected by the Philadelphia entrepreneur's *Apology for Printers*. To Milton, Truth and its messengers are sacred. In Franklin's epistemology, the True and the Useful are mongrelized by economics. Franklin's power-knowledge is calculated in cash. But Milton's epiphany is also petition. The anti-Papist pontificates against a second tyranny of ecclesiastics (this time a presbytery of Protestants). Yet, his poesy delivers the Manna of God to poets—to men whose work may be a "dictate of divine spirit"—without any cautions against possibilities of a third tyranny; without any recognition of "the iron molds" that word-masters can *fabulate*.

Where Franklin is a guileless apologist of his trade defending his wares, Milton is more circumspect. He withholds evidence. No reading between the lines is required to determine that the blind are to be admitted to the divinely elected circle of Areopagites; but no Jews, Turks, Katholicks, Hereticks, Commoners, Vernacularists, Tradesmen, or Women can qualify.[24] Some reading between the lines is required to explain why Milton invokes the war-god, Ares. For he does not tell us that he is fresh from battle with the censors. He equivocates: "to what an author this violence hath been lately done, and in what book of greatest consequence to be faithfully published, I could no instance, but shall forbear till a more convenient season."[25] Like Franklin, Milton had interests to protect: literary property rights, a position among his contemporaries, and a reputation for posterity.

Areopagitica (1644) has been plundered, eulogized, and canonized by Milton's epigones, who also have had interests to defend. The *philosophes* used it to help craft a revolution. We use it to feather our own nests: to protect our *right* to freedom of inquiry and to the jobs and royalties that are its rewards in a capitalist society. We read Milton (as we read Franklin) selectively. We suppress (censor) awareness that Milton's petition can also be read as personal and sectarian pleading: as a lobby for special privileges for authors who belonged to certain Puritan churches. We do not like to be reminded that in "Of True Religion, Heresie, Schism, and Toleration" (1673), Milton maintained that Latin "which the common people understand not" would be a solution for having issues "discust among the Learned only."[26] Or, that this apostle of Liberalism served as a Censor to Cromwell's government. We are puzzled, but forgiving. We have become accustomed to posturing and pretense (hubris).

We are more baffled by the frankness of the author of "Fart Proudly": by his crass (uncensored) apologetics for acquisitiveness— even though we live in a thoroughly acquisitive culture. Perhaps "our eyes are bleared and dimmed with [the] prejudice and custom" of an age saturated with the disclaimers and dis-information of the advertisings of monopolists? My double-reading of *Areopagitica* views it as an eloquent critique of official censorship and an elitist apology for intellectual privilege.

The canon of knowledge that secured the power of the *philosophes* and *ideologues* was more cosmopolitan (less sectarian) than that defended by Milton, and more pretentious (less frank) than that celebrated by the Philadelphia businessman. Yet there are continuities. Like Milton, the Encyclopedists and their followers believed Areopagites were the vanguard of a new world order. Thus Diderot's first and primary collaborator, D'Alembert, described the calling of the new priesthood of the word in these terms:

> Happy are men of letters, if they recognise at last that the surest way of making themselves respected is to live united and almost shut up among themselves; that by this union they will come without any trouble to give the law to the rest of the nation in all affairs of taste and philosophy; that the true esteem is that which is awarded by men who are themselves worthy of esteem. . . . As if the art of instructing and enlightening men were not, after the too rare art of good government, the noblest portion and gift in human reach.[27]

In theory, at least, Jews, Hereticks, Turks, and Katholicks, who were qualified by talent and favored by environment, could be included in the secular priesthood of *philosophes*. For, like Franklin, the ideo-logical architects of the French Revolution were materialists; advo-cates of the rights of man and rights of property. Franklin defended the advantages of cosmopolitanism directly: it pays well. The En-cyclopedists defended it ideologically invoking freedom, equality, and brotherhood. They ennobled it and themselves.

Diderot, personally, was motivated by opposition to persecution, not profit. He apparently earned only 60,000 *livres* from his twenty years work on the *Encyclopédie*—as much, according to Voltaire, as an army contractor could make in three days. But the "Encyclopédie Wars" were not Diderot's first battles with the Censors. Prior to his association with the project, the Parliament of Paris had ordered one of his books burned (*Pensées philosophiques*), and had imprisoned him for another (*Lettre sur les aveugles*). Diderot saw himself as a Martyr of Reason—a modern Socrates:

> ... to abandon the work is turning our back on the breach, and to do
> precisely what the villains who persecute us desire.... Do what be-
> comes men of courage,—despise our foes, follow them up, and take
> advantage, as we have done, of the feebleness of our censors ... I am
> over forty. I am tired out with tricks and shufflings. I cry from morning
> till night for rest, rest ... One must work, one must be useful, one
> owes an account of one's gifts, etcetera, etcetera. Be useful to men!
> ... there is much difference between the philosopher and the flute-
> player ... The Athenians were never wickeder than in the time of
> Socrates, and perhaps all that they owe to his existence is a crime the
> more. That there is more spleen than good sense in all this, I admit—
> and back I go to the *Encyclopédie*.[28]

Others associated with the *Encyclopédie* used more 'good sense' than Diderot in their practical applications of materialism. Voltaire's protest was as profitable as his army contracting. He published abroad and skillfully manipulated the Tacitean principle to his commercial advantage in the clandestine markets of Paris. Le Breton, Diderot's publisher and sponsor of the project, furtively arranged to have his printers expurgate any passages in the last ten volumes that might offend the censors in order to avoid any further interruptions in the flow of profits. And, like official censors, these pioneers of market censorship committed the original manuscript and proof-sheets to the cleansing rites of the stove. When Panckoucke took over Le Breton's rights to the *Encyclopédie*, he planned to bowdlerize, reprinting in order to gain permission to sell the *Encyclopédie* in 1768. Nine years later, when controversy promised to make the *Encyclopédie* the best-selling book of the century, Panckoucke scrapped plans for a revised edition and entered into negotiations in which he bartered his monopoly over printing rights for a larger cut of the subscriptions. Business historians regard the Panckoucke management of the *Encyclopédie* as one of the great success sagas of early modern capitalism:

> ... the quarto *Encyclopédie* sent repercussions into the remotest sectors of the economy. For it to come into being a whole world had to be set in motion: ragpickers, olive growers, financiers, and philosophers collaborated to create a work whose corporeal existence corresponded to its intellectual message ... Its publishers probably spent too much time calculating costs and profits to entertain such lofty thoughts. The *Société Typographique* estimated the total revenue of the enterprise at 2,454,092 *livres*, the total cost at 1,117,354 *livres*: a return of one hundred twenty per cent on expenditures. No wonder they considered this affair the most beautiful ever to be done in publishing ... [29]

Diderot was a poor businessman: either unversed in contractual law or lacking in personal acquisitiveness. Nevertheless he had a keenly developed sense of literary property rights. Grimm reports that Diderot never forgave Le Breton and repeatedly reviled the publisher for his treachery:

> For years, you have been basely cheating me. You have massacred, or got a brute to massacre, the work of twenty good men who have devoted to you their time, their talents, their vigils, from love of right and truth, from the simple hope of seeing their ideas given to the public, and reaping from them a little consideration richly earned, which your injustice and thanklessness have now stolen from them for ever ... [30]

The Diderot–Le Breton alliance was negotiated under royal printing privileges which ensured state censorship and provided the crown with a small share in printing revenues.

Copyright law was an extension of censorship law. Early copyrights were printing rights.[31] They provided printers, not Areopagites, with exclusive (monopoly) rights to literary properties. Copyrights were designed to protect capital investments from piracy *and* free competition. Copyright law left printers free to make their own deals with authors: to buy them off if they could. Areopagites like Macaulay bitterly opposed introduction of copyright laws as prostitution of God-given talents. But the penny novelists of Grub Street, lacking Macaulay's independent means, eagerly took their payoffs. Copyright law was still in its infancy during the Diderot–Le Breton conflict, but nothing in the emerging conventions justifies Diderot's conception of author's rights. Diderot's view was more consistent with the logic of royal patronage systems than the logic of capital. Rights of capital are easier to measure and parcel than rights of genius. And rights of capital have naturally prevailed in bourgeois courts. The law was on Le Breton's side even in pre-Revolutionary France.

But few publishers today would regard Le Breton's *coup* as an exemplar of self-censorship. Diderot's dilemma reflects a basic contradiction in modern society's Culture Industry. Publishers (and the state) do require the services of Areopagites. But Areopagites resist *total* subservience to the logic of capital. Market censorship cannot always constrain them. They are frequently obstreperous. They tend to believe their own press releases: that genius has a logic of its own. They pay occasional homage to *Sancte Socrates* and to the priesthood of Milton, D'Alembert, and Diderot. Most require special handling, and some command generous salaries.

My double-reading of the interests of the Encyclopedists suggests that Diderot was a Martyr of Reason *and* a Martyr of Capital; and that the "Encyclopedie Wars" were effective revolutionary actions against the Church-State monopoly of censorship powers as well as an elitist apology for Areopagite privilege.

vi

Diderot and Company

Areopagites claim that books caused both the French Revolution and Russian Revolution. This is undoubtedly a self-serving exaggeration of the power of the pen. Human misery, crop failures, recession, carnivals, royal hubris, personal opportunism, careful planning, fortuitous events, grand ideals, and arbitrary censors have places within the vocabulary of motives which can be plausibly linked to the storming of the Bastille. Within this vocabulary, however, incidents related to publication, public reception, and suppression of Diderot's *Encyclopédie* do play an important role.

The *Encyclopédie* project envisioned by Le Breton was little more than a French translation and adaptation of Ephraim Chambers's

1727 English *Cyclopaedia*. However, in Diderot's *salon*, the project was transformed into a grand philosophical undertaking. All the finest writers of France contributed. Diderot and Company saw their task as nothing less than reconstruction of the structure of human consciousness. Voltaire effused: "Men are on the eye of a great revolution in the human mind, and it is to you [Diderot and D'Alembert] to whom they are most of all indebted for it."[32]

As soon as the first volume was delivered to subscribers, French authorities recognized the subversive character of the project. The "Preliminary Discourse" profoundly challenged the prevailing cosmology. It discredited both orthodox Thomism and neo-orthodox Cartesianism, and asserted that the only viable alternative was the scientific world-view outlined by Locke and Newton. The Encyclopedists maintained that traditional learning amounted to little more than prejudice and superstition. Thus they called for an irrevocable break with the past. This breach was described as an essential precondition to Enlightenment and Progress. Darnton succinctly summarized the radical politics of the *Encyclopédie*:

> ... the book was dangerous. It did not merely provide information about everything from A to Z; it recorded knowledge according to philosophic principles expounded by D'Alembert in the Preliminary Discourse. Although he formally acknowledged the authority of the church, D'Alembert made it clear that knowledge came from the senses and not from Rome or Revelation ... Thus everything man knew derived from the world around him and the operations of his own mind. The *Encyclopédie* ... rearranged the cognitive universe and reoriented man within it, while elbowing God outside ... beneath the bulk of the *Encyclopédie*'s twenty-eight folio volumes and the enormous variety of its 71,818 articles and 2,885 plates lay an epistemological shift that transformed the typography of everything known to man.[33]

The *Encyclopédie* was an immediate success among the intellectual vanguard of Paris. Subscriptions rose with each succeeding volume. Civil and religious authorities denounced Diderot, D'Alembert, Voltaire, Rousseau, and Buffon as architects of a clandestine league of revolutionaries committed to undermining public tranquility and conspiring to overthrow society.

Within a year of its publication (1751), Volume I was ordered suppressed, and the printing of Volume II was prohibited by a decree of the King's Council. This censorship was intended to mollify the Jesuits, who were apparently jealous of Diderot's success. Diderot was compelled to turn over all the papers, proof-sheets, and plates in his possession. The Jesuits intended to produce the succeeding volumes of the *Encyclopédie*. However, as Grimm notes, they were unable to take possession of Diderot's brain, and consequently they were unable to continue the project. With public interest piqued, the King's Council relented. They appealed to Diderot and D'Alembert to continue their work. Volume III was made ready in short order with another provocative "Introduction" by D'Alembert. The "Introduction" concluded with a fable from Boccalini: "A traveller was disturbed by the importunate chirrupings of the grasshoppers; he would fain have slain them every one, but only got belated and missed his way; he need only have fared peacefully on his road, and the grasshoppers would have died of themselves before the end of a week." Even Enlightened censors would not fully master D'Alembert's intelligence until long after the technology of the Panopticon was complete. But in spite of D'Alembert's taunt, the next four volumes were published without interruption. However, in Volume VII, D'Alembert once again confronted authorities: this time with a parable in which the tolerant Socinians of Geneva are contrasted, by implication, with the cruel and arbitrary ecclesiastics of France. The storm over this article coincided with the controversy surrounding publication of Helvetius' *De l'esprit* which authorities claimed was merely a one-volume abridgement of the *Encyclopédie*. The Council of State prohibited sale of all seven volumes as well as printing of any future volumes. At this point (1759) D'Alembert left the project, but Diderot pursued it alone for seven more years. Le Breton's betrayal came in 1764. Yet Diderot persevered, concluding the text in 1765 and the plates seven years later. In 1765 the *Encyclopédie* was brought out under the forged colophon of Samuel Faulche of Switzerland. It was common knowledge that the *Encyclopédie* was in fact being printed in Paris by Le Breton with the tacit consent of Malesherbes's successor, Sartine. A friend of Diderot's, Sartine allowed distribution of the "forged" *Encyclopédie* under police supervision. The clergy at once leveled a new decree against the *Encyclopédie*, but the parliament quashed it.[34] Nevertheless, the King's forces ordered all copies confiscated from subscribers by the police. At this point, the outlaw books were actually confined in the Bastille. After expurgation they were eventually returned to their owners who were, after all, prosperous and influential citizens. Mass circulation was not achieved until the last quarter of the eighteenth century.

Assessing the victory of Diderot and Company in the "Encyclopédie Wars," Morley maintains, "it was the flagrant social incompetence of the Church which brought what they call Philosophy, that is to say Liberalism, into vogue and power."[35] Throughout the censorship battles, Diderot and Company had skillfully pitted Church against State in ways that were calculated to win parliamentary tolerance. The 'Enlightened' State Censor, Malesherbes, interceded on behalf of the Encyclopedists at several critical junctures. The Church, plagued by the internecine battles of the Jesuits and the Jansenists, responded in ways that rendered its posture even more absurd than the Encyclopedists' caricatures of it.

French censorship was perhaps more arbitrary, capricious, and irrational than any other. The Inquisitors of Spain and Portugal were at least consistent in their malevolence. In contrast, French censors were wholly unpredictable. They tried to prohibit printing entirely in the sixteenth century to forestall Reformation. When this prohibition proved unenforceable, they proscribed all books on theology published after the fateful events. Later, however, ignorant censors would pass the Koran on the grounds that it contained nothing offensive to the established Church of France. The bureaucracy that dispensed permissions to print was not only quixotic, but also complex, redundant, and painfully slow. Thus a manuscript could emerge from three years of deliberations with an approval, only to be suppressed upon publication. Sometimes authorities would condemn a book in a formal decree, but give verbal *permission tacite* for its sale in the clandestine markets of Paris. Police were known to carry out midnight raids in which illicit books would be confiscated from one dealer only to be resold to another for a tidy profit. Punishments were also impossible to anticipate. Officially they ranged from fines, confiscation of books, burning of books, loss of printing permits, suspension of business, confiscation or destruction of equipment, to banishment, corporal punishment, pillory, imprisonment, the galleys, and execution. But prosecutors might condemn a violator to the wheel one day, and the next commit him to comfortable quarters, provide him with quill, secretarial services, and fine wine, until a politically expedient release could be arranged. Heretics were still burned at the stake or stretched and quartered in the public square well into the eighteenth century. As Morley put it, "The Church had not yet, we must remember, borrowed the principles of humanity and tolerance from atheists."[36] Between 1660 and 1756, some 869 prisoners were confined to the Bastille for violations of censorship laws. It is estimated that prisoners-of-the-plume made up 10 percent of the total population of French prisons from the seventeenth century to the time of the Revolution. Roquain lists 368 titles condemned to the fire between 1715 and 1798. His list is not exhaustive. But it is known that the thoughts of Des Perier, Pascal, Rousseau, Beaumarchais, Raynal, Voltaire, D'Holbach, Montaigne, and Etienne Dolet joined those of Diderot in the fraternity of the fire.[37]

All printers were harassed. Large capital investments could be wiped out by the momentary whim of a petty official. Illegal operations were not much riskier than legal businesses, but the profits were far more lucrative. Police corruption tacitly encouraged clandestine presses and international smuggling networks. In 1798 there were more than one hundred secret presses operating in Paris. Prices were not fixed in the illicit market. Controversy increased demand and prices. A hundred-fold return on an investment in a proscribed title was possible. Pirated editions were also common. In short, the clandestine book trade of eighteenth-century Paris was as near as publishing has ever come to being a 'free market of ideas'—albeit an underground market. Versions of press freedom subsequently institutionalized by Liberal societies were considerably more circumspect. Pottinger underscores this fact in his criticism of the free-wielding tactics of the Parisian entrepreneurs of the *ancien régime*:

> There is little to indicate that the book-sellers and printers felt any deep responsibility for the maintenance of the standards set up by the laws. *They had none of the ethical vision which leads the reputable publishing houses of our time to exert a fundamental censorship by refusing to issue manuscripts of a seditious, libelous, scandalous, or immoral nature.* Indeed the publishers were quick to recognize and exploit the fact that suppression was a powerful form of advertising that usually resulted in greater sales and higher prices. Authors like Voltaire aided and abetted them in securing the condemnation of books with just this object in view.[38]

The liberalism of Censor Malesherbes anticipated the *imprimatur* of the Panopticon. He was an Enlightened bureaucrat: a pioneer in the technology of administrative rationality. His *sub rosa* system of tacit-permissions and permissions-of-tolerance was double-edged. It was not just an attempt to open up the tightly controlled legal market. It also was an attempt to colonize and control the unrestrained freedom of the illicit markets. Similarly Malesherbes's lobbying to save the *Encyclopédie* was probably motivated as much by a desire to keep the profits in France as it was to keep the seat of Enlightenment there. Production of the *Encyclopédie*, with its extensive graphics, was too large an operation to be undertaken by the midnight presses.

Voltaire, like most of the prominent French writers of the period, published most of his work outside France. He repeatedly urged Diderot to avoid the censors by taking the *Encyclopédie* abroad. Presses in The Hague, Amsterdam, Liège, Neuchâtel, Lucerne, Geneva, Berne, Copenhagen, and London stood ready to produce quality editions of the great work if the French censorship proved intractable. Foreign publication would have meant a significant capital outflow. The reversal of the 1852 decree of the King's Council and subsequent toleration of the first six volumes of the *Encyclopédie* is probably better understood as a function of the financial acumen of Malesherbes than of his love of humane letters.

Some writers, like Diderot and Voltaire, thrived as voices-in-opposition. Persecution redoubled their resolve. Others were undoubtedly cowed into conformity, or retreated from the craft of writing entirely. Dissimulation, *double-entendre*, and satiric irreverence are so closely identified with French literary style that critics tend to forget that they had their genesis in persecution. Even an author-*engagé* like D'Alembert who openly taunted the censors was wary enough to cover himself with a shield of irony. Some of the most radical entries in the *Encyclopédie* require reading-between-the-lines. In a letter (1857) to Voltaire, D'Alembert described the architecture of this equivocation:

> No doubt we had bad articles in theology and metaphysics, but with theologians for censors, and a privilege, I defy you to make them any better. There are other articles that are less exposed to the daylight, and in them all is repaired. Time will enable people to distinguish what we have thought from what we have said.[39]

But if the cosmological mess-makers who composed the *Encyclopédie* were careful with specifics (with incriminating details), they made no attempt to disguise the epistemological basis of their attack on the old order. If censors were occasionally deceived, sympathetic readers were not. Morley affirms,

> ... the veil imposed by authority did not really serve any purpose of concealment. Every reader was let into the secret of the writer's true opinion of the old mysteries by means of a piquant phrase, an adroit parallel, a significant reference, an equivocal word of dubious panegyric. Diderot openly explains this in the pages of the *Encyclopédie* itself. ... This way of undeceiving men operates promptly on minds of the right stamp, and it operates infallibly and without any troublesome consequences, secretly and without disturbance, on minds of every

description. "Our fanatics feel the blows," cried D'Alembert compla-
cently, "though they are sorely puzzled to tell from which side they
come."[40]

A typical example (albeit one discovered and excised by the censors)
is a fable telling of the destinies of three brothers in the afterlife: one
had died in infancy, one had lived a righteous life, and the one had
been a criminal. The story was designed to discredit belief in Divine
Providence and wisdom. It ended with the remark, "Behold three
brothers very troublesome to an optimistic philosopher or to God."

The conspiracy-of-the-plume generated a unique bond between
authors and readers. Those who could 'crack the code' shared a sense
of fraternity and élan. The tenor of the letters exchanged by the
Encyclopedists suggests that as Areopagites (craftsmen) they de-
lighted in the challenge of ironic word-mischief. They frequently engaged it when it was not needed to assure the survival of a text. Irony
was their code of emancipatory communication. It allowed them to
function as "unacknowledged legislators of the world": the role the
Encyclopedists believed *philosophes* should play in an Enlightened
social order.[41] In their struggles, administrative inconstancy, not
irony, tyrannized. It was covert, not overt, censorship—petty ma-
nipulations, humiliating cat-and-mouse-games, 'red tape,' disinfor-
mation: in short, the tactics of the Enlightened administration of
Panopticonism that finally wore down D'Alembert's resolve. "I am
worn out," he wrote, "with the affronts and vexations of every kind
that this work draws down upon us . . . the new intolerable inquisition
that they are bent on practicing against the *Encyclopédie*, by giving
us new censors who are more absurd and more intractable than could
be found in Goa; all these reasons, joined to some others, drive me
to give up this accursed work once for all."[42] D'Alembert forthrightly
identifies the authors of the campaign of dis-information: "the people
with the power in their hands." But who are the "new censors who
are more absurd and more intractable than could be found in Goa?"
The People! Ordinary folk who listened to sermons and read the
penny-papers instead of subscribing to costly encyclopedias. The
'common man,' laudable in the abstract (re: in tracts on 'the Rights
of Man'), proved a bully and a nuisance in the flesh. For Panopticons
had discovered what Areopagites already knew: Public Opinion can
usually be mobilized molded, manipulated, and orchestrated. They
realized—too late for the *ancien régime*—that the bounty of sover-
eigns could also be secured by the power-knowledge articulated by

the Encyclopedists. Napoleon would be one of the first to capitalize on, and benefit from, this intelligence.

Full exposure of the elitist heart in the humanist body of the work of the Encyclopedists would not be completed until almost a century later, when Karl Marx would disclose the secret of the Encyclopedists in the penny presses and pamphlets of the common man. But being human, Marx would also have some secrets of his own. . . .

CHAPTER FIVE

Marx's Critique of Bourgeois Censorship: Clubs Instead of Needles

i

Introduction

Although more has been written about Karl Marx than anyone except Jesus Christ, Marx's career as a journalist/editor has received very little attention.[1] Yet this experience conditioned Marx's conceptions of freedom and censorship, and provided him with the communicative competence which made his ideas the founding premises of world communism. This gap in the historical record is neither incidental nor accidental. It is a socially structured silence which serves the interests of both apologists and adversaries because it removes the ambiguity from Marx's position and promotes ideological orthodoxy. It permits elevation or reduction of Marx's ideas to what Richard Weaver calls "ultimate words": "God" and "Devil" terms.[2] It excuses friends and enemies from seriously confronting the unsettling epistemological implications of Marx's cosmological mess-making. It keeps things tidy.

Filling the gap requires us to recognize Marx as a powerful practitioner of journalistic sensationalism but a poor rhetorician—if we understand rhetoric as "a way of knowing": "a means for generating understanding."[3] It requires us to see Marx as neither God nor Devil but as a producer of texts on freedom and censorship which are pockmarked with fateful contradictions, ambivalences, and anomalies.

This chapter examines Marx's texts on free speech and censorship, the contexts which produced them, and the epistemological knots which sustain them.[4] I argue that there are both repressive and liberating elements in Marx's conceptions of freedom and censorship, and that, consequently, both doctrinaire Marxist-Leninism and Critical Humanism are legitimate emendations of Marx's texts. I maintain that Marx both defended and betrayed humanistic values, that he was a freedom fighter and a totalitarian, a champion of free speech and a censor. In sum, I conclude that the jury at Cologne erred when it found Marx innocent of *outrages par paroles*.

ii

Contexts: Rights-of-Man/Rites-of-Property

Before 1848 Germany was an underdeveloped country. Rigorous. censorship laws had existed since the Diet of Worms. A popular phrase of the time, "The German Destitution," suggested ironic counterpoint between German backwardness and the Enlightened ideas of the French Revolution. Both Kant and Hegel—whose ideas became the Archimedean points of nineteenth-century German thought—had been profoundly influenced by the writings of Diderot, Voltaire, Rousseau, Condillac, and Helvetius. Progressive Germans of Marx's generation regarded France as "The Future": "the great laboratory where world history is formed and has its fresh source."[5]

Consequently Marx regarded inquiry into the failure of the emancipatory project of the French Revolution as the essential critical task confronting his contemporaries. The *philosophes* maintained that the praxis of revolutionaries combined with Jacobin opportunism to betray their principles. Marx felt the problem went much deeper: that there was something fundamentally awry in the *philosophes'* conception of freedom. He believed that the breakdown of feudalism had been marked by a profound rupture in the basis of civil society which the bourgeois order could not replace. He maintained that the transition from feudal to bourgeois society had not brought liberation:

> ... man was not freed from religion; he received religious freedom.
> He was not freed from property. He received freedom of property.
> He was not freed from the egoism of trade but received freedom of
> trade.

Marx characterized the rights of man—defined by Diderot and Company and legitimated by the French Constitutions of 1791 and 1793— as egoistic and anti-social. He contended that these rights were "not based on the association of man with man but rather on the separation of man from man." They were atomizing, not community-founding: rights of "self-interest" through which "every man find[s] in other men not realization, but rather the limitation of his own freedom."[6]

iii

Texts

Marx began his career as a working journalist in 1842 with an essay on censorship that was censored by German authorities. It was published a year later by a German exile press in Switzerland. The political orientation of this essay, "Remarks on the Latest Prussian Censorship Instruction," has been described as "intransigently liberal" and Spinozian. In his essays on the free press, Marx's essential concern is not to refute Liberalism but to expose "pseudo-liberalism."[7]

At the time the French press was generally regarded as the freest (most Liberal) in Europe. It was not as free as the North American press, but, in the view of many influential Germans, it was nevertheless too free. Karl Marx did not share this opinion. He asserted,

> The French press is not too free; it is not free enough. It is not subject
> to intellectual censorship, to be sure, but subject to material censorship,
> the high security deposit. This affects the press materially because it
> pulls the press out of its true sphere into the sphere of big business
> speculations.[8]

Marx was intensely critical on Destutt de Tracy's ideologizing of property rights as extensions or projections of ego or personality. Tracy maintained, "nature has endowed man with an inevitable and inalienable property, property in the form of his own individuality."

According to Tracy, this equation invalidated communist and socialist ideas: "It is therefore quite futile to argue about whether it would be better for none of us to have anything of our own."[9] But Marx argued that Tracy had the terms of the equation reversed: "The philosophers would only have to dissolve their language into the ordinary language, from which it is abstracted, to recognize it as the distorted language of the actual world, and to realize that neither thoughts nor language in themselves form a realm of their own, that they are only *manifestations* of actual life."[10] In Marx's view, then, the *philosophes'* concept of 'nature' is a foil for an interest in preserving property rights.

Marx-the-revolutionary devoted his life to disproving the validity of Tracy's equation as a founding premise for civil society. Yet Marx-the-intellectual and embattled journalist tacitly accepted its utility as a premise of the craft of writing:

> My *style* is my property; it is my spiritual individuality. *Le style c'est l'homme.* Indeed! The law permits me to write, only I am supposed to write in a style different from mine! I may show the profile of my mind, but first I must present it in prescribed mien . . . I am humourous, but the law commands that I write seriously. I am daring, but the law commands that my style be modest. Gray on gray is to be the only permissible color of freedom . . . You conceive the truth abstractly and turn the mind into an inquisitor who drily records the proceedings.[11]

Marx did not regard this double-reading of the character of property rights as a contradiction because he saw himself as a servant of Truth, and Diderot and Company as servants of Property. Irony and daring were not the only distinctive features of the property—the style—of the much-censored journalist and father of world revolution. David McLellan notes,

> Marx's articles [his early journalistic writings] have a marked style that recurs in all his subsequent writings. His radical and uncompromising disposition, his love of polarisation, his method of dealing with opponents' views by *reductio ad absurdum* all led him to write very antithetically. Slogan, climax, anaphora, parallelism, antithesis and chiasmus (particularly the last two) are all employed by Marx to excess.[12]

Marx was a sensationalist. His antithetical framing of truth and boredom is pushed to the limit. It violates the canons of scholarly discourse. Marx may be correct in asserting that truth cannot always be captured in moderate terms. But he adds, truth is *never* prosaic.

It is Marx-the-journalist, sensitive to circulation rates, not Marx-the-scholar, who unconditionally endorses Voltaire's irony: "Tous les genres sont bons excepté le genre ennuyeux" ("All species of people are good, except the bores").[13] Marx's combative style—his preference for verbal clubs instead of needles—caused him censorship problems throughout his journalistic career. It made him the most censored author of modern times. And, conversely, it is responsible for the fact that he is perhaps rivaled only by Jesus Christ in terms of the frequency with which his name has been invoked to justify censorship. Marx was an skilled analyst of market censorship and a master salesman.

iv

Marx's Battles with the Censors

At twenty-four, Marx was already a battle-scarred veteran of the censorship wars. He had been permanently disbarred from a professorial appointment by an "intellectual censorship" that purged anti-religious forces from German universities. And he had already entered his apprenticeship in "material censorship" as a reporter and soon-to-be-editor of the newly established Prussian newspaper *Rheinische Zeitung*. Like Diderot and his associates, Marx would suffer most, professionally and personally, from the repressions of official censorship. Indeed, fewer than six months after he became editor of *Rheinische Zeitung*, not only would the newspaper be suppressed by Prussian censorship, but Marx would be deprived of his citizenship.

Rheinische Zeitung was a partisan paper backed by Cologne's progressive elements: Western-minded and capitalistically oriented lawyers, doctors, bankers, and business leaders who regarded the central Prussian state as a feudal anachronism attempting to impose alien ways on Rhinelanders. It was certainly not a communist paper. Young Marx was not particularly sympathetic to communist ideas prior to his Paris exile. But *Rheinische Zeitung* was considerably to the left of other Prussian newspapers, which Marx regarded as "merely mindless amalgam(s) of dry reporting and base flattery." From the beginning, Marx was required to submit his daily proof-sheets to a slow-witted censor, Laurenz Dollenschall, who would not permit "making fun of divine things." Dollenschall maintained that when it came to his "bread and butter," he would "strike out everything." Even though he boasted that he had repressed more than 140 articles in his brief tenure as censor of *Rheinische Zeitung*, Dollenschall was no match for a master of Aesopean language like Marx. Dollenschall's successor, Censor Wiethaus was, in Marx's opinion, "an honorable man." But eventually *Rheinische Zeitung* was placed under double and then triple censorship. Marx complained, "we are burdened from morning to night with the most frightful censorship harassments, ministerial scribblings, gubernatorial complaints, Landtag accusations, stockholders' screams, etc., etc." Although he characterized a censored press as an "ogre of unfreedom," "a civilized monster, a perfumed abortion," Marx nevertheless practiced greater discretion in an attempt to appease the Prussian censors.[14] In a letter to Arnold Ruge, Marx acknowledged that he had been accused of conservatism by some of the other young Hegelians who demanded that *Rheinische Zeitung* do "the *UTMOST*" in the battle with the censors:

> You already know that the censorship is mutilating us pitilessly every day, so that the paper can hardly appear. In this way a mass of articles by the 'Freien' was eliminated. As much as the censorship itself, I myself took the liberty of cancelling them, since Meyen and Company sent in heaps of scribblings pregnant with world revolution, written in slovenly style, permeated with atheism and communism (which the gentlemen have never studied)...I no longer considered myself obliged to allow this urine as before. This omission of a few unreliable productions of 'freedom,' a freedom which by preference strives 'to be free from all thought,' was thus the first ground for a darkening of the Berlin sky...I demanded less vague rationalization, fewer high-sounding phrases and self-complacent preening, and more precision, more penetration into concrete conditions, more expertise in their analysis. I said that smuggling communist and socialist dogmas—that is, a new *Weltanschauung*—into incidental theater criticisms, etc., was improper, indeed, unethical, and asked for a quite different and more thorough discussion of communism, if it was to be discussed at all... Finally, I demanded that if philosophy is to be discussed at all, there should be less dallying with the *Firma* (business) of 'atheism' (which is being like children who tell everybody who will listen that they are not afraid of the boogeyman), and more content for the people. *Voilà tout.*[15]

Even this editorial quality-control could not save the *Rheinische Zeitung*. Ironically, the complaint that moved the King and his ministerial council to ban *Rheinische Zeitung* came from Czar Nicholas I of

Russia, who was outraged by the attack on Czarist military despotism. Two weeks before its scheduled demise, Marx resigned as editor of the *Rheinische Zeitung*, which completed publication under the editorship of a banker.

Marx moved to Paris, where he and Ruge founded the *Deutsch-Franzosische Jahrbucher*, a liberal anti-communist literary journal. After one issue, this project was abandoned. Marx freelanced and immersed himself in the radical philosophy of the German expatriate community. In Paris, Marx formed his lifelong friendship with Engels, became interested in the French workers' movement, and developed an abiding interest in economics. But it was Marx's brief affiliation with the ill-fated anti-communist *Deutsch-Franzosische Jahrbucher* that earned him a place on the Prussian proscription list and eventually led to his expulsion from Paris.

Marx was allowed to enter Belgium on the condition that he sign a pledge not to write anything about contemporary Belgian politics. Engels joined Marx in Brussels. There they wrote *The German Ideology*, the *Manifesto of the Communist Party*, and nothing about contemporary Belgium politics. During the revolutions of 1848, Marx urged German workers to join the demonstrators in Belgium and Paris. He also contributed 5000 francs to buy arms. As a result, he was immediately jailed and subsequently expelled from Belgium.

He was allowed to return to Paris under the Provisional Government. But when revolution broke out in Germany, Marx went to Cologne, where he and Engels founded the *Neue Rheinsche Zeitung*. The editorial policy was very different from that of its namesake. *Neue Rheinsche Zeitung* was a revolutionary newspaper committed to proletarian democracy. Troubles with authorities began with the first issue. Engels was forced to leave Cologne under order of arrest, but continued his contributions from abroad. When revolt broke out in Cologne, *Neue Rheinsche Zeitung* and other radical newspapers in the city were suspended by martial law for two weeks. Shortly thereafter, Marx received the first in a series of court summons which provided him with a public forum for a dramatic defense of freedom of the press. Ultimately he was indicted for *"outrages par paroles."* These outrages included insulting the police, satirizing the Junkers, and inciting rebellion by supporting advocates of a tax revolt. The trial of Marx and his publisher took on a theatrical quality, and drew capacity crowds. A jury found them not guilty. But three months later Marx was expelled from Cologne by police order, and the *Neue Rheinische Zeitung* ceased publication. Ultimately, Marx made his way back to Paris, where he lived under an assumed name until he was served with another order of expulsion. After a brief exile in Brittany, the man-without-a-country emigrated to London, which was at the time a refuge for Continental dissidents. From London, Marx launched a new phase in his journalistic career. For a decade (1852–62), he would serve as London correspondent for the *New York Daily Tribune*, and, with the assistance of Engels, contributed approximately 356 articles to the American publication. During his association with the *Tribune* (which later became the conservative *New York Herald Tribune*), Marx encountered no significant problems with censorship.

V

Values: Why Censorship is "Bad" and Press Freedom is "Good"

Marx wrote "Debates on Freedom of the Press and Publication" in 1842 before he formulated his dialectical theory of history. Therefore he dismissed as an "illogical paradox" the idea that the cause of freedom could be advanced through conflicts with censorship:

> The greatest orator of the French Revolution, whose *voix toujours tonnante* (ever thundering voice) is still reverberating in our time . . . —Mirabeau—trained himself in prison. Are prisons therefore the colleges of oratory.[16]

But Marx's own censorship trials subsequently became colleges of freedom which trained his *voix toujours tonnante* into an impressive testament for press freedom—a testament which Shlomo Avineri describes as "a classic in the modern literature on the freedom of the press."[17]

Marx-the-journalist takes the position that censorship is always bad and a free press is always preferable. He does not root this judgment in naive realism, nor does he place his faith in the free market as an arbiter of truth. Rather Marx maintains that censorship is bad because it protects the interests of entrenched elites. It perpetuates the domination of the powerless by the powerful. If the ruling ideas of every epoch are the ideas of the ruling class, then the class which has control over the means of material production also has control over the means of mental production. Control over the means of mental production includes control over the prevailing canons of censorship:

> Lowly opinions, personal chicaneries and infamies, these the censored press shares with the free press. That it produces individual products of this or that sort does not, therefore, constitute its distinction as a species; even in a swamp, flowers grow. The question here is the essence, the inner character, that separates the censored press from the free press.
>
> The free press that is bad does not correspond to the essence of its character. The censored press with its hypocrisy, its characterlessness, its eunuch language, its doglike tail wagging, embodies only the inner conditions of its existence.
>
> A censored press is still bad even when it produces good products, for these products are good only insofar as they exhibit a free press within a censored one, and insofar as it is not in their character to be products of a censored press. A free press is still good even when it produces bad products, for these products are apostates from the nature of the free press . . .
>
> The essence of a free press is the characterful, reasonable, ethical essence of freedom . . . freedom is, after all, the essential species of the whole intellectual existence, hence also the press.

In Marx's view, free expression is natural: a realization of inner laws. Censorship is unnatural: arbitrary "administration of mind."[18]

But the canons of natural rights theory are not the only grounds securing Marx's belief in the superiority of the free press. He also relies upon the testimony of history. He maintains that the American experiment proves the efficacy of press freedom: "You find the natural phenomenon of freedom of the press in North America in its purest, most natural form." Marx's conception of the free press, unlike his idea of democracy, is distinctly Western, American, Jeffersonian. Like the architects of the American Revolution, the father of world revolution conceived of the social role of the press in revolutionary terms. The press is to serve as a 'watchdog.' Echoing Jefferson, Marx maintains,

> That freedom of the press as it exists on the official side, and censorship too, also need censorship. And who is to censor the government except the people's press?[19]

Under representative democracy, Marx contends, the only protection people have against the emergence of a secret government within their parliament, court system, or administrative bureaucracies is a free press. This was an alien idea in Imperial Germany. Marx's advocacy makes this clear: "Keep in mind that the German knows the state only from hearsay, that closed doors are not eye glasses, that a secret political system is not a public political system, and do not consider the fault of the state the fault of the newspapers, a fault which the newspapers, in fact, seek to correct."[20]

Marx conceived of the free press as a cutting edge for enlightened ideas. He maintained a free press is good because it is "the intellectual mirror in which a people sees itself, the self-viewing [that] is the first condition of wisdom." A censored press is bad because it "kills the political spirit." A free press creates critical publics. A censored press creates apathy: it turns the people into a "private mob." The free press can serve as a revolutionary catalyst. Under conditions of tyranny, like the conditions of feudal Prussia, Marx contended (as Jefferson had contended vis-à-vis British colonialism): "The first duty of the press, therefore is to undermine the foundations of the existing political system."[21]

Although Marx shared many of the ideas of the American revolutionaries, his defense of the free press was diametrically opposed to Benjamin Franklin's. Contra the Philadelphia printer, whose *Apology for Printers* defended the free press as a species of free trade, the editor of *Rheinische Zeitung* maintained that,

> To make freedom of the press a class of freedom of the trades is to defend it in such a way as to kill it with the defense . . . *The first freedom of the press consists in not being a trade.* The writer who reduces it to material means deserves as a penalty for this inner unfreedom the outer one, censorship; or rather, his very existence is already a penalty.

Like Milton, Marx abhorred the commodification of thought. Defending freedom of press as a trade reduces it to cost accounting. Profit becomes the measure of truth when "relations of buying and selling have been made the basis of all others."[22]

Marx contended that censorship not only demoralizes the public sphere, it also corrupts the arts. He expressed contempt for writers-in-uniform: for "authorized writers." Whether it is the uniform of a tradesman, mandarin, or government agent that carries the authorization, the effects of the "oligarchy of mind" on aesthetics are equally pernicious. Marx pointed out that it was "unauthorized writers," not commercial lackeys or civil servants, who produced the great traditions of German literature.[23]

Marx maintained that censorship laws are bad because they punish thought instead of action. "Laws that make as their chief criteria not the *action as such* but the *sentiment* of the acting person are nothing," Marx asserted, "but positive sanctions of lawlessness." Further, censorship laws suspend due process: "The censor . . . is plaintiff, defendant, and judge combined in one person." Marx contended that the "radical cure of the censorship is its abolition" for "it is a bad institution, and institutions are more powerful than men."[24]

vi

Criticism as Censorship

In arguing that institutionalized censorship (official censorship) is always bad, Marx faces a dilemma. He has also argued that consciousness is always interest-bound maintaining that, "From the start the 'spirit' is afflicted with the curse of being 'burdened' with matter." So that, "Consciousness is, therefore, from the very beginning a social product, and remains so as long as men exist at all."[25] Thus he contends that social intercourse itself is rooted in constituent censorship; Promethean images of truth are, at best, the hollow promises of false consciousness.

The dilemma is Faustian. What is the individual who becomes conscious of this fundamental censorship to do? Passive submission would chain his or her destiny to blind necessity. Yet no one can ever be completely emancipated from constituent censorship. The best the Faustian individual can do is to consciously—reflexively—assent to the most rational form of censorship: *criticism* grounded in *public* canons of knowledge. This stance requires self-conscious awareness of the existence of unlighted corners in one's own mind. It requires recognition of the fact that censorship is not just something that others do, but also something I must do and you must do if we are to create order and achieve communication and community.

Marx maintained that a free press maximizes opportunities for reasoned consent because no oligarchy of mind secures the privileges of an elite at the expense of the people:

> True censorship, rooted in the very essence of freedom of the press, is criticism; that is the court the press creates out of itself. Censorship

is criticism as government monopoly; but doesn't criticism lose its rational character when it proceeds not openly but secretly, not theoretically but practically; when it does not judge parties but becomes itself a party; when it does not use the sharp knife of reason but the blunt scissors of caprice; when it wants to apply criticism but does not suffer it; when it disavows itself while offering itself, it is so uncritical as to confuse individual with universal wisdom, dicta of power with dicta of reason, ink spots with sun spots, the crooked lines of the censor with mathematical constructions, and striking blows with striking arguments?[26]

Since "censorship is official criticism," Marx asserts, "its norms are critical norms which therefore must not be withheld from criticism, a field to which they belong." Critical norms, freely arrived at, impose a legitimate discipline. Thus Marx is forced to acknowledge reluctantly that official censorship could achieve a provisional legitimacy if it were based upon objective (public) standards and subject to regular judicial rules. Such censorship would at least be open to criticism. Conversely, he maintained that the worst form of censorship—the most complete administration of mind—"would be for the censorship also to be censored, by some director of a Superior Commission, for example."[27] According to Marx, then, the worst tyranny would be a tyranny of concealed rules.

vii

Clubs Instead of Needles

Until recently, Western Marxists, with few exceptions, have claimed that Critical Marxism was betrayed by the praxis of Russian Revolutionaries. (In the same spirit, apostles of the Enlightenment claimed that the principles of rationalism were betrayed by the praxis of French Revolutionaries.) To be sure Lenin and Stalin, like Napoleon and Guizot, were not friends of press freedom or critical reason. All were censors. All were practical politicians who were quick to suspend criticism and purge freedom fighters when their own dicta of power were in question. Marx, however, was not the innocent this line of defense implies.

Marx's style was his "property": his *imprimatur*. The jury in Co-

logne found him innocent of *outrages par paroles*. But posterity has
found him guilty. Both disciples and opponents have found it necessary to expurgate Marx. The Soviets have routinely censored parts
of Marx's corpus. His warnings against the Russian Menace in Europe, his analysis of the Asiatic mode of bureaucratic control, and
his exposure of the irrationality of official censorship, are all anom-
alous to Soviet power-knowledge. Anti-communist dragon-slayers
have also systematically suppressed or depreciated Marxian sub-texts
which are not readily conflated into "devil terms": his humanism, his
defense of the free press, etc.

Marx was a pamphleteer. He loved combative metaphors and
hyperbole. He hated "gray on gray": moderation (*"moderation.
Only a 'scamp' is moderate, says Goethe"*). He was an impatient
prophet:

> It is bad to perform menial services even for freedom, and to fight
> with needles instead of clubs. I became tired of hypocrisy, stupidity,
> raw authority, and our cringing, bowing, back turning, and word
> picking.[28]

Marx's "property"—his sensational style—betrayed Critical Marxism. It invited excess. Striking arguments were not offered as alternatives to striking blows, but as incitements to them. For example,
with characteristic polemical extravagance Marx advocated "revolutionary terrorism": "there is only one way to shorten, to simplify,
to concentrate, the murderous death pains of the old society and the
bloody birth pains of the new society: only one way—revolutionary
terrorism."[29]

The reductive premises of historical materialism imply far greater
consistency in Marx's work than can actually be found there. Sen-
sationalists can seldom afford the luxury of consistency. Lukacs,
Gramsci, and members of the Frankfurt School faulted the incom-
pleteness of Marx's renderings of 'spirit,' 'superstructure,' and 'ideology.' The adequacy of these theoretical constructions can also be
faulted. They are riddled with contradiction. Like bourgeois economists who conceive of the marketplace as the measure of all things,
Marx embraced an economistic model of humankind: a model that
does not take into account humankind's art, erotic nature, sense of
play, or spirit of adventure.[30] Like Diderot, Tracy, and other sons of
Enlightenment, Marx offered a program for moral reform which separated justice from utility, and substantive rationality from instrumental rationality.

viii

The Original Sin of Marxism

Marx's critique of censorship is incisive, historic. It is one of the great documents in the West's struggle for free speech. Yet, Lenin's advocacy of censorship is as much exegesis of Marx as betrayal. Lenin's reading is also secured in authentic Marxian texts: texts in which Marx, the sensationalist and propagandist, speaks with more resonance than Marx, the Critical thinker. Thus, for example, in the *Manifesto of the Communist Party*, Marx and his collaborator, Friedrich Engels, forcefully assert that a strategic measure essential to achieving communism is "Centralization of the means of communication and transport in the hands of the state." To be sure, "means of communication" had different connotations in 1847 from what they do today. For Marx, these means were closely related to the productive process; they included technologies of transportation as well as communication (railroads, steamships, telegraphy, mail); they were instruments for the circulation of money and messages:

> Circulation is the great social retort in which everything is thrown, and out of which everything is recovered as crystallised money. Not even the bones of saints are able to withstand this alchemy; and still less able to withstand it are more delicate things, sacrosanct things which are outside the commercial traffic of men.[31]

It is unclear whether Marx intended his advocacy of revolutionary state control of the means of communication to include the press.[32] But it is clear that Marx's antithetical writing style—his fondness for polarization, climax, slogans, anaphora, and chiasmus—permitted his disciples to claim he did.

"Revolutionary terrorism" and "bones of saints": there is very little "gray on gray" in the texts of Marx and Engels. Scientific principles are weapons: rhetorical clubs for battering the bourgeois and securing the future for socialism. The disciples of the fathers of world revolution did not have to press this precedent very far to produce warrants for scientism and vanguardism: warrants which placed their claims to scientific authority beyond criticism. These warrants held an especial appeal for disciples of Marx and Engels in Russia, where historical and cultural traditions favored censorship.

Like all ingenious cerebrations, historical materialism offers us a way of seeing by not seeing. The conundrums within Marx's writings are not just disparities between the thought of the young Hegelians and the mature historical materialist. They are the contradictions and tensions that are necessarily present in all comprehensive cosmologic adventures: all system-building and world-building, all effective forms of power-knowledge.

If all communication, except perhaps some of the babblings of babes, ravings of the mad, mumblings of the introverted, or repetitive tunes of the distracted, are attempts to control, influence, persuade, incite, annoy, refute, correct, pacify, enchant, or otherwise connect with others, then all communication aspires to create power-knowledge. All power-knowledge is interest-bound; skewed by a spiral of perceptual, linguistic, organizational, and hierarchical priorities. All knowledge, including Marxism, bears the *imprimatur* of the original sin of consciousness.

CHAPTER SIX

Censorship in Socialist Societies

i

The Negation of Critical Marxism in Revolutionary Marxism

Khrushchev liked to tell the story of Stalin's decision to arrest a famous Ukranian actor for treason.[1] According to Khrushchev, Stalin had watched the actor, Buchma, portray a traitor on a television show. Captivated by the effectiveness of the performance, Stalin concluded that only an actual traitor could play the part so well and demanded that the appropriate measures be taken against the "traitor," Buchma! Other reports confirm Stalin's intense preoccupation with the arts. On more than one occasion, he took so great an interest in theatrical productions that he attended more than a dozen performances of a play before rendering a definitive ideological critique. Stalin's biographers claim he harbored poetic aspirations. In spite of his protests to the contrary, Stalin also fancied himself to be a perceptive literary critic. He personally read manuscripts of well-known authors prior to publication and suggested both editorial and substantive changes. With bitter irony, Roy Medvedev remarked, Stalin "left a very great mark on our literature."[2]

In the West both orthodox and neo-Marxists claim that Stalinism should not be equated with socialism. The former regard Stalin's extreme methods as a betrayal of both the theory of Marx and the *praxis* of Lenin. The latter do not speak with a singular voice but

insist on the prefix, 'neo' precisely because they want to distance
themselves from Stalin's fanaticism. For some, the distancing effect
extends to Lenin's revolutionary program and even to Marx's ideal-
ization of the proletarian future.

Socialism is not synonymous with Stalinism, just as capitalism is
not synonymous with Hitlerism. Stalinism and Hitlerism are extreme
forms: perversions of the structures in which they took root—perversions not anticipated by Karl Marx or Adam Smith.

Nevertheless Stalin's interference in the arts was not a perversion
of Marxian theory. It was a logical extension of the principles of
Marxist-Leninist aesthetics which conceive of control of communications as an essential step in the development of a socialist culture.
Stalin's actions were, of course, also pragmatic responses to the very
real and very severe domestic and international problems the Soviet
system confronted during and immediately after World War II: enormous wartime casualties, failures in Soviet agriculture and collectiv-
ization programs, counter-revolutionary activities, the development
of the atomic bomb by the United States, and the international ideological and economic victories secured for the U.S. by the Marshall
Plan and NATO. However, Stalin's theoretical and pragmatic responses to the challenge of advancing the cause of socialism in a
hostile world created a powerful centralized state bureaucracy in the
Soviet Union. Official censorship became a necessary constituent
principle for the maintenance of that state. This constituent principle
was foreshadowed in and rationalized by the revolutionary theories
of Lenin *and* Marx.

Nevertheless censorship does not officially exist in Russia. The
Constitution of the Union of Soviet Socialist Republics does not
authorize the restrictive or prescriptive control of literature. According to the procedural fictions of Soviet legalism, submission of manuscripts to the Chief Administration for Literary Affairs, *Glavlit*, for
editorial and ideological criticism prior to publication is a purely
"voluntary" decision of writers. Officially, then, *Glavlit* is regarded
as a kind of state service supplied to authors committed to building
social democracy.

Censorial measures were introduced by the Bolsheviks just ten days
after the overthrow of Kerensky's government. Lenin enfranchised
Glavlit in 1922 as a "temporary measure," a revolutionary expedient.
Revolutionary expedience was soon replaced by the expedience of a
civil war which Lenin saw as a "necessary" precondition to reconstructing Russian society according to the blueprint of Marxist-Len-

inism. As a result, the temporary measure of 1922 became a permanent feature of the reconstruction process.

Western Marxists, schooled in Socratic and Liberal texts, frequently try to explain away the betrayal of "critical Marxism" by actually existing socialism as a distortion produced by peculiarly Russian conditions, e.g. an underdeveloped economy, a strongly entrenched historical tradition of censorship, etc. Certainly the accounts of those who experienced Czarist censorship, like Stepniak (pseud.) and Aleksandr Nikitenko, document its harsh and arbitrary character.[3] Moreover, even an outspoken dissident like Andrei Sinyavsky (Abram Tertz) affirms that there is a certain amount of historical continuity between Czarist and Soviet censorship.[4] Yet it can also be argued that censorship under the Czars was not significantly more repressive or capricious than the censorship of royalist France.

But such apologetics are irrelevant if the *Manifesto of the Communist Party* is taken seriously; regarded, that is, (as Marx regarded it) as the definitive constitutive statement of the principles of revolutionary socialism. In calling for the centralization of control of the means of communication in the hands of the state, this programmatic document unambiguously authorized and legitimated Lenin's directives.[5]

The negation of "critical Marxism" is implicit in this thesis of revolutionary Marxism. *This paradox is a problem for all Marxists.* Soviet censorship is not merely predicated upon Czarist censorship. Soviet censorship is both qualitatively and quantitatively different from the censorship described by Czarist 'dissidents.' Where Czarist censorship was only restrictive, Soviet censorship is both restrictive and prescriptive. Moreover, the scope of Czarist censorship is dwarfed by Soviet censorship. This quantitative difference is graphically described by Michael Heller:

> . . . after the 1905 revolution and the easing up of censorship, when all the works of Russian writers previously banned were published, they would have fitted into one volume. Today they would fill a library.[6]

To view the repressions of really existing socialism (RES) as a Russian problem is to evade the essential issue. State censorship appears to be a necessary consequence of state *monopoly* of the means of communication. Until the impasse posed by this paradox in Marxist-Leninism is resolved, all briefs for humanistic Marxism will be regarded with skepticism by serious litterateurs.

Indeed, even covenants for democratic socialism which claim non-

Marxist lineage (e.g. certain strains of Eurosocialism) must share the onus of skepticism. None has convincingly demonstrated that the formal distinctions drawn between state 'ownership' and state 'control' of communications are not useful fictions easily abrogated in times of crisis—witness Britain's long-term censorship of B.B.C. coverage of hostilites in Northern Ireland, as well as its censorship of both print and electronic media during the invasion of the Falkland Islands in 1983; witness, too, Canada's suspension of constitutional provisions, declaration of martial law, and censorship of coverage of Quebeçois separatism, in response to violent assaults on government officials in 1974. Even where ownership of communications facilities is in private hands, governments use the cover of crisis to censor media, as in the United States' censorship of press coverage of its invasion of Grenada in 1983.

However, within systems of power-knowledge like that of the Soviet Union, where prescriptive as well as restrictive controls of communications are concentrated in state hands, censorship does not have to be justified. Crises do not have to be declared or created. Intervention by state censors is routine operating practice.

ii

Literary Freedom and Restrictive Censorship Under the New Economic Policy

In Czarist Russia, as in royalist France, literary censorship served as a school for revolutionaries. Russian litterateurs, like French Encyclopedists, played a vital role in translating private outrage into public contempt for the prevailing powers. Solzhenitsyn exaggerates little when he claims that prerevolutionary litterateurs rocked the foundations of the Czarist state: "Russian literature, no other, nurtured all those young people who conceived a hatred for the Czar and the gendarmes, took up revolution, and carried it through."[7] Indeed, the literary underground gave birth to *Pravda*.

But where the French Revolution was preceded by an acceleration of state control of literature and the press, the period immediately prior to the Russian Revolution was the only time in that nation's history that literature and the press were relatively free of government supervision. So if the French experience demonstrated that severe repression can compress the power-knowledge of litterateurs into the cadences of revolution, the Russian experience affirmed the inflammatory power of unfettered protest.

The French and Russian Revolutions also assigned different roles to litterateurs in securing post-revolutionary order. Unlike the French Revolution (but more like the American Revolution), the Russian Revolution placed the reins of power directly in the hands of "philosophes," the revolutionary intellectuals who forged the ideals that ignited the violence. Under the New Economic Policy, NEP (which lasted until 1929), this cadre of intellectuals was preoccupied with state-building and increasingly agricultural production but it did not have a coherent cultural policy.

The devastation of World War I and the aftershocks of the revolution and civil war left openings between the "no longer" of Czarism and the "not yet" of Marxist-Leninist statism. So that even as "émigrés and renegades" were establishing a post-revolutionary literature in exile abroad and the first shadows of Soviet *gulags* began to darken the face of revolutionary hopes, the Party formally maintained a protectionist policy toward "reactionary" elements within the literary community. It restrained the more zealous and impatient apologists for proletarian literature from succeeding in attempts to impose literary policies that would have irrevocably alienated individualists, idealists, disciples of various Western avant-garde movements, bourgeois literary specialists, fellow-travelers, and other intellectuals who had established public reputations under the ancien régime. The Party's stance toward these "reactionary" elements was frankly proselytic. It sought to "win them over." During this period of dialectical conversion, cultural matters were under the authority of A.V. Lunacharsky, who was himself a successful writer and thus sensitive to the issues confronting litterateurs under conditions of post-revolutionary tumult. Indeed, until the end of NEP, independent literary and artistic organizations were permitted, and even a number of semi-autonomous publishing firms operated without state interference.

To be sure, there was censorship. Lenin's "temporary measure" had bureaucratized restrictive censorship. But during these early years, *Glavit's* function was to prevent publication of overtly counter-revolutionary works, not to articulate aesthetic canons or establish an "oligarchy of mind." The first major policy statement on literature was issued in 1925. Entitled "The Policy of the Party in the Field of Artistic Literature," it noted the existence of a plurality of literary trends corresponding to the diverse material conditions of the NEP period. In essence, it endorsed non-intervention:

> ... the Party absolutely cannot commit itself to any one trend in the sphere of literary form. While controlling literature in a general way, the Party can no more give support to any one fraction (fractions being classified according to differences of view about *style* and form) than it can decide by resolution questions of family life ... There is every reason to believe that a style consonant with the new era will be created, but it will be created by different methods, and so far there is no sign of a solution of this question. Any attempt to tie the Party down in this respect at the present stage of cultural development must be rejected.
>
> Therefore, the Party must declare itself for free competition between the various groups and trends in this field. Any other solution of the question would be a bureaucratic pseudo-solution. In exactly the same way it would be inadmissible to ordain by Party decree the legalized monopoly of literature and publishing by any one group or literary organization.[8]

Max Hayward refers to the NEP as "relatively mild, in retrospect almost idyllic."[9] The recent surge of *tamizdat* ("published there," in the West) on life in the early camps underscores the fact that such judgments can, at best, be rendered only in relative terms. If Stalinism is taken as the plane of comparison, the assessment, stripped of the effusive term, 'idyllic,' may have some accuracy. The 1920s were at least a time when, as Michael Heller put it, "some people still had the right to whisper."[10] Heterodox political and aesthetic ideas did circulate. Gorky's critical essays on the brutalities of bolshevism and on Lenin's dogmatism enjoyed a certain popularity in the early twenties. The writings of G.V. Plekhanov were widely influential through the NEP period. Plekhanov argued for a sociology of knowledge, rooted in the principles of historical materialism; but he maintained that the spirit of scientific criticism is inimical to attempts to establish extrinsic prescriptive controls over literature.[11]

Idyllic or despotic, NEP ended in 1929 with Stalin's decision to tighten Party control of all aspects of Soviet life. Like other workers, artists, writers, and intellectuals were to be "bolshev- ized" and proletarian literature—or, as it would soon be known, "socialist realism"—was to become the only acceptable genre of cultural service.

iii

The Marxist-Leninist Paradigm of Power-Knowledge as Auspices for Prescriptive Control of Literature

The great purges of litterateurs and the singular commitment of the Party to Socialist Realism did not take place until the thirties. Therefore the part Lenin played in setting the stage for Soviet "administration of mind" is open to question. Lenin's epigones in the U.S.S.R. quoted chapter and verse in their apologetics for prescriptive control of literature. But Western Marxists frequently dismiss the repressive doxology produced by such exegesis as a Stalinist perversion. Their own hagiography glosses over Lenin's role in establishing Party control of culture. In part, this whitewash stems from excessive dependence upon the texts of Trotsky and Trotskyites. Certainly, Stalin betrayed and falsified the humanistic elements in the writings of the young Marx *and* the young Lenin. But there is also a logical and historical continuity in the programs for cultural renewal outlined by Marx, Engels, Lenin, Trotsky, *and* Stalin.

Marxist-Leninist eschatology is inherently intolerant of heterodox ideas. For if culture (the superstructure) reflects economic conditions (the substructure), and if proletarian revolution is taken as the inevitable goal of historical progress, then intellectual or artistic currents which impede progress toward that goal can only be seen as "deviations" which reflect survivals of "reactionary" economic interests. At best, this world-view may lead administrators of RES to grant a certain amount of indulgence to late-bloomers and half-wits who are slow in discovering the path to true consciousness. As we have seen, this was the expressed intent of the relatively lax literary policy of NEP.

Lenin himself was no champion of literary freedom—not even for those who were unquestionably committed to furthering the cause of proletarian revolution! Lunacharsky made this clear at a meeting of the Central Committee's Press Section in 1924 when he acknowledged:

> He [Lenin] feared Bogdanovism, feared that the Proletkult might give rise to all sorts of philosophical, scientific, and ultimately political

deviations. He did not want the establishment of rival worker's organizations alongside the party ... For this reason, he personally directed me to draw the Proletkult closer to the government, to subject it to control.[12]

Lenin's 1905 essay "Party Organization and Party Literature" is cited by friend and foe alike as paradigmatic of the revolutionary leader's views on toleration of deviations. The essay focuses on Party literature and the need to maintain Party discipline. On the one hand, Lenin seemed to endorse literary autonomy: "it is absolutely necessary to provide a broad scope for individual initiative, individual inclinations, scope for thought and imagination, form and content." He warned that literature must not be "mechanically identified with the other parts of the party affairs of the proletariat." On the other hand, however, Lenin maintained that literature "must become party literature"; that it "must become a part of the general proletariat cause ... a part of organized, systematic, united Social Democratic party work." He contended that writers "must without fail enter party organizations" and called (as Marx and Engels had called) for Party control of communications facilities like newspapers, libraries, and publishing houses. Unlike Marx, who was ambivalent in his attitude toward Western concepts of 'style' and 'freedom,' Lenin dismissed the cherished 'freedom' of bourgeois liberalism as "only disguised dependence on the moneybag." He maintained that real freedom will only come when the writer is "openly bound to the proletariat."[13] He re-read the individualism of Marx's defense of 'style' in collectivist terms: as auspices for developing a policy statement on the *correct style* to be used by proletarian writers. In another essay from the same period, "What Is To Be Done?," Lenin equates 'freedom,' 'diversity,' and 'criticism' with 'opportunism':

> He who does not deliberately close his eyes cannot fail to see that the new 'critical' trend in socialism is nothing more or less than a new variety of *opportunism* ... 'Freedom' is a grand word, but under the banner of freedom of industry the most predatory wars were waged, under the banner of freedom of labour, the working people were robbed. The modern use of the term 'freedom of criticism' contains the same inherent falsehood. Those who are really convinced that they have made progress in science would not demand freedom for the new views to continue side by side with the old, but the substitution of the new views for the old.[14]

Lenin posits his views under the warrant of scientific reasoning. But his linguistic analysis of the vocabulary of motive of his critics (especially Bernstein, Vollmar, and Millerand) undermines the role critical reason conventionally plays in grounding scientific knowledge. Lenin does not refute his critics. He invokes scientism to silence them. Lenin's *Censorship of criticism* is a direct inversion of the principle of *Censorship by criticism* defended by Marx as a young journalist.

Lenin believed that "words are action," and that literature had a revolutionary mission to fill in the creation of proletarian culture. Therefore he regarded literature as too important to be left in the hands of litterateurs. Lenin conceived of literature and the press as essential instruments of development.

Lenin's theses on the social functions of the press were anti-theses. Western capitalist concepts of press liberty provided the 'from' for Lenin's 'to.' Lenin maintained that what capitalists call "freedom of the press" consists "in freedom of the rich systematically, unceasingly, and daily in the millions of copies to deceive, corrupt, and fool the exploited and oppressed mass of people, the poor." He identified the essential feature of the constitutive censorship of the capitalist press—its "holy of holies"—and outlined very different constitutive principles for a Soviet press:

> In the 'good old bourgeois times' the bourgeois press never referred to the 'holy of holies'—the internal state of affairs in private factories, in private enterprises. This suited the interests of the bourgeoisie. But we must radically dissociate ourselves from this. We have not dissociated ourselves from it. The type of our newspapers has not yet changed in the way it should change in a society which is passing from capitalism to socialism.

The 'to' of Lenin's critique asserts that all newspapers are political whether their political franchise consists in protecting the 'holy of holies' of capitalist or socialist interests. In short, he maintained that there is no such thing as a neutral press. Lenin therefore concluded that the press should play a pro-social role in the development of socialism. He maintained that, "A paper is not merely a collective propagandist and collective agitator, it is also a collective organizer." That is, the press should not merely "propagandize" (disseminate the views of the Party elite) or "agitate" (motivate the masses to pursue Party goals); it should also be an "organ" organizing society along socialist lines and cultivating a socialist consciousness. Lenin's pro-social concept of the press does not preclude all criticism, but it does preclude criticism of the goal of establishing socialism. Nevertheless Lenin's charge to the periodical press included the responsibility to act as a forum for self-criticism (*samokritika*): criticism of the means used to achieve socialist goals.[15] In practice, this has produced extensive networks of peasant or worker correspondents and development of 'letters to the editor columns' that are far more serious and extensive than such forums in Western newspapers.[16] Institutionalization of prescriptive censorships of literature and the periodical press in the thirties was a logical extension of Lenin's pro-social and pro-socialist concept of the press.

iv

Socialist Realism and Leninist Linguistics

According to André Gide, Party member and tourist of the revolution, no traces of the influence of "critical Marxism" could be found within the official culture of the Soviet Union by the early thirties.[17] By that time prescriptive controls for "the administration of mind" had been firmly established.

At the close of NEP, there existed two main literary organizations: the All-Russian Union of Writers, an apolitical group composed of fellow-travelers and members of the older generation including the best known writers of the day, and the Association of Proletarian Writers (RAPP), a militant collective of writers who claimed proletarian origins or at least strong solidarity with the interests of workers and peasants. Members of RAPP regarded themselves as the vanguard of socialist culture. After 1929 the Party gave RAPP control of the campaign to bring about conversion or submission of remaining reactionary elements within the literary community. Under the tight reigns of the fanatical leadership of RAPP, terror, inquisition, villification, and scapegoating replaced persuasion. The leadership and as many as half of the members of the Writers' Union were expelled during the RAPP-sponsored purges.

In 1932 the Central Committee of the Party announced that Soviet writers would henceforth be consolidated into a single organization, the Union of Soviet Writers, and that membership would be compulsory for anyone who wished to pursue the craft of writing. Two years later, the Union of Soviet Writers would be furnished with a unitary theory for the practice of their craft.

Maxim Gorky played an essential role in the process. Gorky's writings, along with those of Pushkin, Gogol, Belinsky, Chernyshevsky, and Mayakovsky were among the celebrated texts of Russian literature that nurtured those young people "who conceived a hatred for the Czar and the gendarmes, took up revolution, and carried it through." A vehement critic of Lenin during the revolution, Gorky was nevertheless persuaded or coerced into collaborating with Stalin in promulgating the dogma of socialist realism. Together they outlined the calling of litterateurs in building proletarian culture. Writers were to become "the engineers of the soul" who would construct "a new life, in the process of 'changing the world'."[18] Gorky introduced this motif in his resolution on "Soviet Literature" at the first Soviet Writers' Congress in 1934. At this meeting Gorky, André Zhdanov, Karl Radek, Nikolai Bukharin, and others laid the epistemological foundations for the prescriptive control of literature.

The Congress repudiated Plekhanov's version of historical materialism and replaced it with a Leninist aesthetic. Plekhanov and Lenin had agreed that the goal of a literature, informed by historical materialism, should be the discovery of objective truth. And both agreed that 'realism' is the appropriate genre for achieving that goal. However, Plekanov's sociology of knowledge also contained a brief for 'critical realism' and protected the use of equivocal language. Members of the Congress regarded 'critical realism' and the equivocations of Aesopean language as outmoded tools: useful in undermining Czarism, but useless in building a new order. In the words of Gorky's resolution: "Without in any way denying the broad, immense work of critical realism, and while highly appreciating its formal achievements in the art of word painting, we should understand that this realism is necessary to us only for throwing light on survivals of the past, for fighting them, and extirpating them."[19] In place of this negative and destructive form of individualism, the Congress endorsed Engels's exhortation that the artist should depict "typical characters" in "typical circumstances."[20] Gorky pointed out that the folklore which united primitive peoples (that is, members of tribal societies and religious groups) into unified human communities was based upon "typicalness." However, he maintained that under the selfish competition of capitalism; the principle of "typicalness" had become truncated. It survived only in the methodology of the experimental sciences. As a result, he contended, bourgeois society had "completely lost the capacity for invention in art." Serious literature had become hermetic. Modern ("decadent") poets wrote only for other poets (e.g. Symbolism). Literature for the people had lost its epic quality. Commercialism had reduced it to the heroism of the comic book.

In contrast, Gorky called upon socialist realists to reintroduce "the logic of hypothesis" into art:

> Myth is invention. To invent means to extract from the sum of a given reality its cardinal idea and embody it in imagery—that is how we got realism. But if to the idea extracted from the given reality we add—completing the idea, by the logic of hypothesis—the desired, the possible, and thus supplement the image, we obtain that romanticism which is at the basis of myth and is highly beneficial in that it tends to provoke a revolutionary attitude to reality, an attitude that changes the world in a practical way.[21]

The typical heroes of the new mythology were to be proletarians: peasants, factory workers, construction technicians, soldiers, etcetera. And the typical circumstance was to involve the triumphant resolution of class struggle. According to Gorkian epistemics, the past as well as the present was to be brought under the discipline of socialist realism. Gorky asserted, "We do not know the history of our past—not in the way it has already been narrated, but as it is illuminated by the teaching of Marx, Lenin, Stalin. . . . "[22] He called for the formation of a militia of hundreds of literary craftsmen dedicated to the Herculean task of rewriting world history.

The official definition of social realism ratified by the Congress was:

> Socialist realism is the basic method of Soviet literature and literary criticism. It *demands* of the artist the truthful, historically concrete representation of reality in its revolutionary development. Moreover, the truthfulness and historical concreteness of the artistic representation of reality *must* be linked with the task of ideological transformation and education of workers in the spirit of socialism.[23]

Three terms summarize the essential constituents of socialist realism: *partinost, ideinost*, and *narodnost*: the truthfulness (in terms of historical materialism) and Party-mindedness of a work's portrayal of reality, the work's pedagogic potential, and the accessibility of its form and content to the broad masses.

Because writers were required to belong to the Soviet Writers' Union and because the Writers' Union was under Party control, the Congress's endorsement of sociorealism was not merely the statement of an aesthetic ideal. It secured a statutory prescription which required conformity. Non-conformity would result in expulsion from the Writers' Union, and in some cases even criminal liability for "anti-Soviet activities." The writer was not free to remain silent. He could not choose to become an "internal émigré" as dissident writers have done throughout history. He was required to produce for the state.

Obviously, this created a dilemma for writers who still resisted the Marxist-Leninist doxology. Gorky *et al.* anticipated this problem. The Congress's resolutions provided an epistemological warrant for the literary purges undertaken by the Stalinist state. Thus, Gorky's speech called for the forceful removal from Soviet Literature of all the remaining "pernicious toxins" of philistinism:

> The Party leadership of literature must be thoroughly purged of all philistine influences. Party members active in literature must not only be the teachers of ideas which will muster the energy of the proletariat in all countries for the last battle for its freedom; the Party leadership must, in all its conduct, show a morally authoritative force. This force must imbue literary workers first and foremost with a consciousness of their collective responsibility for all that happens in their midst. Soviet literature, with all its diversity of talents, and the steadily growing number of new and gifted writers, should be organized as an integral collective body, as a potent instrument of socialist structure.[24]

The administrators of sociorealism soon discovered, however, that even the "new and gifted writers" of the proletkult, who accepted the wisdom of Marxist-Leninism without reservation, could not always be relied upon to produce truthful renditions of reality if left to their own devices. Two facets of the craft of writing make its practitioners peculiarly vulnerable to deviations. First, writing is a solitary task: lonely and isolating. Thus, it is easy for writers to slip into unacceptable (anti-social) departures from sociorealism. Second, language itself is infected with the "pernicious toxins" of the past.

The "Party leadership of literature" attempted to meliorate the effects of the writer's isolation by giving the censor a broader warrant. Under sociorealism, the censor could make aesthetic judgments: render the kinds of evaluations that had formerly been the exclusive prerogatives of editors and literary critics. Thus a work could be rejected by a censor not only because it explored forbidden themes, contained false information, or was considered dangerous to the power or interests of the state (or even just the personal interest of one of its functionaries); but also because the censor regarded the portrayal of the "positive hero" as too weak or unconvincing, or the plot in which the "positive hero" was enmeshed as too tedious, or the ideas too subjective, or the setting too florid, or a secondary

character too sketchy or too sinister or not sinister enough . . . Sim-
inov's *Smoke of the Fatherland*, for example, was condemned because
the basic ideas of the book were not presented in vivid artistic images
and because the positive hero was a "moralizing *intelligent*" (member
of the intelligentsia) rather than a fully developed three-dimensional
character.[25] Karl Radek provided authors with a simple formula for
self-censoring the subjectivist temptations of their craft: "When it
seems to a person that he is defending only some individual shade
of opinion against it [the Party], it will always become apparent on
the basis of a political test that he is defending interests alien to the
proletariat."[26]

Purging language of its toxins proved a more difficult problem. It
necessitated a full-scale criticism of established schools of linguistics
and the creation of a theory of language based upon Marxist-Leninist
principles. Marx's theory of sub-structural dominance and Lenin's
criticism of empirico-symbolism provided the foundations for the new
linguistics. Contra philosophical idealism, Marx maintained, "ideas
do not exist separately from language": "Language is the immediate
actuality of thought."[27] In his view, word and thought are integral
and inseparable. Marx did not regard language as an autonomous
phenomenon. He treated it as a dependent variable—a facet of the
superstructure which is both a reflection and projection of the organization of the powers of production within the substructure (or
material base) of a society. Thus, according to Marx, *Homo sym-
bolicus* is really only *Homo economicus* in drag. In *The German
Ideology*, Marx and Engels describe bourgeois language as thoroughly
"distorted" by relations of buying and selling. Indeed, they suggest
that not merely convention and usage are skewed by commercial
relations; but that the very categories of language and thus the "deep
structure" of the thought processes themselves reflect and support
this deformation. Whether or not it was the intent of the original,
this conception of language can clearly be interpreted by pragmatists
and copyists as authorization and warrant for linguistic intervention
and reform in a post-revolutionary context. Especially when it is tied
to a program for accelerating the process of eliminating residues of
"false consciousness!" Lenin, Stalin, and their apologists interpreted
it in this way.

Lenin's biographers claim he displayed an early predilection for,
and lifelong interest in, language study. Indeed, we are told that
Lenin was, in his own way, an Encyclopedist who conceived a massive
project for the standardization and codification of the modern Russian

language. The project, which has occupied Soviet linguists and lex-
icographers for over a half-century, was designed not only to bring
the language up to date but also to eliminate slang words as well as
regional and local usages. If Marx wanted to show that thinking is
not possible outside of its "material linguistic envelope," Lenin
wanted to hermetically seal the envelope by eliminating all "superfluous" usages.[28] Thus he rejected formalist and phenomenological
theories of language on the grounds that they denied the connection
between word and thought. Because it was the preeminent school of
linguistic philosophy when Lenin undertook the project of empirico-
criticism, Lenin singled out Carnapian formalism as an especially
virulent species of reactionary thought. Carnap's linguistics reduced
cognition to the logical syntax of language. It tried to articulate a
systematic exposition of the rules governing relations among symbols.
Lenin maintained that Carnapian formalism empties symbols of all
content and tries to replace them with an artificial language of logical
signs. Thus it is totally cut off from the discipline of history and
necessity. The attempt to "dematerialize" language is responsible for
such modernist tendencies in art as expressionism, surrealism, symbolism, imagism, etcetera—tendencies which negate the social purpose of art by shutting ordinary people (narodnost) off from art.
Inherently anti-democratic, these trends reflect, preserve, *and* disguise exploitive productive relations.

In place of the power-knowledge of Carnapian linguistics, Lenin
posits a formula for Soviet power-knowledge. He believes that if the
language of art was to be made accessible to the people, it would have
to be stripped of subjectivist uses of symbolism. Consequently, he
maintains that post-revolutionary culture would have to be founded
upon an aesthetic which polices equivocation. Otherwise decadent
trends would be reintroduced into a society which had transcended
them. Vladimir Shcherbina outlines Lenin's theory of symbols:

> Lenin rejects symbols that substitute meaningless subjective signs, ci-
> phers, for cognition of the external and man's inner world. The symbol,
> he insisted in his criticism of Helmholtz, can stand for not only existing
> things, but for purely phantasmogorial, religious, pathological con-
> cepts, experiences, etc.[29]

Lenin, then, distinguishes between symbols which are rooted in historical necessity ("what is") and symbols which violate or negate this reality with counterfactual images ("what was" or "what might be"). He
contends that the former enrich life, while the latter produce a cleav-

age between art and life. Thus equivocal symbols (metaphors, hyper-bole, etcetera) are permissible only if they are firmly anchored in the soil of reality. Symbols are evaluated in terms of their instrumental value: their social utility in building the new culture (*ideinost*). Marx-ist-Leninism rejects the doctrine of "art for art's sake" because it was created by "superfluous men": bohemians and outsiders like Baude-laire and Mallarmé who had no role to play in the productive processes of bourgeois society. In contrast, it claims that within a socialist con-text, artists and litterateurs play an integral role in the production of culture. They are no longer superfluous. But an essential category of bourgeois and classical art—the beautiful—does become superfluous.

The prescriptive warrant for Marxist-Leninist linguistics precludes irony, satire, double-entendre, the utopian, allegory, non-essential use of foreign terms or foreign settings, all unnecessary departures from the economy of discursive language, virtually anything that could be interpreted as a possible index of deviationist tendencies. *If* this warrant could be enforced, sociorealism would be the most readily censorable form of art ever invented by humankind. Not only do the epistemics of sociorealism contain an explicit apology for external con-trol by administrative rationality (*partinost*), but they also attempt to silence the rebellious element inherent in the double-edge of the ironic base of language. Sociorealism instructs the writer to speak in the uni-vocal language of theory (*ideinost*) and to purge all devices of equivo-cation (all symbols of transcendence). It eliminates the cosmological mess-making of artistic creation by forcing its expressions into the al-ien voice of scientific discourse. Stalin's epistemological policemen had become so adroit at enforcing this methodology for "administra-tion of mind" that, as we shall see later, Stalin himself ultimately found it necessary to intervene on behalf of "idealism" in order to avoid total suffocation of the creative spirit in the Soviet Union.

v

Purges of Zamyatin and Pilnyak; Blight of Zhdanovism

Mayakovsky committed suicide in 1930, two months after his capit-ulation to RAPP's demands for a "consolidation of all forces of proletarian literature."[30] The death of the poet who some claim single-handedly caused a revolution with his verse coincided with the beginning of an ice age for creative freedom in the Soviet Union that would continue uninterrupted for over two decades. Nineteen-thirty has been called the "Year of Acquiescence." That year RAPP's campaign against "neo-bourgeois" elements in Soviet literature reached full intensity.

The purges that followed cannot be fully catalogued. Isaac Babel, Osip Mandelstam, and Mikhail Kolcov are among the best known of the estimated six thousand writers who perished in Stalin's gulags. However, the cases of Yevgeni Zamyatin and Boris Pilnyak are examined in some detail here for two reasons.[31] First, because they were the first public purges and in many ways the most dramatic. Second, because they were paradigmatic: that is, they set the pattern for the dramaturgy of subsequent purges. Zamyatin and Pilnyak were singled out for a public campaign of villification because they were regarded as the leading "neo-bourgeois" elements in the Union of Writers. They were charged with allowing publication of their writings abroad without prior approval by *Glavlit*. The incidents in question had occurred long before the furor. They were the result of the failure of the Soviet Union to enter into international copyright arrangements, not from any culpable action on the part of Zamyatin and Pilnyak. Nevertheless the authors were attacked in the press for "treason" and "traffic with the enemy." Statements condemning their "traitorous behavior" were solicited from many writers, including Mayakovsky. Both were expelled from the Writers' Union. In addition, Pilnyak was humiliated into a groveling public recantation; and the work which had been the object of the controversy, *Mahogony*, was transmogrified into a "Five-Year Plan novel."[32] Zamyatin proved more recalcitrant. He presented convincing evidence that he had tried to prevent publication abroad of his novel, *We*; but he refused to renounce the work itself. Instead, he wrote a strongly worded letter of protest directly to Stalin. Incredibly, Zamyatin avoided trial and was allowed to emigrate as a result of the personal intervention of Gorky. Others who emulated his example were not so lucky, as the texts of *The Gulag Archipelago* document. In the purges that followed, Pilnyak's example was the preferred mode: the response that best served the interests of the persecutors and the comfort of the persecuted.

Zamyatin occupies a special place in Soviet demonology. He is still cited by apologists for *Glavlit* as exemplifying the kind of "anti-Soviet renegade" who cannot be tolerated by actually existing socialist systems.[33] Throughout the twenties, Zamyatin resisted dialectical conversion. Indeed he conceived of the calling of the artist as diametrically opposed to state service. In his essay, "I am afraid," written in 1921, Zamyatin claimed that literature can only be dissident: "True literature can never be produced by efficient, reliable civil servants; it can only be produced by madmen, hermits, heretics, dreamers and rebels."[34] Zamyatin was a cosmological mess-maker of the *first order* who posed a direct threat to the emergence of the hegemony of the Soviet State. Like the medieval witches who had to be ritually exorcised, Zamyatin's ideas required special coding as 'evil,' 'unnatural,' 'irrational' (read: "neo-bourgeois," "anti-Soviet," "treasonous"). In Michel Foucault's formula for describing the "anatomy of power," Zamyatin represents the archetypal "condemned man": "In the darkest region of the political field the condemned man represents the symmetrical, inverted figure of the king." His purgation made perfect sense from the perspective of Soviet power-knowledge. It set boundaries and established the parameters within which the groundings of socialist realism could be articulated. Zamyatin's *We* was placed beyond the limits of permission. Its theme betrayed (exposed) the interests of the State. The question it posed could not be accommodated within the assumptions of the constitutive principles of the Stalinist state. *We* committed epistemological treason. It provided testament against messianic statism: against a society which sacrifices the present to the future and the individual to the collective. It is also a protest against centralized planning in politics, economics, language, and literature. In Zamyatin's anti-utopia, human autonomy is destroyed by prohibiting the individual to say 'I.' A "double language" is mandated in which spies and informers, the pariahs of all former human societies, become the "lily-whites" of the new order.[35] George Orwell described Zamyatin's novel as the inspiration for, and prototype of, his own anti-utopian works, *Nineteen-Eighty-four* and *Animal Farm*—works which, like Zamyatin's *We*, are still banned in the U.S.S.R.

The purges of Pilnyak and Zamyatin signaled an expansion of the role of the state in the restrictive control of literature. The purges were followed by a decree of the Council of People's Commissars in 1931 which considerably broadened the franchise of Lenin's "temporary measure" of 1922. *Glavlit* was given authority over all "manuscripts, drawings, paintings, broadcasts, lectures and exhibits to be printed, made public and disseminated."[36] It was empowered to circulate secret lists of items (*perechen*) which could not be published, and to prepare indexes of previously published works which were to be banned or expurgated. Revised "to eliminate typographical errors" became the operative euphemism! Further controls were added in 1934 to cover broadcasting and film as well as all public performances, including theater, ballet, opera, and even circus acts. In the same year, of course, the Soviet Writers' Congress secured the prescriptive controls of socialist realism.

During World War II, there was a slight relaxation in literary controls. However, the devastation of the war—which left twenty-million Soviet citizens dead, the atomic bomb securely in the hands of the U.S., and all of Western Europe aligned with the U.S.—also left the U.S.S.R. isolated, alone in a hostile world. It was a difficult and dangerous time for the Soviets. Stalin's overseer of the arts, Andrei Zhdanov, responded to the danger by introducing a "fifteen year plan" for literature which conscripted all litterateurs into state service. Zhdanov's decrees prepared the way for a new series of purges and public attacks on established writers. The Zhdanovian inquisitions effectively intimidated writers, who quickly translated the instincts of self-preservation into the imperatives of self-censorship.

Writers retreated to the safe formulas of the "illustrating literature" of the prewar era. Schematism, repetition of stale themes, exaggerated didacticism, total avoidance of anything that might be interpreted as subjectivism, cosmopolitanism, or aestheticism characterized the literary output of the period—an output Malenkov would describe in 1952 as "mediocre, dull works" afflicted by "grave shortcomings."[37] The artistic sclerosis of Zhdanovism was particularly acute in dramaturgy because empty theaters, unlike full book repositories, could not be kept a state secret. Consequently, the Council of Ministers curtailed financial supports for theatrical productions in 1948. Drama critics were accused of trying to create an "anti-Soviet literary underground" by slandering dramaturgy from the viewpoint of "aestheticism." But if empty theaters required scapegoats, they also alerted Party officials to the limits of Zhdanovism—limits that were underscored by the revenue sheets of the publishing industry and the circulation records of lending libraries.[38] These indicators set the stage for revisionism in Soviet literary politics.

In 1952 Stalin modified the 1930 plan for the Soviet administration of mind not because it was unsuccessful, but because it was too successful. Total administration of mind precluded discovery in science and novelty in literature. Soviet science stagnated or even regressed, as in the case of T.D. Lysenko, who under Party auspices, repealed the laws of Mendelian genetics, with disastrous effects for Soviet agriculture. The Soviet reading public abandoned its authors in favor of the classics, or, still worse, foreign or clandestine literature.

Zhdanovism had revealed an essential principle for the articulation of power-knowledge within an industrial context: it must meet "surplus demand," it must provide channels for "making it new" (or seeming to).[39] Thus Stalin attempted to cut some windows through the hall-of-mirrors he had created without endangering the larger structure of Soviet power-knowledge. He set in motion an "artificial dialectic" which he could control by foreclosure if its development threatened to betray Party interests.[40]

In his first linguistic letter (1952), Stalin authorized more "criticism and self-criticism" in the sciences. He affirmed that, "It is generally recognized that no science can develop and flourish without a battle of opinions, without freedom of criticism." Stalin charged that, under the tutelage of N.Y. Marr, Soviet linguistics had violated this tenet of scientific inquiry and, as a result, had become a moribund discipline. The stated purpose of Stalin's letters was to breathe new life into linguistics.

Marr was an eminent ethnographer who had done pioneering work in recording the grammars of several regional languages. He exercised enormous influence in Soviet linguistics. Marr was also the author of a "Marxist" theory of linguistics. This theory was relatively straightforward and predictable. Marr contended that language was part of the superstructure and therefore reflected the base, the organization of the means of production. He cited precedence in the works of Marx, Engels, and Lenin to support this contention. The domestic political implications of this theory were, however, extremely problematic. They seemed to imply that with the securing of a socialist base, linguistic diversity would disappear and regional or "zonal" languages would be replaced by one language. This inference was consistent with Leninist linguistics which maintained that the international triumph of socialism would produce one world with one culture and one language (not Russian or German or French or English but an entirely new language). In the early 1950s, however, there was little to indicate that the triumph of international socialism was near at hand and much to indicate that the domestic acceptance of the Soviet way of life would be seriously imperiled by attempts to impose one language upon peoples of great ethnic and linguistic diversity.

Stalin was concerned about stagnation in linguistics but this concern was secured in the realpolitiks of the historical moment. Contra the prevailing dogma in linguistics, Stalin decreed language *not* a part of the "superstructure":

> . . . language radically differs from superstructure. Language is not a product of one or another base, old or new, within the given society, but of the whole course of the history of society and the history of bases throughout centuries. It was created not by any class, but by all the classes of society, by the efforts of hundreds of generations. It was created for the satisfaction of the needs not of only one class, but of all society, of all the classes of society . . . Language, on the contrary, is the product of a whole number of epochs, in the course of which it takes shape, is enriched, develops, and is polished.

Stalin concludes his discourse on the relation of language to super-structure with two forceful assertions:

> a). A Marxist cannot regard language as a superstructure on the base;
> b). To confuse language and superstructure is a serious error.[41]

Stalin did not intend to release literature from state service. Never-theless publication of his linguistic letters combined with the Party's public repudiation of the ultra-orthodox literary critic A. Belik to expand the limits of permission. It gradually allowed litterateurs to discard exhausted themes in favor of previously proscribed topics.

vi

Clandestine Literature in the U.S.S.R.: Samizdat, Tamizdat, and the Emergence of the Dissident Movement

If prisons are schools for revolutionaries, under the Soviet system they have also become colleges of poetry. Andrei Sinyavsky, like Aleksandr Solzhenitsyn, a former prisoner, maintains that the pop-ulation of the camps has not only included an exceptional number of actual poets, internal émigrés who could not confine their voices to the metier of sociorealism, but also verse-makers without any special gifts who have taken up poetry as a form of protest against the extreme isolation and dehumanization of camp life.[42] Among the latter were "the caption writers": men who used knives or pieces of glass to tattoo messages on their foreheads, typically "Soviet Slave." Sinyavsky claims that caption writing spread rapidly in the camps until the authorities attached the death sentence to this form of protest.

But even under Zdanovism not all dissidents were confined to the camps. Like Mayakovsky, many writers "stamped on the throat" of their own songs and served sociorealism.[43] Unlike Mayakovsky, however, dissident "engineers of the soul" practiced this self-censorship reluctantly. In silent protest, they struggled to maintain the integrity of their private thoughts and waited for a break—a 'thaw'—in the repressive regimen of state censorship. When it finally came, they retrieved fugitive manuscripts from "hidey holes," "lightened" their dissent or encoded it in the cryptography of Aesopean language, and submitted it to the editors of "enlightened" publications like *Novy Mir*.[44]

A "thaw" finally came in 1956. It lasted only a few months. Like the purges of the early thirties and mid-forties, it was orchestrated from above. It too can be viewed as an attempt, albeit a faulty one, to shape public opinion through the dramaturgy of an "artificial dialectic."

The "thaw" did not result from a relaxation of state interference in the arts. To the contrary, the work which more than any other served as a harbinger and symbol of a change in Soviet literary politics, Solzhenitsyn's *One Day in the Life of Ivan Denisovich* was published only because Nikita Khrushchev's advisers believed it could be useful in consolidating their power. They saw it as engineering of the soul which could be an effective tool in their campaign against "the cult of personity" of the Stalinist era. Unlike his predecessors Khrushchev claimed no expertise in literary affairs and, in fact, personally preferred to get information from films. However, his adviser and personal secretary, V.S. Lebedev, read Solzhenitsyn's story to Krushchev. The chairman not only approved its publication in *Novy Mir*, but endorsed it from the platform of the plenary meeting of the Party as important and much needed. The prescriptive *imprimatur* of the party leader made *One Day in the Life of Ivan Denisovich* required reading for all delegates to the plenary sessions. They returned to the provinces with two books, a red one containing the materials on the agenda of the Party meetings, and a blue one (*Novy Mir*, Number 11).

Ironically, the same political considerations which made possible the publication of *One Day* required banning of Victor Nekrasov's *In the Trenches of Stalingrad*, the foremost Soviet war novel which had been studied in Russian schools for years. These political considerations also set in motion the chain of events which led to Khrushchev's denunciation of modernist artists. Nevertheless, approval of Solzhenitsyn's story marked a radical departure from the established imperatives of *partinost*. It contained the first public acknowledgment of the existence of the camps in which millions of political prisoners had died, and thereby lifted the interdictions surrounding discussion of the most extreme mechanism of Soviet power-knowledge. It released a floodgate of reaction far beyond anything anticipated by those who had set this particular round of the "artificial dialectic" in motion: a floodgate which briefly crashed through the barriers of artificiality and produced a short-lived but very real and significant "thaw" in the Soviet administration of mind. The thaw made possible the emergence of a dissident democratic movement in the Soviet Union which continues to this day. Indeed Solzhenitsyn contends that it would have been possible for him to publish anything, even the texts of *The Gulag Archipelago*, during the period immediately following the appearance of *One Day*. His own caution and that of his editors prevented it, not Soviet censorship.[45]

One Day fit into the pragmatics of Khrushchev's policy precisely because Solzhenitsyn conformed to the strictures of sociorealism. Ivan Denisovich was a peasant and thus filled the prerequisites of a "positive hero." This was especially appealing to Nikita Khrushchev, peasant *cum* Party chairman. Solzhenitsyn authentically reproduced the details of camp life. Moreover, he included a labor scene. Khrushchev was particularly pleased with Ivan's meticulous workmanship in which he was as the chairman put it, "so careful with the mortar."[46] But Solzhenitsyn's long apprenticeship in the camps enabled him to encode a message of liberation between-the-lines of Ivan's story. He created a "typical hero" in a "typical situation." Even the title (suggested by the editor of *Novy Mir*) underscored the "typicalness" of Ivan's experience. Ivan, however, was a positive hero in a negative situation. The camp motif was powerful stuff to a reading public used to the tepid gruel of Zhdanovism. If the didactics (*ideinost*) of Ivan's case were clear to Khrushchev and his advisers (repudiation of Stalin's errors), they were more ambiguous to relatives and survivors or pre- and post-Stalinist *gulags*. With the ban lifted, even *Izvestia* immediately printed a camp story. Editors were soon deluged with manuscripts exploring the new theme, and it began to seem as if every former prisoner had secreted away a personal cache of tales of terror—tales encoded in the power-knowledge of opposition.

Khrushchev could not close the Pandora's box he had opened even though he later expressed regret that he had ever gotten involved in the Solzhenitsyn affair.[47] His successors, however, declared the camp theme "exhausted," and quickly constricted the limits of permission. But even Shelepin, the "Iron Shurik" of the K.G.B., could not silence the literary underground that was born during the months of the "thaw."

Solzhenitsyn's work no longer passed censorship. It was not even acceptable to the editors of *Novy Mir*. Shelepin's men searched the author's quarters and those of his friends. Manuscripts that he had secreted away were discovered and confiscated. Very incriminating manuscripts! Yet Solzhenitsyn was not arrested. He was an author protected by a theme. Ivan Denisovich kept his creator from returning to the camps. The old dramaturgy of literary purges could hardly be invoked in the immediate wake of the Politburo's condemnation of Stalin's methods. This unanticipated twist in the outcome of the "artificial dialectic" produced a kind of moratorium on public purgation of well-known writers and intellectuals which lasted until the trials of Sinyavsky and Daniel in 1966. For the decline of European colonial powers and the emergence of the Soviet Union as a major world power transformed the old rhetoric of Communist internationalism into the imperatives of *Realpolitiks*. The "artificial dialectic" became an export commodity. Its dramaturgy had to be scripted for consumption in Asia, Africa, and Latin America. The doctrine of Polycentrism facilitated this scripting, but it also created openings for more exposure of Soviet intellectuals to heterodox ideas. Soviet expansionism required a continued presence abroad. Travel restrictions had to be moderated. Soviets increased their participation in international scientific meetings and cultural exchange programs. The Soviet decision to flex its new muscles on the world stage also paradoxically contributed to creating the preconditions for emergence of an *organized* democratic movement within the Soviet Union. The end of Soviet isolation did not end the persecution of dissident writers and scholars within the U.S.S.R., but it did signal the beginning of coverage of those persecutions in international media as well as the beginning of international human rights activism.

Thus the Pasternak affair, unlike the earlier persecution of Mandelstam became an international *cause célèbre*. Boris Pasternak was among the many Soviet writers who ceased to exist in the official annals of Soviet literature after 1928—censored from the great Encyclopaedia conceived by Lenin and brought to fruition by the literary proletariat of the Stalinist era. Except for a brief interlude during the war, Pasternak was not allowed to publish. When his masterwork *Doctor Zhivago* was denied the Soviet imprimatur in 1956, the author, who had always prided himself on his refusal to collaborate with "them" (the Soviet authorities), arranged to have the book published abroad. Pasternak was denounced as a "traitor," a "malevolent philistine," a "decadent formalist," and even a "nestmesser." He was expelled from the Writers' Union and threatened with exile. Pasternak's *tamizdat, Doctor Zhivago*, was awarded the Nobel Prize for Literature in 1958.

When Pasternak died two years later, his funeral at the writers' colony of Peredlkino was the scene of a spontaneous demonstration—an act of resistance—in which students, workers, and well-known writers paid tribute to the fallen freedom fighter. Sinyavsky and Daniel were pallbearers. The pianist Sviatoslav Richter paid a musical tribute and the philosopher V. Asmus delivered a funeral oration. A few months later, Pasternak's friend Olga Ivinskaya and her daughter were arrested and sentenced to labor camps. The Party was wholly unprepared for the protest that followed. In an effort to placate world opinion and silence internal dissidence, Khrushchev's successors released Ivinskaya and halved the sentence of the real-life model of Pasternak's Lara.

A period of relative moderation, a second "thaw" ensued. During this period, officially sanctioned writers like Illya Ehrenberg and Yevgen Yevtushenko pushed the limits of permission further than they ever had before—although not as far as Solzhenitsyn had, and not as far as he thinks they could have.[48] In 1964 the non-conformist poets Kazakova and Akhmadova were allowed to hold a poetry recital before an audience of almost two thousand. This unprecedented event was followed by an unprecedented two-part article by the editor-in-chief of *Pravda*. Contra sociorealism, the editor, A.M. Rumjancev, argued:

> Genuine creativity is possible only in an atmosphere of searching, of experimentation, of the free expression, and mutual clashes of opinion. A salutary development of art demands the presence of different schools and directions . . .[49]

Stalin's First Linguistic Letter had specifically authorized the end of isolationism in science. In 1958 the theory of relativity and quantum physics were legitimated. In 1964 biology and genetics were released from Lysenko's law of heredity; and in 1955 the All-Union Congress of scientists held discussions on logic, pathology, cybernetics, and scientific methodology. Because of their quasi-scientific status, economics and sociology enjoyed some of the benefits of the moderating climate. Philosophy and history, however, remained barren monuments to Zhdanovism. Because they are indispensable to a technological society, scientists and engineers enjoyed greater privileges than litterateurs. Indeed, before his internal exile in 1979, the atomic scientist Andrei Sakharov enjoyed far greater freedom to express dissident ideas than any other Soviet citizen. And it was engineers, not litterateurs, who turned critical Marxism against official Marxism in a widely circulated 1965 *samizdat, The Bell,* which bore the epigraph: "from the dictatorship of the bureaucracy to the dictatorship of the proletariat."

With the Soviet invasion of Czechoslovakia, the second thaw abruptly ended. The limits of permission tightened. Domestic purges were used to refract criticism of foreign adventurism. Pasternak's pall-bearers, Daniel and Sinyavsky, were convicted of publishing in *tamizdat* and sentenced to long terms in work camps. Tvardovsky, the editor of *Novy Mir* who had arranged publication of *One Day* lost his membership on the Central Committee of the Party and barely retained his editorial post. *Junost,* the second most liberal Soviet journal, underwent "self-criticism." *Pravda*'s lone defender of literary freedom had long since been reassigned to the Academy of Sciences. But this time the dissidents were organized. They could withstand the assault. The trials of Daniel and Sinyavsky did not cow dissidents into submission. To the contrary, they consolidated the forces in opposition.

Alexander Herzen once described described Russian literature as "one continuous indictment of Russian reality."[50] Litterateurs like Pasternak and Anna Akhmatova, who refused the uniform of sociorealism, proudly referred to their writings as Russian literature, not Soviet literature. They saw their work as the true heir of the classic tradition in Russian literature.

After 1934 the classics became the only window to the past that was not papered over by socirealism. Gorky's aesthetics had, of course, subordinated historiography to the imperatives of *partinost, ideinost,* and *narodnost.* But no amount of expurgation could fully eliminate the ironic disjuncture produced by confronting the achievements of Soviet literature with the achievements of Czarist literature. No amount of censorship could silence the oral tradition of Russian literature which circulated the forbidden verses of Pasternak and Akhmatova. And after the imprisonment of Daniel and Sinyavsky, no amount of K.G.B. harassment could stop the flow of *samizdat* and *tamizdat*.

Today many of the supporters of Daniel and Sinyavsky are in exile, in prison, or in the new *gulags* of the Soviet state, the psychiatric clinics. But they have left their imprimatur. For the first time in the Soviet Union, public opinion exists. To be sure, the weight of this opinion has not rallied behind the democratic movement, but neither is it marching passively to the old cadences of *partinost*.

Today there are three categories of literature in the Soviet Union: official literature, dissident literature, and mass literature. The first is little read but highly rewarded. The second is technically not illegal but frequently confiscated, supported only by donations, and subject to corruption because it must be laboriously reproduced by carbon copy since the K.G.B. regards duplicators and copying machines as "quasi-military objects." The earliest *samizdat* were underground high school newspapers in which the dictates of sociorealism were parodied. They were followed by overtly apolitical journals of aesthetic protest like Aleksandr Ginsberg's *Sintaksis*. Harassment politicized the largely apolitical aesthetic journals and radicalized political *samizdat* like *Feniks* into revolutionary tracts. When the Central Committee issued its 1968 order to begin an "offensive against bourgeois ideology (an effort to rid the U.S.S.R. of *samizdat*), Sakharov issued a counter-statement in *tamizdat, Progress, Peaceful Co-Existence and Intellectual Freedom*. This courageous move gave birth to the *Chronika Tekuschich Sobytij* (Chronicle of Current Events): the primary *samizdat* of the democratic movement which has published in *samizdat* and *tamizdat* on a regular basis ever since. The Chronicle reports Soviet persecutions (arrests, forced emigrations, and involuntary confinements to mental hospitals) of democratic, aesthetic, and *ante-bellum* humanists, as well as Christian, Jewish, Ukranian, and other ethnic dissidents. The dissident intelligentsia who publish in *samizdat* represent three distinct currents of opinion: (1) "true" Marxist-Leninism; (2) Christian ideology; and (3) liberal ideology.[51] They have been welded together by censorship, but speak in unison only in their opposition to the current dictatorship of the bureaucracy.

The third class of literature, "mass literature," is seldom mentioned in official publications, but it is now the most widely read of all.[52] It is of poor literary quality and, unlike sociorealism, makes no elevating claims. It is presented as entertainment. And, like bourgeois mass literature, it is designed to appeal to the lowest common denominator of the largest possible audience. In this case, fear is the numerator. Like much of Soviet television, the new genre of popular culture is intended to serve the interests of the bureaucracy by acting as an "opium of the masses." The "typical hero" is a secret agent working behind enemy lines. The world depicted in these detective novels is one in which Soviet citizens are surrounded by menacing forces which can only be exorcised by the heroism of the K.G.B. agent. This reactionary, quasi-bourgeois literature returns the Soviet reader to the spiritual womb of Stalinism: to the 'good old days' of the Cold War when black was black and red was red: when dissidence was treason, and when soldiers were celebrated for distinguished service in repelling the fascist invader, not quietly dispatched to crush insurgence in Czechoslovakia, Hungary, or Afghanistan. This literary genre disguises purgation in the trench-coat of a thriller *cum* morality play. The message of these detective novels is overtly anti-intellectual. For the Party, once so eager to establish spiritual bonds between litterateurs and proletarians, is now keenly atuned to the dangers implicit in such alliances.

My analysis does not suggest that the *samizdat* or *tamizdat* poses a serious threat to the survival of the Soviet system. To the contrary, the Soviet state is an insular steel giant with all the hardware necessary to repel a foreign invasion or a domestic uprising. It does suggest that the Soviet state is a giant that does not trust its own strength. And that consequently it will probably continue to enforce censorship and engage in periodic rites of purgation.

There are alternatives. The Soviet bureaucracy could transcend this primitive technology of control by making further compromises with bourgeois values: it could sponsor a mass literature and electronic culture sophisticated enough to refract the resonance of the radical power-knowledge of dissident literature. Or it could rediscover its revolutionary mission! With the ascent of a younger, better educated cadre of Party leaders, the Soviets could institutionalize a thawing process which would empower movement from the "dictatorship of the bureaucracy" toward a "dictatorship of the proletariat." This genuinely revolutionary alternative would, however, require a radical restructuring of Soviet power-knowledge.

At the time of this writing (1987) the Soviet Union, under the leadership of Mikhail Gorbachev, is making unprecedented moves in the direction of liberalization ("Reconstruction"): endeavoring to restructure the Central Committee of the Party by introducing "democratization," experimenting with market-style economics, making tentative moves to develop the infrastructure of an information society, releasing Andrei Sakharov from internal exile, inviting performing artists who left the Soviet Union to escape censorship to return as guest performers, taking initiatives in expanding cultural and scientific exchanges, permitting some public criticism of the K.G.B., allowing some U.S. media figures and public officials to engage in open dialogues on Soviet television, and relaxing some controls over publication. Gorbachev maintains that a national party conference in 1988 will "impart a mighty charge" to his efforts. While Gorbachev's reforms will retain the one-party state system, he has nevertheless announced that, "Now, it is time to raise the level and effectiveness of control from below so that each executive and each official constantly feel their responsibility to and dependence on the electorate."[53] To date, Gorbachev's initiatives have apparently met significant resistance from old-line conservatives in Party councils. But the public at large has responded with indifference to these changes, and Gorbachev has openly expressed his frustration with the apathy of Soviet citizens to "democratization."

vii

Polycentrism: Alternative to or Extension of Official Censorship?

Russia is not Hungary, Yugoslavia, or Poland. National traditions, officially dissolved by Leninist aesthetics, have in fact preserved a heritage of freedom among the peoples of these lands. The limited pluralism that has sporadically existed within these countries reflects colonial resistance to Russian hegemony rather than integral movements toward more humanistic socialisms. Similarly, the polytheism of the epigram of Mao's cultural revolution, "let a thousand flowers bloom," only resonated long enough for a few buds to form before it was suppressed by its author.

The analogy between Marxist-Leninist doctrine and religious dogma has been drawn so frequently that it is perhaps over-worked, albeit most eloquently in Sinyavsky's eulogy on the god-hunger of the Russian people.[54] It will suffice here to point to the structural congruences between the system of power-knowledge which secured the medieval Church and that which secures the Soviet system: the bureaucratic organization of censorship; the periodic issuance of indices of forbidden books; the insistence on the authority of certain selected texts from a larger corpus (Paul, not Barnabus; *The Manifesto*, not the essay on the Russian Menace to Europe); the hierarchical enfranchisement of authorized interpreters and correspondent devaluation of "protestant" readings based upon individual conscience; reliance upon the Domitian strategy to suppress forbidden books; the use of periodic ritual purgations to achieve congregation through segregation; the inability to deal rationally with the Tacitean effect and the consequent resort to easily discredited counter-measures; the generation of a radicalized dissident literature abroad resulting in creation of a lucrative domestic black market; and a chronic vulnerability to irony created by the disjunctures between the humanistic visions of their respective founding texts and the rigid bureaucracies which have displaced these visions.

The Soviet system has provided workers with a form of job security they do not have under capitalism. But slaves and serfs also have job security. The Soviet system made possible the rapid industrialization of Russia. It has brought the benefits (and hazards) of a technological society to its citizens. It has improved national health. It has created a quasi-equalitarian system in which a *muzik* like Khrushchev can rise to Party Chairman. It has provided women with broader educational opportunities than have Liberal societies, but it has not modified the patriarchal authority structure of family or state. It has provided a level of state support for the arts unprecedented in modern times—support which produced the blight of Zhdanovism but also the splendor of Bolshoi. But it has built its achievements upon a foundation of enforced silences: prior censorship, denial of dissent, travel restrictions, abridgment of all "rights" to free public assembly. The *gulag* is the inverted figure of the *politburo*. The Soviet system requires state censorship. Soviet officials freely admitted this during the 1980 Polish workers' strike.

Fifty years after the fact, socialist realism provides the critic with an easy target. Literature by five-year plan or fifteen-year plan was bound to produce more bad work than good. But historical amnesia encourages us to forget that in the 1930s the power-knowledge of world domination was encoded in conceptual categories different from what it is today. The world was in the grips of a capitalist depression. Fascism was ascendant in Spain, Germany, and Italy. To many writers in the U.S.S.R., Europe, and the U.S., socialist realism appeared to offer an authentic vocabulary of resistance. It appeared to be the 'or' in the 'either/or' of an equation that included fascism, *cum* 'futurism.' The 'proletarian movement' in American literature, which attracted well-known writers like Dos Passos, Steinbeck, Farrell, Anderson, and Gold, was an attempt to realize the emancipatory potential of this dimension of sociorealism. Such modern classics as *U.S.A., The Grapes of Wrath*, and *Studs Lonigan* reflect the influence of socialist realism. Its influence is also evident in the portrayal of the typical anti-heroes in the dramas of Arthur Miller and Eugene O'Neill. The protagonists of these works were ordinary folk (*narodnost*) locked in a struggle for survival in an oppressive world. Sociorealism's "logic of hypothesis" empowered critical dialogues on the crisis in American capitalism and, for a time, provided a politic for resisting fascism. Yet American literary critics still view the impact of sociorealism on American literature through the frames of unreconstructed Cold War cant. They still dismiss it as a blight.

Like any compelling system of power-knowledge, sociorealism is both a way of seeing and a way of not seeing. In the hands of talented enthusiasts it opened a window to the artistic evocation of a world generally disdained by the elitist conventions of aristocratic and bourgeois literature: the world of the ordinary working man and woman. In the hands of conscriptees and Party hacks, however, it became an aesthetic straitjacket.

viii

Socialist Institutions

Socialism in a *good idea*. It seeks equality and justice for all. And it tries to eliminate poverty and greed.

Some of the evils of the Soviet system were produced by the culpable acts of opportunists. Good ideas *and* good people are necessary to secure human freedom.

But they are not sufficient to sustain it. In his much censored *Memoirs*, Ilya Ehrenberg cited a passage from an unidentified French author: "The unfortunate thing about despotism is not that it does not love people, but that it loves them too much and trusts them too little."[55]

Human freedom can only be sustained by *Good institutional structures*. Good institutional structures do not, as conservatives often imply, merely save the masses from one another. They save them from their leaders—from their commissars *and* yogis, legislators *and* corporate controllers.

It remains to be demonstrated whether any socialist state can institutionalize viable mechanisms for "self-criticism." Lucien Goldmann's judgment of socialism has not yet been disproven:

> ...it remains true that the experience of forty years [now seventy] of socialist society proves that the abolition of exchange and market production in a society with an economy entirely planned by the central authority poses a most serious threat to freedom, equality, toleration— all the great values of the Enlightenment.
>
> Although these values have been rightly stigmatized in the socialist camp as purely formal and devoid of content; although freedom loses much of its meaning when it becomes, as Anatole France put it, "freedom for the millionaire to sleep in a palace and the beggar to make his bed under a bridge," and when those who have the money have the power to direct public opinion by means of the Press, the radio and every medium of propaganda; although equality is critically weakened if it becomes mere equality 'before the law' and has no economic reality; although toleration is practiced only in the domain of religion, since religion plays no significant part in the capitalist world, despite all this, western people in general, and particularly the educated classes, even the socialists among them, have become aware of the immense importance to human life of preserving the values of the Enlightenment. The right to express and defend opinions in all social and political circumstances, in books and newspapers; respect for all men as possessing equal rights in law; toleration in religion and social philosophy: these give the life of society a fundamental structure which, even if realized only in formal terms represents an immeasurable historical advance that cannot and must not lightly be thrown away.[56]

CHAPTER SEVEN

Censorship in Capitalist Societies

i

Democracy and Capitalism: the Two Faces of the American Republic

Outlaws—rebels, freethinkers, pirates, and pornographers—invented the idea of a free press. For them, prisons were "schools of freedom." Hemlock, not olive branches, inspired Plato's *Apology for Socrates*. Milton's *Areopagitica* was written to protest a fine levied against him for literary crimes. The pragmatic warrant for free speech forged by the clandestine book merchants of Venice bore the mark of the Inquisitor's sword. Franklin's *Apology for Printers* was a response to a series of harsh encounters with censors in Boston and Philadelphia. Tom Paine wrote parts of *The Age of Reason* in Robespierre's prison under sentence for high treason. The British Stamp Act of 1765, which imposed taxes on all printed materials circulated in the American colonies, provided the animus for the illicit birth of the Sons of Liberty.

Covenants forged by outlaws are never dispassionate. They always bear grudges. They are designed to settle old scores. Their theses are anti-theses. Their power-knowledge is contingent: battle-scarred. Only dependents can articulate declarations of independence.

The history of the emergence of concepts of free speech and free press in America has been extensively and effectively recorded by others.[1] I am not prepared to offer a revisionary interpretation of this history. My intentions are more limited. I seek only to fill some of the blank spaces in the narrative structures of the classic texts.

A. Freedom and Control

Worms and fires in Washington do not account for these blank spaces. They were created by semantic organizations of the past that stressed the 'from' of American libertarian concepts more than their 'to.' My own restylization of the past emphasizes the dual, sometimes competing, contingencies which shaped the contexts in which these concepts were articulated. It stresses the fact that libertarian ideals arose under conditions of colonial repression and matured in consonance with the maturation of industrial capitalism. The first contingency— the role British tyranny played in shaping American ideas of liberty— has been widely chronicled and celebrated by Liberal historians. The second contingency—the role industrial capitalism has played in shaping the institutional framework through which libertarian ideas could be realized—has not been fully recorded.

This gap in the historical record is not incidental. It is a socially structured silence produced by the conflation of libertarian and commercial interests in the articulation of American power-knowledge. Some of the precedents which legitimated this silence can be identified.

First, by stressing the adversarial role of a free press—its Promethean spirit—the Revolutionary covenant provided an epistemological warrant for historical and cultural studies which would perceive the subsequent development of U.S. press institutions as well as the commodities they produced as autonomous expressions: free and independent in the fullest meanings of those terms. This deflected attention from institutional analysis. It inhibited the use of totalistic perspectives which would have seen press practices as embedded within a holistic network of political, economic, technological, and social structures, values, and actions. It prepared the way for the development of the professional code of journalistic objectivity, and for the emergence of traditions within literary criticism, such as the New Criticism, Practical Criticism, and Literary Structuralism which treat texts as wholly independent of the social situations in which they were written. It allowed editors and publishers to deny the political and class basis of literary trends, styles, and concepts of merit. In sum, it separated texts from their contexts.

Second, Jefferson entrusted the free press, especially newspapers, to serve as the "watchdog" of American democracy. But, to his own later regret, he provided no means for citizens to watch the watchdogs. Abuses of press freedom eventually led to movements toward self-censorship and professionalism within journalism. Journalistic professionalism succeeded in reducing the visibility of abuses of the free press. But it also disenfranchised lay criticism by fostering the impression that members of the public lack the expert technical and managerial knowledge necessary to comprehend and debate competently issues involving editorial decision-making. This limited the warrant for press freedom to professionals and secured hierarchical principles in the creation and distribution of information in America. It left professionals free to articulate and enforce their own limits of permission. It ensured that the only dogs licensed to watch the press would be guard dogs of professionalism. Citizens retained rights to legal redress in cases of libel or slander; but there was no redress (beyond refusal to purchase an offensive publication) if the practices of professionals systematically ignored, discredited, or suppressed minority views. In sum, professionalism in journalism and publishing placed professionals beyond the scrutiny of lay criticism.

Third, the unique combination of talents and structures of opportunity in journalism and publishing have made journalists and publishers both the makers and keepers of the history of press freedom in America. The resulting record is an insiders' account or "captive history" which reflects the interests, priorities, and values of media professions and institutions and their patrons.[2] It is, in a sense, an official history. Insider accounts are valuable accounts: authentic accounts. But they are also partial accounts. They do not tell the whole story. They must be supplemented, enlarged, criticized, and contextualized before a creditable history can be written. The blank spaces they have left in the historical record result from the fact that insiders have been in the best position to know and care about the development of media institutions in America, and from the fact that professional historians have shown little interest in this development and have thereby, in effect, surrendered the territory to the insiders. The result has been the creation of an historical record which is largely silent about the business side of media institutions: the ways in which they have used their power to maximize profit, expand markets, and circumvent competition. In sum, insider accounts of the history and practices of media institutions are self-serving: they stress the freedom of the Liberal press from government control but gloss over its subservience to the imperatives of profit.

Fourth, the combined effects of these precedents have sanctioned analogies which equate 'truth' and 'profitability.' The "free market of ideas" is the best known of these analogies. Using market mechanisms to determine the logic or merit of ideas reduces ideas to commodities. When this happens the circulation of ideas is determined by their sales profiles. The 'consumer' is described as voting for the products of the *Consciousness Industry*[2a] with his or her dollars (consumer sovereignty). Such metaphors suggest democracy and freedom of choice. They deflect attention away from the tightly controlled decision-making processes that actually determine what ideas will gain entry into the commodity system. That is, they render the control system of the capitalistic consciousness industry invisible and thereby permit subterranean censorship based upon both market and political considerations. In sum, they permit elites to rule but preserve the semiotic of democracy.

The cumulative effect of these socially structured silences is to render the system of control of industrial capitalism extremely resistant to criticism. They permit industrial capitalism to function with impunity—even where it violates the promises of the democratic covenant.

My re-reading of this history indicates that American capitalism has not only been guilty of violating the promises of democracy, but that such violations have become frequent, systemic, and intractable. Contra Liberal histories, which portray democracy as the theory and capitalism (cum 'free enterprise') as the practice, my analysis suggests that industrial capitalism routinely abridges free enterprise as well as freedom of the press. It affirms the cogency of Theodore Dreiser's 1925 diagnosis of "the American tragedy" as an essential conflict between democratic principles and corporate practices. And it asserts that this historic conflict is currently being projected onto the world stage in the tragic failure of the Liberal Enlightenment: its collapse into an engine of cultural imperialism.

Established conventions of political discourse in America treat 'democracy' and 'capitalism' as nearly synonymous. Political speech has been compared to prayer.[3] In the prayers of capitalists, 'the American way' is their way, the 'free world' is the capitalist world, 'democracy' is capitalism. . . . These conventions allow no critical distance and acknowledge no disparities in the two agendas. However, my analysis indicates that these terms are not interchangeable: that they have different historical origins and denote different practices. It further indicates that these practices frequently conflict, and that the basis of the conflict is deeply rooted. It attributes the conflict to the fact that the two systems embody radically different solutions to the problems of social order. The disparities in these solutions are underscored by Bowles and Gintis in the following description of the contrasting priorities of democracy and industrial capitalism:

> ... the central problems of democracy are: insuring the maximal participation of the majority in decision-making; protecting minorities against the prejudices of the majority; and protecting the majority from any undue influence on the part of an unrepresentative minority.
> ... Making U.S. capitalism work involves: insuring the minimal participation in decision-making by the majority (the workers); protecting a single minority (capitalists and managers) against the wills of a majority; and subjecting the majority to the maximal influence of this single unrepresentative minority.[4]

In sum, democracy opposes *all* arbitrary exercises of power; but capitalism permits arbitrary exercises of power in the pursuit of profit.

Where Liberal historians maintain that the American Revolution is distinguished by the absence of a Thermidorean purge, my analysis suggests that the emergence of corporate capitalism was in a sense the American Thermidor. Corporatism domesticated the radicalism of the American covenant. It eclipsed the Natural Law concepts upon which the Bill of Rights had been secured and reversed much of the egalitarian thrust of the Jacksonian era. In short, it made Americans "citizens of government but subjects of corporations."[5]

B. The American Thermidor

My re-reading of the history of American press freedom does not attribute the failure of the Liberal project merely to crass motives, although I acknowledge that the American Revolution produced its share of war profiteers and that some of those profiteers are now venerated as patriots. Rather I ascribe the failure of the Liberal Enlightenment to the convergence of a number of historical and economic factors. Some of these factors have their genesis in the way the founding fathers conceived the American Republic: in their utilitarian economic philosophy which led them to a facile equation of free expression and free trade; in their radical individualism ('freedom from') which easily translates into a warrant for selfishness; in their implicit acceptance of a double-standard of morality which allowed them to separate public (official) and private (personal and business) conduct; in the explicit patrician elitism of their paternalistic attitudes toward "the people," especially the people without property, education, white skin, Christian ancestry, or male gender; and, in their class and personal economic interests. But the limited vision of the fathers of the Republic only prepared the ground. That ground was cultivated by a series of profound structural transformations in nineteenth- and twentieth-century capitalism.

These transformations allowed industrial capitalism to assert the primacy of its *formally totalitarian* principles of social organization and quietly to negate much of the emancipatory potential of the democratic covenant. These structural changes made the Panoptic discipline and hierarchical controls of the factory and office the *paradigm for all social relations* in industrial society including the relation of a citizen to his or her government.

The Consciousness Industry—press, advertising, public relations, mass entertainment, and organized leisure—played a decisive role in securing the new paradigm. It cultivated allegiances to the new order within the authority structures of people-producing agencies: families, schools, churches, and the body politic. For industrialism not only required reorganization of work, it also required resocialization of workers and creation of consumers. Industrial America did not repudiate the democratic covenant, it ideologized it. The terms of the bargain were changed. The free press was not crushed, it was sold. Free speech did not lose its franchise, it lost its resonance. The publics it had once addressed were transformed into audiences (markets) for mass communications. These communications were scripted to sell products and a new social order. The terms of the new bargain were sealed in the vernacular of democracy. The symbols of the Republic were recast as corporate logos: 'Liberty' became an insurance company; 'American,' an airline and an automobile manufacturer; and the 'New Freedom' a beltless sanitary napkin. . . .

C. Liberalism and Resistance

My narrative does not deny the emancipatory achievements of libertarian power-knowledge. Even Karl Marx described the American press of his day as the freest press in the world. But my rereading of American history does stress the duality of Liberal power-knowledge: its hidden conservative agenda and system of control. This duality is not a simple charade—a mere lie. Contra conventional Marxist interpretations, my analysis suggests that even today Liberal power-knowledge is more than ideology. It is more than a reflection of the interests of capitalists—more than just a smokescreen to cover their dirty deeds. It is also the moral authority which defines and proscribes those deeds as 'dirty': an authority which has sometimes empowered pockets of democracy within corporate structures (e.g. collective bargaining, employee profit-sharing, etc.). Liberal power-knowledge provides the people with the basis for struggle and resistance. When the people protest corporate practices (e.g. when utility companies increase their rates or parent companies shut down a local plant), they invoke principles of equality and fair play. When women and minorities demand redress for their historic exclusions from the rewards of Liberalism and capitalism, they cite the Jeffersonian promise of freedom and justice for all. When Third World liberation movements articulate their resistances, they frequently secure them within natural rights theories derived from the Western Enlightenment. Even within the consciousness industry itself, the dialectic of freedom has not been fully harnessed. Given the broad warrant to create an oligarchy of mind that industrial capitalism has provided the U.S. Consciousness Industry, it is remarkable how many—not how few—journalists have tried to remain faithful to the Jeffersonian trust. Their restraint and integrity are authentic souvenirs of the emancipatory stage of Libertarian power-knowledge. They demonstrate that Liberal ideals still resonate in the margins of corporatist control, but they do not erase the imprimatur of capital from the products of contemporary journalism.

My narrative seeks to empower criticism of corporatist control, not because I believe that either corporations or control can (or necessarily should) be eliminated. But because I believe in democratic control which is open, subject to criticism, and amenable to redress, and I oppose all systems of control which are secured by secrecy. Since the corporation under industrial capitalism has in many respects become "a body politic," I contend it should be brought under the discipline of democratic control.[6] In sum, I support Jefferson's admonition that, "no government ought to be without censors."[7]

D. Colonizing Resistance:
The Consciousness Industry

This argument assumes a special urgency today because American capitalism is currently undergoing a radical structural transformation. This transformation has been widely noted, and its implications variously defined.[8] In my judgment, the structural features of this transformation can be described in relatively simple terms.

The decline or collapse of the public sphere in capitalist societies has long been predicted and eulogized. I believe we are now witnessing removal of the last vestiges of social pluralism and the emergence of a monolithic society in which the *market is the measure of all things*. That is, America is at last fulfilling Adam Smith's vision of a society in which the rules of the marketplace become the rules of civil society. It is "creating the first purely capitalist society in world history."[9] We are entering the era of ultracapitalism.

Realization of the capitalist's *wildest dream* is at last possible because the buffers that once cushioned and resisted the impact of the marketplace—religion, the family and, less consistently, the state—have lost their capacity to protect citizens from the imperatives of profit and loss. The 'conservative turn' [*sic*] of U.S. politics in the 1980s has accelerated the transfer of power from public to private interests, but it did not initiate it. And a return to the nominal liberalism of Democratic party politics cannot reverse it. The change I am describing is not ephemeral. It is not a simple swing in the pendulum of political sentiment. And it is not in any sense 'conservative'! It entails a radical (root) change in the dynamics of capitalism.[10]

This change has made the Consciousness Industry the linchpin of the new monolithic market system. Mass media, especially electronic media, prepared the way for the current removal of institutionalized resistance to the discipline of the marketplace. They permitted corporations to bypass and usurp the power of patriarch, priest, and party boss. They rendered "two-step" models of opinion formation obsolete. They allowed direct access to the individual. They used this access to set the agenda for discussion of public issues and to define the legitimate alternatives for action. In the words of Dallas Smythe: "Their purpose is to set a daily agenda of issues, problems, values, and policies for the guidance of other institutions and the whole population."[11] Within the new order, the corporate controlled consciousness industry itself becomes the only mediator separating the citizen from the vicissitudes of the market. The Consciousness Industry uses this mediation to attempt to manage consumer demands for commodities including soap suds, golf balls, and automobiles, as well as ideas, candidates, and lifestyles. Because the products of the Consciousness Industry are marketed throughout the world, the prescriptions they carry—their messages about commodities and consumption—bear the imprimatur of cultural imperialism. They prescribe global realignments in the relations of power and knowledge: realignments which would translate the imperatives of the hierarchical relations of U.S. capitalistic production into global imperatives.

E. Securing the Capitalist's Dreams: Demand Management and a Permanent War Economy

Demand management streamlines production. The 'law' of supply and demand is repealed: the supplier of commodities now also produces the demand for those commodities. The risk factor that was so characteristic of the entrepreneural stage of capitalism is removed from the equation when "what the public wants is not felt, until supplied."[12] Risk is transferred from producer to consumer. The consumer pays for design and production errors and assumes the hazards of a life of counterfeit pleasures.

But management of consumer demand is not the only measure American capitalism relies upon to insulate itself against financial risk. Since 1940 burgeoning military and welfare budgets have also served this function. Government has become the largest single consumer of corporate production. Military spending now plays such an integral role in stabilizing the American economy that some critics assert, "Capitalism leads to war"![13]

In sum, demand management and a permanent war economy make the productive process more efficient and profitable. Risk no longer disturbs the capitalist's sleep. He is no longer "surrounded by unknown enemies" who are "driven by want, and prompted by envy, to invade his possessions."[14]

F. Democracy's Nightmare: Terms of the New Cosmological Bargain

Realization of the capitalist's dream is the nightmare of democracy. Freedom of expression is reduced to a caricature by the myth of consumer sovereignty. Demand management places in the corporate trust power that is analogous in scope (though not in kind) to the power that Stalin placed in the hands of his overseer of the arts, Andrei Zhdanov, who created a system for the total administration of mind that was so effective that even Stalin found it stifling.

Such concentrations of power are dangerous in any age. In a nuclear age when rot just citizen or nation but the entire planet is placed in jeopardy, concentrating so much power in so few hands in especially perilous. When those hands are private hands—hired hands—operating outside of the legislative process, it is a grotesque inversion of democratic principles.

The Consciousness Industry has already rendered criticism of its control system impotent by conditioning intellectuals to produce and consume criticism rather than to act upon it. If the new market system succeeds in establishing the dominion of its monolithic power-knowledge, market censorship will not only become more pervasive, it will become even more resistant to criticism. The preconditions for the emergence of authoritarian (or fascist) tendencies within capitalism will then be fulfilled in the U.S. These tendencies are already emergent in many corporate occupied-zones in the Third World.

At present, domestic resistance is colonized by consumerism or pressed to the margins and ghettoized. The new market system will significantly enlarge these margins as the principle of capitalist accumulation exercises its imperative: 'The rich will get richer, and the poor will get poorer.' This will produce a formidable challenge for the Consciousness Industry. It will have to convince the new poor that their deprivations are the price that must be paid to secure the new cosmological bargain. If the Consciousness Industry fails to meet this challenge, guns and chains could replace Whoppers and Super Bowls as artifacts of corporate control.

In this chapter I will attempt to fill some of the gaps in the historical record by examining the development of the American press and Consciousness Industry within the holistic perspective of institutional analysis. My remedial effort will (1) review the nexus through which commercial and ideational networks intersect in America, and (2) examine the ways American political, economic, religious, educational, and familial institutions have promoted and resisted the emergence of elite control in America. It will require inquiries into the foundations of American concepts of free speech and free press in the Revolutionary covenant, the role of moral values in securing that covenant, the hidden hierarchical assumptions of the founding fathers, the early emergence of monopolistic tendencies within communications industries, the roles played by advertising and public relations in securing political capitalism, the social stratification of information in the U.S., and the role of electronic media in the cultivation of consent.

ii

The American Enlightenment: Censorship and Press Freedom in the New Republic

Like revolutionaries everywhere, the American insurrectionists backed into the future. Their concepts of freedom were forged from the metal of their own immediate experiences of unfreedom. Even Thomas Jefferson acknowledged this. Forty years after the Revolution, he wrote, "In truth the abuses of monarchy had so much filled all the space of political contemplation, that we imagined everything republican which was not monarchy."[15]

The early politics of the Republic were anti-politics. Whatever the monarchy had favored, the Republic opposed. Monarchy had controlled the press, the Republic tried to set the press free. Monarchy had censored objectionable reading matter; the Republic allied itself against censorship. Monarchy had supported theocracies; the Republic endorsed religious freedom. Monarchy had been secured by the "tinsel" aristocracy of birth; the Republic celebrated the "natural aristocracy of mind." Monarchy had regulated, taxed, and expropriated the fruits of industry; the Republic declared men "free to regulate their own pursuits of industry and improvement."[16]

Because the gravestones of monarchy formed the cornerstones of American democracy, the patriots' campaign to rally popular support for independence greatly exaggerated the tyranny of the crown. The Declaration of Independence was an integral part of this campaign. Historian Clinton Rossiter describes this hallowed document as combining "truth and distortion in amounts calculated to convince the irresolute of the evil designs of the mother country." He maintains that, "This effective piece of propaganda was, like the Revolution itself, the work of a determined minority that could hardly have afforded to be more straightforward and moderate in statement."[17]

If the founders of the Republic exaggerated the crimes of the crown, they also exaggerated the universalism of their own libertarian commitments. Their dictions are contra-dictions punctuated with hidden terms and unexamined assumptions. They promised more than they could deliver.

A. Colonial Censorship

Colonial censorship policies were harsh but inconsistent. The Royal Instructions to Governors required licensing and control of all presses. Governor Berkeley of Virginia outlawed printing presses entirely on the grounds that, "learning has brought disobedience and heresy and sects into the world; and printing has divulged them and libels against the government."[18] The first colonial newspaper, *Publick Occurrences* (1690), was suppressed after its premiere issue in Boston.

In early America, censorship controversies were centered primarily on the periodical press. Newsletters, newspapers, and pamphlets addressed issues of immediate relevance in an expanding empire. The book industry developed much more slowly and remained an ancillary enterprise. Early American booksellers simply relied upon the mother country to supply their stocks. Consequently the great battles against censorship and for press freedom in America were waged by publishers and printers of periodical literature. These battles were in many respects rehearsals for the Revolution. They defined, clarified, dramatized, and polarized the antagonisms that would later fracture the British colonial empire in North America. The also forged a fateful alliance between apologists of press freedom and apologists of free trade.

The colonial struggle for press freedom was essentially a a struggle against England's monopoly control over public information resources in America. Colonial shippers, merchants, and farmers agitated for the right to have their positions on controversial issues represented in the press. The dispute between colonial entrepreneurs and royalists was also at the heart of the Zenger case. Peter Zenger's *New-York Weekly Journal* was closely aligned with the interests of prosperous colonial factions and opposed to the governor and his council. Newspapers throughout the colonies carried accounts of the Zenger case. Zenger's vindication was a critical victory for colonial entrepreneurial interests and a compelling testament to the power of the press to propagandize for those interests.

This power asserted itself with full force when the British announced the Stamp Act of 1765. At that point the colonial press became an opposition press. So much so that one historian maintains the newspapers declared war on the British more than a decade before the Declaration of Independence![19]

The Stamp Act was designed to raise revenue to pay the debts incurred by the crown in the war against the French. It required newspapers to use only paper which had been stamped as duty-paid in order to assure the mother country a monopoly over paper manufacture. It also imposed a stamp tax on all documents, books, playing cards, licenses, and advertisements. The Stamp Act hit printers hardest, extracting most of its revenue directly from their pockets, but it also had a direct impact on lawyers. Newspapers throughout the colonies villified the impending law not merely as discriminatory, but as an attempt to place shackles on the minds of Americans. When the "fatal *black-act*" went into effect, some newspapers appeared with black borders and illustrations featuring skulls and crossbones.[20] They announced they would cease publication until the Stamp Act was repealed. Other papers continued to publish unstamped. A few even appeared with symbols of Liberty in their logos. But the Sons of Liberty did not extend their commitment to press freedom to the loyalist press. It was regarded as the enemy press. During the Revolution, freedom fighters under the banner of liberty raided the shops of loyalist publishers and printers, smashed their presses, and burned the offending papers.

B. Press Freedom in America: Three Perspectives

The "determined minority" that promoted revolutionary sentiment in America was made up of men who had held prominent positions within the colonial ruling class. It was comprised of a prosperous class of traders, investors, and landholders, as well as a new class of mental workers: lawyers, postmasters, administrators, clerks, professors, and publishers. Both groups championed press freedom in principle and on pragmatic grounds. The emergent commercial class saw abridgment of press freedom as an abridgment of man's Natural Right to free trade and a violation of the property rights of those who owned presses. Their pragmatic interest in press freedom derived from their desire to sway public opinion on issues of commercial policy in directions favorable to their interests.

The second group, publicans or Aeropagites—men who made their livings by reading, writing, calculating, and managing the affairs of others—saw abridgment of press freedom as an abridgment of man's Natural Right to Enlightenment and a barrier to social and scientific Progress. Their pragmatic interest in press freedom was immediate. Their power-knowledge was secured by print. They shared Jefferson's convictions that "Science is progressive," and that "Science had liberated the ideas of those who read and reflect."[21] They were readers, thinkers, scientists, litterateurs—men of Enlightenment. They be-

lieved that science had liberated them. They considered themselves
the vanguard of the new world order: charter members of "the aristocracy of mind."

A third group, "the Mechanicks"—small tradesmen, artisans, day
laborers, longshoremen, mariners, and printers—were also instrumental in bringing about the Revolution. Their daily bread depended
upon the prosperity of the commercial class. The printers were directly affected by the Stamp Act, and they immediately turned the
tools of their trade—ink, pulp, and press—into instruments of revolution. More than 400 pamphlets on the Stamp Act were published
between 1760 and 1776. Paine's *Common Sense* went through twenty-
five editions and sold over 100,000 copies in 1776. The pamphlets,
posters, and broadsides produced by the mechanicks were so effective
in generating populist support for independence that David Ramsay
concluded, "In establishing American independence, the pen and the
press had a merit equal to that of the sword."[22]

The alliance of the mechanicks, the businessmen, and publicans
was an uneasy one. The mechanicks had neither formal education
nor, in most cases, property. They were "The People" celebrated in
the abstractions of the Age of Reason; but in flesh-and-blood they
proved less malleable. They had minds, interests, and methods of
their own. They did not share the businessmen's respect for property
or the publicans' regard for law, order, and sophistry. Moreover their
resentment of British wealth and privilege easily spilled over and
soured into resentment of the wealth and privilege of colonial entrepreneurs and publicans. These were ready Sons of Liberty who believed their courage in action entitled them to full voices in articulating
the new order. They were the first American unionists, the "mobs
in the cities," the "unknown enemies," the proletariat who would
henceforth disturb the slumbers of capitalists and publicans.

The mechanicks' theory of press freedom was largely derivative.
It reflected their dependence upon the emergent commercial class.
Their radical egalitarianism was their single addendum. Ben Franklin's *Apology for Printers* became the Bible of the Printers' Union.
Franklin's concept of press freedom as a form of trade freedom con-
cisely defined the parameters of the theory of press freedom endorsed
by the commercial class and the mechanicks during the Revolutionary
era. Both defined press freedom as a property right. The businessmen
saw it as a Natural Right of ownership, a right of investors to receive
a fair return on their capital. The mechanicks saw it as the Natural
Right of craftsmen to market their labor, skills, and industry at a fair

return for time and energy invested. Neither group was willing to surrender or compromise these rights by assenting to the demands of the crown.

At this juncture in American history, businessmen's and mechanicks' conceptions of 'fairness' were more closely aligned than they are today. Both were living off of the accumulated spiritual capital of Calvinism. They viewed commerce in moral terms. They saw 'industry' as a great leveller: an enemy of hereditary privilege as well as a prophylaxis against personal vice. Within their vocabulary of motives, industry was a personal attribute or virtue. It denoted "skill, assiduity, perserverance, diligence, not a set of institutional arrangements."[23] Money, but also integrity, respect, and perhaps even Grace, were regarded as the just rewards of industry. In contrast to the Tories who lived off of hereditary wealth, the fortunes of the commercial classes were new: fresh fruits of industry. The link between the businessman's industry and his prosperity was immediate. Mechanicks were encouraged to believe that they too could forge such links. Ben Franklin, cum Poor Richard, was the proof in the pudding. By trade a mechanick—by industry the founder of the first major newspaper 'chain,' the father of modern advertising, scientist, inventor, litterateur, educator, statesman, and revolutionary—Franklin provided a larger than life prototype of the rags-to-riches scenario that would continue to be mythologized by the Horatio Alger parables long after the Protestant ethic had been overpowered by the spirit of capitalism. But on the eve of the Revolution, the two emergent classes of industrialism—capitalists and workers—were briefly united in opposition to the hegemony of the crown. Industry was still an adjective and labor was still a verb, and the founding fathers were still rebellious Sons of Liberty.

C. Publicans' Theory, Traders' Practices: Press Freedom as a Property Right

Neither the mechanicks nor their business associates had much interest in exploring the epistemological implications of their warrant for press freedom. They were practical men, manual workers and traders, not philosophers. Nevertheless Franklin did articulate a crude version of the 'free-market-of-ideas' thesis in his analysis of the success of *Poor Richard's Almanack*. He equated truth with popularity (sales) and professed faith in the judgment of the people (consumer sovereignty). But with a quick sardonic twist of his pursestrings, Franklin also saluted the power of advertising as a means of ensuring that the judgment of the people and the judgment of the marketeer will be the same (demand management).[24]

The publicans' defense of press liberty has received extensive coverage in the history books. The traders' interests in advancing the cause of press freedom has received much less attention. Yet institutionalization of press liberty in America was actually more successful in securing the traders' interests than in keeping the publicans' promises. This was already apparent to Tocqueville in 1831 when he wrote, democracy "introduces a trading spirit into literature," and described, in pejorative terms, the commodification of literary and artistic production in America. No egalitarian revolution or publican counter-revolution has removed the trading spirit from the American publishing industry. The Jacksonian revolution removed property requirements for suffrage, *but the poll tax on press freedom remains in effect.* Press freedom is a property right restricted to owners of presses and their hirelings.

Jefferson and Madison are the most widely celebrated defenders of the publican theory of press freedom. Jefferson's salutary description of the mission of the free press has become a sacred canon of the professional ideology of journalism: "The basis of our government being the opinion of the people, the first object should be to keep that right; and were it left to me to decide whether we should have a government without newspapers or newspapers without government, I should not hesitate to prefer the latter." Jefferson, like Milton, Voltaire, and Diderot, assumed the keepers of the opinion of the people would be Areopagites/publicans. But unlike his European counterparts, Jefferson was strongly committed to universal literacy. As a result, he added a singular qualification to his brief for an unrestrained press: "that every man should receive those papers and be capable of reading them." This was a major advance over the elitism of European humanism. But it was far from an endorsement of the egalitarianism of the mechanicks.

Jefferson provides revisionists with an easy target. But he is no strawman! Jefferson's blind spots were the blind spots of his generation and his class, not the narrow prejudices of a mean-spirited hypocrite. It is for this reason that they are significant. Jefferson was a great humanist, rationalist, and democrat. The racist, classist, and sexist shadows at the edges of Jeffersonian Liberalism are not idiosyncratic. These pockmarks in the democratic covenants forged by the Age of Reason mirror the dualism of the hierarchical assumptions taken for granted by eighteenth-century publicans and traders.

This dualism muted expectations for consistency between public and private behaviors. It produced patterns of inconsistency in all the institutions fabricated by publicans and their business partners. The resulting incongruities were integral, not incidental, to the structure of power-knowledge in the American Republic. The principle of inconsistency secured the liberties of publicans and entrepreneurs at the apex of a finely articulated pyramid of denial. Within this pyramid, the freedom of whites was supported by the subjugation of non-whites; the power and prosperity of businessmen and publicans were secured by the political and economic subordination of the mechanicks, strollers, and vagabonds; and the sovereignty of males was assured by the servitude of females.

The conundrums in Jefferson's humanism illustrate the double standard of Enlightened morality. Jefferson agonized over the morality of slave-holding, but of course held his own slaves in bondage throughout his lifetime. Jefferson professed faith in human reason: faith in the universality and perfectibility of man's rational powers. His agrarian ideal celebrated "the people" as "the origins of all just power," but Jefferson dismissed the urban masses as debauched "mobs." He proclaimed the rule of law but advocated placing any white woman who gave birth to a child of mixed race "out of the protection of the laws." Jefferson regarded education as the road to equality, but proposed a two-tier system of education which would ensure that "the laboring classes" are educated to follow and that the "learned classes" (professionals and the independently wealthy) are educated to "share in conducting the affairs of the nation." Jefferson maintained that he was "really mortified" to be told that in the United States of America a civil magistrate could order a book suppressed, and he asserted that it is the "duty" of every patriot "to buy a copy [of the censored book], in vindication of his right to buy, and to read what he pleases." But Jefferson advocated prohibiting females from reading all novels except selected works by Marmontel, Edgeworth, and Gentilis, and he advised severe restrictions on their intake of poetry. He believed that reading would undermine the moral virtues of women, fill their heads full of ideas, and render them unfit for their domestic and maternal duties. Jefferson is a patron saint of press freedom, but when that Freedom was invoked in criticism of President Jefferson's policies, he expressed the conviction that "a few prosecutions of the most eminent offenders would have a wholesome effect in restoring the integrity of the presses."[25] The dualism which underwrote Enlightened power-knowledge did not just permit Jefferson to cook the morality books. It required it! The 'bad' (double-dealing) Jefferson made the 'good' (libertarian) Jefferson possible. Similarly the 'bad' (racist, sexist, and classist) angles at the base of the pyramid of Enlightened power-knowledge made the 'good' (rationalist, libertarian, and democratic) peaks at its apex possible. The principle of incongruity is a fundamental law of the architecture of Panopticonism. The American Revolution secured this principle, and thereby began the long process of colonizing the hopes and dreams of the repressed—a process that would never *fully* conquer the resistances of "the people" or entirely silence their cynicism.

iii

From Industry to Industrialism

Economists like to use formal models to describe the 'rules' of the marketplace. This formalism endows their rhetoric with the authority of science. But it also endows those 'rules' with an aura of naturalism and determinism. The 'rules' take on a life of their own. They seem to be impersonal, objective, and inevitable.[26]

However, rereading the founding texts—the original articulations of the rules—removes this reifying aura. It restores the human signatures to The Rules. It relocates them within contexts of human history, argument, and decision. It *reminds* us that they are products of human thinking, social constructions, not laws of nature. It encourages us to recognize that what humans have made, they can unmake or remake. It reaffirms the fact that the men who wrote the social contracts by which we live regarded them as drafts, and that others have rewritten them in stone.

It makes the road to corporate capitalism appear far less immutable than either capitalist or Marxist apologetics asserts. It reminds us that there are no forces of production, only men and women who produce; that there is no law of supply and demand, only men and women who make decisions to produce in large or small lots and to create or relieve scarcity. It reminds us that there are no natural resources: that there is only human resourcefulness to nuture, cultivate, conquer, or plunder nature. It reminds us that there are no free markets, only markets controlled by capitalists, kings, communists, or pirates, for markets are complex human organizations which cannot exist without order, hierarchy, power, and control.

In sum, rereading the texts which secured the cosmological bargain under which we now live renders the invisible hand of history visible and accountable. It reminds us that human history is made by humans, not by God, Nature, or Destiny. It purges the ghosts from the machine of historical interpretation and permits us to ask, 'What if?' It encourages us to sort through the wastebasket of history: to examine false starts, exhume the remains of defeated arguments, mark radical discontinuities, and visit the graves of lost hopes.

A. Little Republics

Even a casual sorting of the texts of the founders of the Republic makes clear that early American archives are not corporate archives. Suspicion of corporate forms of organization was widespread during the early days of the Republic. Private corporations were illegal before 1807.[27] They did not become the established modus operandi of U.S. business until about 1850. The earliest corporations were chartered companies, political, economic, and religious communities founded in the public interest—Congregational parishes, trading companies like the Hudson's Bay Company, companies founded to provide a public service like the Charles River Bridge Company, and a few early manufacturing companies like the Boston Manufacturing Company which began the textile industry in Lowell, Massachusetts. The fathers of the Republic were profoundly suspicious of corporate charters because they saw them as rival political entities—efforts to conserve or restore aristocratic power and influence.

English Common Law explicitly recognized the political nature of corporations; Blackstone had described them as "little republics." The republican character of the private corporate structure was affirmed by Justice Hornblower in 1834 when he insisted that all stockholders were entitled to an equal vote in corporate decision-making regardless of the size of their holdings.

Paradoxically, the judicial rulings that established the legitimacy of private corporations were decisions designed to curb abuses of power by certain charter corporations which were perceived as failing to act in the public interest. The first decision recognizing the existence of private corporations, *Ellis v. Marshall*, was a punitive decision which prohibited private corporations from requiring individuals to become members. Chief Justice Taney's landmark decision empowering competitive capitalism actually sought to limit the monopoly power of the Charles River Bridge Company by denying it exclusive rights to provide bridge service across the Charles River.

The founding fathers were also deeply concerned about the pernicious effects of hereditary wealth. The patriarchs of the Republic were very wealthy men: George Washington was the richest man in America, Benjamin Franklin had amassed a fortune in excess of $150,000, and Thomas Jefferson had large land- and slave-holdings. Predictably, they strongly opposed property taxes. The sentiments excited by the Stamp Act revolt made such taxes generally suspect. Jefferson regarded property taxes as liens against individual talent and effort. He considered them regressive because he believed they would stifle individual motivation and thereby repress social progress. However, inheritance was also considered a reactionary idea, an artifact of deposed "tinsel" aristocracy. It was regarded as a barrier to the development of an aristocracy of talent. Jefferson proposed abolishing rights of inheritance as a way of raising public revenues and inhibiting the growth of a new aristocracy. *If* this Jeffersonian idea had been empowered, the landscape of the American Republic would have assumed a radically different topography.

B. Collapse of the Little Republics

The Wealth of Nations was published the same year as the Declaration of Independence. Capitalism took hold much more rapidly in America than in any other nation because there were fewer traditional barriers to be removed. Opposition to the "tinsel aristocracy" of birth led the fathers of the American Republic to adopt attitudes toward property very different from those of their European contemporaries. Common Law had conceived of property as a right of lineage linked to both heredity and personality. It treated property rights and inheritance rights as sacrosanct. Blackstone defined the right of property as "that sole and despotic dominion which one man claims and exercises over the external things of the world, in total exclusion of the rights of any other individual in the universe." The entitlements of aristocrats were extensions of their titles to property.

The American Republic affirmed the importance of property as integral to its vision of civic humanism by securing voting rights in property qualifications. But the republican concept of property was far more fluid than the European version for three reasons. First, a land of immigrants systematically driving native inhabitants from their ancestral lands could not effectively seal property rights in history or lineage. Second, many of the largest landholders in states like Maryland and Virginia were royalists. During the Revolution they were treated as enemies and their properties were subject to pillage or confiscation. After the war they were regarded with contempt. Third, in post-revolutionary America, the privileges of property rights were secured against the egalitarian demands of the people by promising free white men access to property through purchase. This meant property would change hands, titles would be transferred, and new land claims would be staked in the westward movement. In sum, property became a medium of exchange, a commodity, rather than an extension of personality or polity. Property assumed a purely economic character.

This transformation of property relations brought about radical changes in corporate structures. The public sphere of the corporation collapsed. Corporations lost their republican character. The one-man/one-vote concept of stockholders' rights forfeited its warrant. Ownership, defined in quantitative terms, replaced citizenship as the basis for distribution of power in corporate decision-making. Corporations were no longer required or expected to act in the public interest. The only legitimate interest of the private corporation became the interest it earned on investment. Because the emergence of the private corporation deposed the entrenched powers of the charter corporations, Liberals hailed it as a triumph of democracy.[28]

C. Industrial Warfare and the Manifest Destiny of Capitalism

The 'rationalization' of the power of capital proved to be a hollow victory for opponents of monopoly control. It cleared the way for ambitious entrepreneurs to form new combinations of capital which would permit them to exercise control over major financial markets in America. This control asserted itself in the formation of joint stock companies to capitalize railroad-building; in the patent control, patent-pooling, and patent monopolies that characterized the electronics industry from its inception; in overcapitalization of industries to eliminate competitors; in the development of trade associations which permitted coordination of business policies; and in the consolidation of the power to set the agenda for public opinion through the alliance of Western Union and the Associated Press.[29] It was evident in the alliance of entrepreneurs who sponsored the "merger movement," which sought to restrain and "rationalize" competition because, as James Logan of the U.S. Envelop Company noted in 1901:

> Competition is industrial war. Ignorant, unrestricted competition, car-
> ried to its logical conclusion, means death to some of the combatants
> and injury to all. Even the victor does not soon recover from the
> wounds received in the conflict.[30]

Monopoly control was achieved early in communications-related industries—railroad, telegraph, and newspapers—because effective coordination   and   guidance   of   industrial   growth   required
"rationalization" of networks for the distribution of information and
commodities.[31] This control was not always successful, but it was
always purposive. It invariably bore the imprimatur of human designs
and human decisions.

There was nothing impersonal about the workings of market
'forces' in the era of the "robber barons." The barons had names
and faces. They engaged in "conspicuous consumption" and invidious
displays" of wealth and power.[32] They were not instruments of capital.
They were capitalists—self-promoters who attributed their successes
to personal character and genius and ascribed their blunders to necessity. While their contemporaries in the university lecture halls
embraced laissez-faire doctrines and encoded their accounts of the
dynamics of the marketplace in the jargon of Social Darwinism, the
barons of big business purposively planned and openly acknowledged
their control over the marketplace. They did not follow the rules of
the marketplace, they made them.

J.P. Morgan's successful marketing of U.S. gold bonds and railroad
stocks in Europe gained him a reputation as a "rescuer of governments." He used this reputation to gain control of U.S. Steel, International Harvester, and AT&T; to arrange financing for Thomas
Edison's researches; and to play a leading role in the formation of
General Electric. The "King of Wall Street" did not deny his achievements or hide his intentions. He defended the practices of stock-
watering and overcapitalization of mergers which destabilized rather
than rationalized markets on the grounds that these strategies enhanced his power and profits. He promoted the merger movement
for the same reasons. Like Charles Francis Adams, president of the
Union-Pacific Railroad, Morgan saw consolidation as expedient.
Adams characterized it as a hallmark of modernity: "The modern
world does its work through vast aggregations of men and capital."
He described consolidation of enterprise as a "sort of latter-day manifest destiny."[33]

Realization of the manifest destiny of industrial capitalism required
the barons—Morgan, Adams, John D. Rockefeller, Jay Gould, Rus-

sell Sage, William Astor, P.R. Pyne, C.P. Huntington, Chauncy Depew, Henry Flagler, Cyrus Field, A.B. Cornell, John Hay, Charles Schwab, and others—to extend the dominion of their control to politics. Hence, paradoxically, the long-term effect of the "rationalizing" process which pushed politics out the front door of the corporation was to slip them back in through the rear!

The Progressive Era brought the process to fruition. It secured the groundings for what Gabriel Kolko calls *political capitalism*: "the utilization of political outlets to attain conditions of stability, predictability, and security—to attain rationalization—in the economy." The Progressive Era did not invent business/government alliances. Joint ventures involving business and government, both licit and illicit, had existed since the early days of the Republic. But political capitalism regularized and formalized the union. It made business a senior partner in government operations. After 1900 neither the legislative nor executive branches of the federal government would make any major political or economic decisions without the advice and consent of business leaders.[34]

The "rescuer of governments" saw business-government alliances as mutually advantageous. The Morgan interests advocated federal government intervention and regulation as a means of rationalizing the economy. They reflected the general consensus of business leaders of the period who assumed that federal regulation, unlike state and local regulation, would be both uniform and uniformly responsive to the interests of big business. The advocates of regulation also assumed that Congress would follow the expert advice of the leaders of industry in drafting its regulations. They were not disappointed. Business leaders met little resistance in negotiating the most important alliance of the merger movement: the merger of business and government.

iv

Securing the Logic of the Free Market

Political capitalism did not immediately surrender the direction of the growth of industrialism to the "logic of the free market." Unlike academic theorists who imputed an impersonal logic to markets, the daily practices of Morgan, Rockefeller, and their allies reminded them that the logic of the marketplace is human logic—the logic of those who control the markets. This logic secured the great fortunes of industrial America. It provided the essential tenets of twentieth-century capitalist power-knowledge. But it was not the logic of the people of the nineteenth century.

Widespread labor violence, ethnic conflicts, urban rioting, and the resistance of certain recalcitrant immigrant groups, particularly the Irish, were distressing reminders of the deep conceptual chasm that still separated the patrons of Progress from the perversities of the people. Concrete historical events, not the immanent unfolding of the laws of capitalism, influenced the decisions of Morgan and associates, events such as: the assassinations of Lincoln, Garfield, and McKinley, the chaos of Reconstruction, the long depression of the 1870s, the great strike of 1873, the Haymarket bombing in 1886, the participation of thousands in demonstrations of the unemployed sponsored by the First International in Chicago and New York during the depression of the 1890s, the Pullman strike of 1894, the Spanish-American War in 1898, the meeting of the "Continental Congress" of the Wobblies in 1905 to emancipate the working class from "the slave bondage of capitalism," the financial panic of 1907, the popularity of Debs's socialism, and the events leading to America's entrance into World War I.

Instead of rethinking the "logic of the marketplace," apologists for big business decided to remake the people—to purge their perversities and retool their conceptual apparatus to fit the specifications of the Progressive blueprint for the future. In spite of its misleading label, this blueprint had a distinctly conservative agenda. The Progress it secured was progress in advancing the Enlightened self-interest of industrialists.

Schoolbook histories portray the Progressive Era as a period of social reform in which monopolistic tendencies in big business were exposed, checked, and outlawed. My double-reading of the reforms of Progressivism, e.g. trust-busting, regards these reforms as acts of self-censorship which served to mark the new limits of permissions and prohibitions, *and* secured the credibility of the power-knowledge of political capitalism among the people. The presidential campaign of the "Trust-Buster," Teddy Roosevelt, was supported by the Morgan interests. Roosevelt assured Wall Street, "I intend to be most conservative, but in the interests of corporations themselves and above all in the interests of the country."[35] The newly elected president kept his promise to Wall Street by closely relying upon advice and counsel of Mark Hanna, Robert Bacon and George W. Perkins of the House of Morgan, Elihu Root, Nelson Aldrich, and James Stillman of the Rockefeller interests.

The foresight and planning of the industrialists of the Progressive Era was not a conspiracy. It did not involve a plot to repeal the Bill of Rights or hijack the ship of state. Their blueprint simply put forth a set of practical strategies designed to routinize, stabilize, preserve, and extend the newly won privileges of industrial capitalism.

The Progressives saw the diversity of the people as the source of their perversity. For the people were not a people at all. They were many peoples of diverse ethnic, racial, religious, geographical, and economic origins. They were not just butchers, bakers, and candlestick-makers. They were Indian braves and former slaves, anarchists and socialists, polygynists and papists, Shakers, Quakers, and Klansmen . . . Pluralism is always troublesome and disruptive of social order. Under conditions of mass production, it is also unprofitable.

The fathers of the Republic had regarded American diversity as an essential anchor of liberty. James Madison maintained that the spread of factions would keep tyranny from taking root in America by preventing any single interest from amassing too much power. The epic poet of American democracy, Walt Whitman, believed that American diversity would produce a new species of humankind: "the Eidolons," a people of unprecedented creativity who would not only cherish liberty but exercise it with wisdom. But the fathers of American industrialism considered the Civil War as decisive testament to the folly of such idealism. They believed that it conclusively demonstrated the dangers of factionalism. The war, which is remembered today largely for the Emancipation Proclamation, was, of course, a war over competing economic interests and technologies of production, not primarily a war for racial justice. The root cause was resistance to the expansion of industrialism by Southern factions. Resistance to industrialism was not just a Southern perversity. Subsequent launderings of history have obscured the fact that resistance to industrial capitalism was widespread in nineteenth-century America. This resistance created a deep tension in the structure of American social life which periodically erupted into episodes of violent conflict.

A. Changing Minds: The Public School Movement

Early industrialists had undertaken sporadic campaigns to eliminate this tension. The public school movement was their most ambitious effort. Sponsored by prominent citizens who sent their own children to private schools, the public schools in the great population centers of the nineteenth century—New York, Philadelphia, Boston, and Chicago—were given a broad franchise. They were expected to "civilize" the children of the laboring classes: to resocialize them to fit the demands of industrial production. In the words of a report of the Boston School Committee, they were expected to take "children at random from a great city, undisciplined, uninstructed, often with inveterate forwardness and obstinacy, and with the inherited stupidity of centuries of ignorant ancestors; forming them from animals into intellectual beings. . . ."[36] The early urban schools resembled prisons and were surrounded by high walls to keep their inmates from escaping. The clock dictated the routines of the school day with the same rigid precision with which it controlled coordination of machine production. Schooling was made compulsory in the cities because many lower-class parents refused to send their children to public schools. Some of these "ignorant ancestors" complained that the schools were being used to teach their children "alien" (WASP) social, economic, and religious values.

Business interests not only organized and directed the operations of the early urban public schools, they also shaped their curricula. The Lancasterian system represented an extreme expression of these efforts; the Lancasterian approach was a nineteenth-century pedagogy which actually organized the physical layout of the classroom and instructional processes to simulate production of commodities within a modern factory. In 1828 the Boston School Committee described the workings of the Lancasterian "manufactures": their "effects on the habits, character, and intelligence of youth are highly beneficial; disposing their minds to industry, to readiness of attention, and to subordination thereby creating in early life a love of order, [and] preparation for business."[37] Standardization, a basic feature of mass production also became a central feature of schooling in the nineteenth century. Testing, grading, separation of pupils by age, credentialing, and mass-produced textbooks acted as quality controls ensuring the uniformity of the schooling process. Standardization was initially introduced by mining companies which developed uniform curricula for schools in mining towns so that employees and their families could be readily relocated. Similarly, vocational education was introduced into American high schools, and standardized curricula for programs in business and manual arts were developed under the sponsorship of the American Association of Manufacturers. In sum, the educational tracking system sanctioned by Jefferson was formalized and given a corporate imprimatur by the public school movement. Children of the privileged classes were educated in private academies so as to assume positions of leadership in American business and government. Children of the laboring classes were educated in public schools to reproduce the labor power of their parents.

B. The Press as an Arbiter of Manners and Morals in Industrial Society

Socialization for industry was not confined to schooling. The nineteenth-century press also played a critical role in articulating the industrial reconstruction of American social realities and in selling the new order to the people. In spite of the egalitarian thrust of the Mechanicks' movement, the American press was an elitist press until about 1830. Early newspapers were addressed primarily to the partisan political interests of publicans—businessmen and Aeropagites. However, after 1830 both the format and audience for newspapers changed radically. Prices were lowered. The so-called penny press, which was overtly less political and placed more emphasis on news, timeliness, and sensation, became the wave of the future. It was heavily subsidized by advertising and had a much larger circulation than earlier papers.[38] Building on the precedents established by Ben Franklin in the *Poor Richard* series and in the anonymous "Silence Dogood" columns which Franklin wrote for the *New England Courant*, the penny presses acted as guardians of the moral authority of industrialism.[39] The penny papers informed readers of new products arriving in the marketplace and advised them on money matters. The most widely respected feature of the *New York Herald*, the best-known penny press of the pre-Civil War era, was its Wall Street Report. But the penny presses also counseled readers on manners and morals. They filled the void left by the decline of ecclesiastical and governmental authorities. They told readers how to live their lives: how to behave in new or novel social situations, how to deal with ethical dilemmas, how to order their domestic arrangements, how to advance in their jobs, etc. For example, the leading female journalist of the day, Sarah Josepha Hale, advised middle-class women—the displaced persons of the industrial revolution—that industrialism had freed them from their economic role in production so that they would be able to pursue their true calling as "God's appointed agents of *morality*." Hale urged them to embrace "The Cult of True Womanhood" by making their homes places of order and moral uplift which would refine man's "human affections and elevate his moral feelings."[40] In short, she told women to keep their husbands sober and to get them to work on time.

The periodical press also advised immigrants of the errors of their regressive foreign ways. Newspapers became the primary vehicles of the "Americanization movement." They counseled foreign-born readers about the rewards of Anglo-conformity: told them how to dress, talk, eat, think, pray, and smell like real Americans. They told them how and where to shop, and what products they must buy to effect the metamorphosis. Editorials, comics, literary serials, didactic columns, and letters to the editor ridiculed "greenhorns" who were too ignorant or undisciplined to adopt American ways. The Society pages made it clear that Poles, Italians, Jews, and Afro-Americans never gave a memorable party or had a proper wedding. The obituaries implied that only WASPS died of natural causes, or scheduled funerals. And, if these lessons did not take, the copy of the crime reporters demonstrated that resistance to assimilation was not just unpatriotic and unprofitable, it was also dangerous. For "in the papers," crime and its victims seldom had real American names.[41]

Press participation in the Americanization process was not confined to mainstream, large circulation, WASP-controlled newspapers. Foreign-language presses were also recruited to the effort through the American Association of Foreign Language Newspapers, an advertising agency formed by a group of large corporations (including Standard Oil, American Tobacco Company, and others) and some members of the Republican National Committee. The AAFLN used its control of advertising revenues to influence and direct the editorial policies of foreign language papers in the U.S. It purged these papers of regressive pre-industrial values and disruptive anti-capitalist sentiments and transformed them into agents of Americanization. It monitered them to ensure that they would not support behaviors or values "so different from our own" as to constitute a threat of "action that is inimical to our national purposes, or that interferes with our social machinery."[42] However, AAFLN did not fully succeed in bringing all foreign language presses under the discipline of the Americanization movement, and socialist, anarchistic, and communist ideas continued to have some circulation in the German, Polish, and Hungarian-American newspapers until World War I.

C. The Ethic of Capitalism
Alliances between Protestant clergy and capitalists continued to prosper even though the moral authority of religion was being undermined

by secularization. Some factory owners required their employees to attend church on Sunday and Bible studies during the week. This was designed not only to encourage regular habits on the part of employees but also to keep factories free of papists and Jews and their foreign ideas. Many companies, large and small, sponsored in-house educational programs for their employees which went beyond training in the skills necessary to do their jobs and often included education in morality, religion, citizenship, diction, nutrition, personal hygiene, and physical education. A pioneer of the industrial education movement, Gertrude Beeks, warned that "the so-called democratic idea should be avoided" in such programs because it poses a threat to order in the factory.[43]

The reading habits and popular entertainments of the laboring classes were also placed under close scrutiny. The clergy displayed little concern over the infection of erotica until it began to spread beyond the elites to the laboring classes. Similarly, civil laws against obscenity were uncommon until the nineteenth century, when increased literacy and lower prices made bawdy novels available to the lower classes. Bourgeois aesthetics could tolerate erotic pictures in museums but not on postcards. Books were confiscated and theaters were raided to protect or correct the morals of the people. The development of electronic communications ultimately enfranchised a formal system of censorship in America. The marriage of theology and capitalism permitted development of a censorial system that was ostensibly designed to protect the morals of the people, but which also protected the property of the capitalists. The Hays Office, which censored motion pictures, came into existence during the depression of the 1930s after a series of gangster movies had been produced to a formula which implied that 'crime pays.' Broadcast Standards and Practices have monitored the listening/viewing of American radio and television users on the grounds of good taste. The power-knowledge mediating the aesthetics of good taste has, of course, been the power-knowledge of the industrial education movement.[44]

Jefferson may have been "really mortified" by censorship in America. Warren Harding was not! President Harding served as honorary chairman of Comstock's New York Vice Society. The same money that supported the great museums and educational institutions of New York—the old money of the déclassé Federalists and the new money of Wall Street—also funded the Vice Society.[45] Comstockery was only the crude visible edge of a pervasive and pernicious attempt to inscribe *The Message to Garcia* within the souls of the people.

D. Progress: Mass Culture as Class Culture

The Progressive younger sons of Poor Richard Improved took the lessons of Franklin, Calvin, Barnum, Morgan, Pinkerton, Hearst, and the Chautauqua circuit to Madison Avenue. They used the prescriptive controls of advertising, public relations, and scientific management to try to convince the people that the corporate way is the American way. In 1929 John Dewey observed, the publicity agent "is perhaps the most significant symbol of our present social life." Publicity—"information with news value issued as a means of gaining public attention or support" (*Webster's New Collegiate Dictionary*)— created the language of twentieth-century business, politics, sport, and entertainment.[46] For industrial progress not only provided the auspices for mass production of commodities, it also made possible mass production of images, ideologies, and constructions of social reality.

The same asymmetrical (undemocratic) organization of the productive process that is used to produce locomotives, light bulbs, and laxatives is also used in the manufacture of the products of the Consciousness Industry: news, advertising, scripts, programs, comics, etc. Both forms of production are structured to assure minimal participation in decision-making by workers, to insulate managers against the wills of workers, and to subject workers to the discipline of managers.

Managers of the Consciousness Industry are further insulated against the wills of workers *and* consumers by advertising, since advertisers, not audiences or subscribers, provide the profits of electronic media, newspapers, and magazines. Advertising thereby removes the element of risk from the productive process in these segments of the Consciousness Industry. It even insulates managers against the mythical "power of the box-office."

In contemporary America, mass communications are therefore corporate communications. Messages, and the social constructions of reality in which these messages are embedded, flow down and out from the company to the people. Mass culture is created for the people, not by the people. Like the curriculum of the public schools or the platform of the New York Vice Society, mass entertainments are manufactured to the specifications of elites who go elsewhere for their own pleasures. In short, mass culture is a class culture. It is a counterfeit but technically superb rendering of social reality which celebrates and legitimates the hierarchical power-knowledge of the "tinsel" aristocracy of industrial capitalism: officials, investors, managers, experts, and the princes and princesses of consumerism—stars, celebrities, and other big spenders. It is Schmidt's and Fritos supplied by devotees of Campari and Häagen-Dazs! Like the pedagogy of 'public' schools, the pedagogy of mass culture is a pedagogy of psychic oppression. Both forms of instruction use the language of democracy to secure and reproduce hidden curriculums of hierarchical control, and thereby reduce the people's power to resist. Resistance does not resonate because, as Max Horkheimer noted, "The patterns of thought and action that people accept ready-made from the agencies of mass culture act in their turn to influence mass culture as though they were the ideas of the people themselves."[47] The louvered shutters in the tower of the Panopticon are replaced with one-way mirrors which not only conceal the controllers from view but also the tower itself.

The pedagogy of mass culture denies, deflects, and defuses resistance. "Public opinion [*sic*]" manufactured by the instruments of publicity—news, advertising, and press agents—is substituted for democratic dialogues and decisions by the people. Political consensus is reduced to political consent. Elites set the agenda for public opinion, define the permissible alternatives, and confine expression of the people's political vision to the parameters of a multiple-choice question.

In *Advertising: The Uneasy Persuasion*, Michael Schudson suggests that advertising is capitalism's equivalent to Socialist Realism. Like Socialist Realist art, advertising simplifies and typifies: "It does not claim to picture reality as it is but reality as it should be—life and lives worth emulating." Schudson maintains that both Socialist Realism and Capitalist Realism present simplified social messages which picture people as representatives of larger social categories, and both forms of realism repress criticism of the system in which their respective messages are embedded.[48] Capitalist Realism is Political Capitalism's celebration of itself: a celebration in which the Party-mindedness of sociorealism is replaced by consumer-mindedness, and the positive collectivist hero is recast in the costume of the Marlboro Man.

Under political capitalism the theory of mass marketing replaces classic theories of democracy. When Philo Farnsworth demonstrated his prototype for the modern television system in 1927, he presented it with a dollar sign on the screen. The symbolism was prophetic. The social organization of television production in America marked a decisive advance in the power-knowledge of political capitalism.

Television not only used publicity as a means of marketing commodities and marshalling support for industrial capitalism, it turned
publicity itself into a highly marketable commodity. The television
business is organized to *"produce* audiences and *sell* them to advertisers of consumer goods and services, political candidates, and groups
interested in controversial public issues."[49] Television producers manage this skin-trade with extraordinary technical and aesthetic agility.
They are the gatekeepers and shamans of contemporary American
culture. Their single-minded commitment to produce audiences and
sell them to advertisers skews the language, storytelling routines,
images, values, dreams, and hopes that make up the common American culture. It transforms the American landscape into a
'mediascape.'[50]

In capitalist economies the organizational structure of television
production, like other forms of production, is formally totalitarian.
It is under the hierarchical control of a corporate elite. This organizational structure inverts the classic democratic principle which
proscribes undue influence on the part of an unrepresentative minority. According to Ben Bagdikian, the unrepresentative minority
who own major U.S. media "have a narrow, common outlook not
out of a conspiracy but because corporations of this size and power
by their nature have common goals and outlooks, particularly in
economics, in politics, and in sustaining the status quo." Like other
individuals and institutions, media owners and media corporations
have self-interests, but they have more power to pursue their self-
interests because they control access to the mediascape.[51]

Television writers, the galley slaves of the system, typically earn
in excess of $200,000 per year. Producers earn much more.[52] Nearly
all are white male college graduates. This "tinsel" aristocracy creates
dreams of consumption, mediates vicarious access to unknown (often
forbidden) worlds, cultivates images of wealth and power, patterns
of language, and social values for the people: the kid in Spanish
Harlem, the unemployed steel worker in Lackawanna, the Hasidic
Jew, the resident of the nursing home, the born-again Christian, and
the typical American worker who earns somewhere between $12,000
and $16,000 per year depending upon his/her sex. In the dreams—
the culture—produced by television these people are "symbolically
annihilated." They are invisible. The fictional world of television is
a homogeneous world. It is a world in which white males, in the prime
of life exercise nearly all of the power. It is a world largely purged
of racial and ethnic minorities, women over thirty-five, the aged, and

physically infirm. It is not a mirror of American society. It is a mirror of the distribution of political and economic power in American society. Significantly, those who are heavy viewers of television are more likely to endorse totalitarian solutions to social problems than people who watch less television. In sum, no hyperbole is involved in the assertion that television is "the cultural arm" of corporate America.[53]

I am not suggesting that corporate control of media precisely parallels state control of media. It does not. Heterodox messages do penetrate the net of corporate control just as they penetrate church and state control. Aesop continues to exercise his wiles. The dialectic of human freedom is not entirely silenced. Even within a tightly controlled production system like network television, creative people sometimes do manage to turn the tables and make monkeys out of the moguls. Moreover, cynical decodings of corporate encodings cannot be fully policed. So that the boy in the barrio or the girl in the ghetto may read the corporate communications of television programming with his or her own crooked smile! S/he may re-create and reconstitute the corporate communications of mass culture into authentic codes of resistance through negation, parody, or other forms of linguistic therapy, rapping or "jiving the man."[54] Moreover, because novelty keeps the commodities moving in a consumer society, corporate control *may* even allow more to "get through" than religious or state censorship. Or at least it may create the impression that it is letting more through. But as George Gerbner points out, corporate production of novelty may involve sleight of hand. It may provide an illusion of the new—an illusion of change, choice, and diversity—which keeps real alternatives from being communicated.[55]

Political capitalism may also permit more to get through because the corporations that control mass media are part of a plurality of elites. Their interests do sometimes compete and conflict with the interests of other corporations. CBS may find that exposing the nuclear industry's abuses of safety regulations attracts audiences. In this case, CBS's profits are made at the expense of the nuclear industry. CBS is not acting at the 'behest' of the nuclear industry but it is acting in 'behalf' of the capitalistic system of profit. What gets through the opening created by this structural contradiction is still under capitalist control. It does sustain residual opportunities for heterodoxy. But these opportunities are only residual. The adversarial relations that arise when conglomerates fight over which one will bank the biggest bucks do not provide a reliable or principled warrant for press freedom. What gets through this structural contradiction is still dependent on the power of the dollar. The Golden Rule of capitalist power-knowledge remains, 'He who has the Gold, makes the Rules.'

Nevertheless these rules do socially stratify access to mass communication in ways that permit those near the top of the pyramid of power-knowledge significant freedom. So that there is more than an element of truth in Liberalism's assertion that intellectuals in capitalist societies are freer to express dissident views publicly than their counterparts in socialist societies. This artifact of elite pluralism enhances public impressions of the credibility of mass media in capitalist societies. But it is not much solace to the boy in the barrio or the girl in the ghetto. The relative freedom of Publicans, cum professionals, and their business partners, is still secured by circumscribing the freedom of the people, cum masses.

In the U.S., mass media have always been closely scrutinized. The organizational charts of American film, radio, and television corporations routinely include offices for epistemological policemen: 'censors' or bureaus of 'standards and practices.' Writers frequently complain about the arbitrary and tyrannical decisions that emanate from these offices.

Yet even the most perceptive critics of American television are hesitant to use the term 'censorship' to describe the totalitarian structure of television production or the skewed images of social reality cultivated by the fictional worlds of television programming. Rose Goldsen came close. She pointed out that, "A political system that offers only these alternatives for making the public will known is called totalitarian." Goldsen noted:

> The term *oligopoly* has been suggested; and it is indeed suitable for the economic arrangements that exist in television. It is unpleasant to the ear, however, and not as widely understood as *totalitarian*. When this country was founded and none of these terms was in current use, the term *established*—as in *established* religion—was used to describe a system which offered the populace an officially approved ideology.[56]

Gerbner follows a similar line of reasoning by comparing the structures of corporate control under capitalism to the structure of control that the orthodoxy of medieval religion exercised over the faithful. Significantly, he also sees a similar structure of hierarchical control operating in industrialized nations under socialism.[57] Dallas Smythe, however, bites the bullet and asserts directly:

The act of modern censorship is essentially a decision as to what is to be mass produced in the cultural area. So long as current cultural production is in the hands of privately owned giant corporations, *they* must also make decisions as to what is to be mass produced in the cultural area and what will not be produced. Because in monopoly capitalism, privately owned giant corporations are regarded as legal persons, we are accustomed to yield them the same privileges to which natural persons are entitled. *It is as accurate therefore to refer to corporate decision making in the cultural area as being censorship as it is to refer to government decision making by that pejorative term.*[58]

Smythe does not confine his indictment to television production, but rather he sees corporate censorship as a pervasive feature of all operations of the culture industry. In my judgment, television production offers the most compelling documentation of his thesis.

When I assert that material censorship is at work in the U.S. Consciousness Industry, I am not suggesting that this censorship is absolute. I am not suggesting that it is always successful, that it is enforced with uniform rigidity, or that it produces a "one-dimensional society." Similarly, when I use the concept 'political capitalism' I am not endorsing the claim of Marx and Engels that "the executive of the modern state is but a committee for managing the common affairs of the whole bourgeoisie." To the contrary, I acknowledge that even under advanced capitalism, residual pluralism, the "plurality of economic elites" remains. In spite of the designs of Morgan and Company, competition has not been eliminated, it has simply been "rationalized" to eliminate most of the wild cards from the game. *Elite pluralism* has replaced democratic pluralism, but competition among elites still permits some slippage in the system of corporate censorship. Nevertheless I affirm, with qualifications, Ralph Miliband's assertion that " 'elite pluralism' does not, however, prevent the separate elites in capitalist society from constituting a dominant economic class, possessed of a high degree of cohesion and solidarity, with common interests and common purposes which far transcend their specific differences and disagreements".[59] Like Miliband, I acknowledge the reality of the cohesion of corporate elites, but I argue that competition among these elites renders that cohesion far more tenuous than Marxist formulations imply. I believe that this competition places the cohesion of elites in constant jeopardy. And that as a result, specters of "unknown enemies" must continually be raised by these elites to re-create and reinforce their own class solidarity as well as to justify their control of the consciousness industry. These specters, in turn, weld the alliance of state and capital.

The specter of communism has been an especially potent force for generating solidarity among American elites as well as for assuring the continuity of political capitalism. If Karl Marx had not existed, capitalist elites would have had to invent him. In 1789 an enraged proletariat raised the Red Flag in Paris. Enraged capitalists have been seeing red ever since. Capitalist hardliners regarded Abraham Lincoln as being soft on communism.[60] And as early as the 1870s the specter of communism was invoked to justify the use of military and law-enforcement agencies in repressing trade-unionism. Since then, it has provided a ready excuse for government intervention on behalf of capital. The Palmer Raids (1919–21), a violent series of raids on the headquarters of dissident groups, led by U.S. Attorney General A. Mitchell Palmer, were, in part, aftershocks of the Russian Revolution. They were also morality plays. Subsequently the repressive character of the Soviet regime under Stalin provided political capitalists with the perfect enemy: in Foucault's terms, it provided them with a symmetrical inversion of the godhead of 'Jeffersonian democracy,' a monster regime which could be invoked, at will, to justify realization of the 'manifest destiny' of the world-system of capitalism.

But the system of control used to secure the power-knowledge of anti-Stalinism in the U.S. after World War II bears the scars of its troubled birth. Stalin's fanaticism provided political capitalists with a warrant for constricting free expression in the U.S. Under the auspicies of the House Un-American Activities Committee, the Truman Doctrine, the F.B.I., the Subversive Activities Control Board, the Internal Security Act of 1950, the Smith Act, a system of loyalty oaths, and other quasi-legal devices, political capitalism created its own monster. The peril of the Red Menace was invoked to purge the U.S. Consciousness Industry of its own cosmological mess-makers, communists, former-communists, fellow-travelers, socialists, left-liberals, revisionists, and fifth-columnists of every imaginable and imagined stripe. Political capitalism purged—smeared, blacklisted, and in some cases tried—thousands of writers, journalists, printers, linotype operators, actors, producers, scientists, educators, and trade-unionists. Some were Stalinist sympathizers. A few were probably Soviet agents. But most of those targeted by this inquisition were not enemies of the principles of Jeffersonian democracy. They were, however, enemies—critics—of the practices of political capitalism. The sanctions against these dissidents were primarily economic. They were far less lethal than the political sanctions invoked by Stalin. Nevertheless they were very effective in silencing domestic opposition to political capitalism's international adventures.

Reliance upon ideological alchemy to produce solidarity within the capitalist class has global consequences. It produces a siege mentality that makes elites in capitalist societies vulnerable to fascist temptations. Moreover it excuses political capitalists who succumb to these temptations by translating their actions into the vocabulary of patriotism. In short, it does not just permit cultural imperialism, it mandates it. Consequently neither the domestic repressions committed by cold warriors nor the foreign ventures undertaken by the hot warriors of twentieth-century American capitalism can be seen as temporary aberrations. They are systemic products of elite pluralism. As a result, censorship enfranchised under the cover of "national security" has become an integral part of the normal functioning of state and corporate control in America. And violations of civil and human rights have become routine practices in policing "the free world."

V

'Information-Capitalism': The New Economics of Market Censorship

Classic Liberal models of democracy were premised upon the assumption that knowledge is a social resource, a public utility, or a collective good. For this reason, free public libraries have been regarded as cornerstones of democracy. Even the much criticized Utilitarian image of "a free-market of ideas" protects the belief that access to knowledge is a right rather than a privilege; it assumes free entry of diverse ideas into a public marketplace which is open to all citizen/shoppers who seek knowledge.

As we have seen, the Liberal ideal of free and open access to knowledge has never been fully realized in practice. What Tocqueville characterized as "the spirit of trade" had already entered the American marketplace of ideas by the 1830s. Artifacts of the spirit of trade like copyrights and patents are abridgments of free-flows of information designed to protect capital investments and thereby ensure reliable supplies of commodities and profits. As a result of Liberalism's compromises with the comforts of capitalism, the institutional structures of Liberal societies have never been as pure as their ideological structures.

Under industrial capitalism, human labor has been the source of 'added' or 'surplus value.' That is, the basic source of conflict between owners and wage-laborers has revolved around the distribution of profits earned from the commodities produced by the muscle and sweat of human labor. Capitalism, however, is currently undergoing a profound structural realignment in which the terms of the equation are being radically altered. Daniel Bell and others see this realignment as signaling the end of industrialism and the beginning of a "post-industrial" socioeconomic system.[61] The "information society" is a buzzword used to describe transformation to the new system of production. Under "information-capitalism," access to control over knowledge becomes a source of surplus value as well as a potential site of social conflict.[62]

Within this new order, knowledge is no longer simply a means or resource used in the production of commodities, it also becomes a commodity. It becomes "cultural capital."[63] As a result, the source of profit is not " 'the theft of alien labour time' but rather the private appropriation of 'accumulated social knowledge'."[64] In sum, under information-capitalism, the marketplace of ideas is no longer a public utility which serves all who seek its goods. Increasingly it becomes a private enterprise which serves only those who can afford to pay a price for the commodities it markets to citizen/shoppers.

Under this new system of capitalism, the production of knowledge becomes a basic industry like the production of oil, steel, and transportation.[65] The shift in economic activity from the production of material goods to the commodity production of knowledge occurs in three ways. First, through automation, especially robotics and other forms of computer-assisted manufacturing which redirect the efforts of the human workforce to research, planning, design, and development of knowledge that is applied in manufacturing of material goods. Second, through the emergence of 'hi-tech' enterprises which specialize in the production and sale of what Tessa Morris-Suzuki calls "commodified 'producer information' " (i.e. design, software, databases, etc.)—information resources which are used by other firms in the productive process. Third, through expansion of the production and marketing of "consumer information" goods such as computers, VCRs, videos, books, magazines, television programs, etc.[66]

The transformation to information capitalism cannot take place without transforming the relationship of the citizen/shopper to knowledge. Unlike oil, steel, or streetcars, knowledge is not consumed. It may be censored, lost, or forgotten, but it does not deplete itself, rust, or wear out. Moreover, once it is produced, knowledge can be copied, pirated, or plagiarized. This creates a problem for producers of commodified knowledge. A specter haunts them. For, at least in theory, a free-market of ideas conceives of knowledge as communal property not as private property. Consequently a free-market of ideas cannot turn a profit. Knowledge can only become a profitable commodity if this specter is removed, that is, if access to knowledge is restricted by: (1) removing it from the public sphere and (2) limiting the channels available for its distribution.

Transfering production of knowledge from the public to the private sphere requires a close alignment of the knowledge-producing facilities of business and government. It requires "privatization of information" because the new information brokers have a vested interest in keeping information secret.[67] As a result, they put pressure on government to stop giving away the goods: to cease producing and distributing information *gratis* (or at cost) through government publications, the Library of Congress, government statistical services, census reports, etc. Since 1980, U.S. government information policy has been responsive to these pressures. It has reduced its information-related responsibilities in the following ways: (1) through "deregulation" which has eliminated much of private industry's responsibility to report its activities to government agencies; (2) by narrowing the federal government's production and distribution of knowledge so that information that was previously gathered and analyzed by the federal government for local governments is no longer provided; (3) through restricting access to previously available information by expanding the range of information protected by government classification; (4) by sharply increasing the price of information available through the Freedom of Information Act; (5) by significantly reducing the number and volume of publications available through the Government Printing Office, and by making future government publication decisions contingent on profitability; (6) by subjecting the writings and speeches of more than 120,000 current or former officials to prior censorship; (7) by restricting access to non-strategic scientific and technological information produced in universities under government contracts and grants; and (8) by reducing the operating budget of the Library of Congress and thereby reducing the services it provides users.[68] Privatization of information means that information that was once available as part of a citizen's right to know is now available only at a price. And, as Herbert Schiller has pointed out, under information-capitalism, information that does not generate a profit will not be produced.[69] Thus, for example, in Britain the self-interest of Margaret Thatcher's government has combined with its responsiveness to market forces in a way that has gradually resulted in the disappearance of poverty statistics.[70]

The deregulation movement has also promoted a shift to information-capitalism by accelerating historical trends toward concentration of ownership within information industries: electronics, telecommunications, publishing, etc. And, this concentration has, in turn, exerted structural pressures toward concentration within those sectors of the economy which have exchanges with information industries: suppliers of raw materials, distributers, and retailers.[71] Ben Bagdikian points out that in 1984 forty-four corporations controlled half of all mass media outlets in the U.S. The historical trend toward concentration is dramatically displayed by changes in ownership of newspapers. In 1900, Bagdikian reports, there were 2,042 daily papers with 2,023 different owners. However, by 1982 there were 760 owners but twenty of these were large corporations which conducted more than half of the business. By 1984 mergers and acquisitions had reduced the number of major corporate chains from twenty to fourteen. Moreover, concentration of ownership has almost completely eliminated competitiveness in the newspaper industry at the local level. As a result, 98 percent of American cities now have only one daily newspaper.[72] In television, ownership is concentrated in the hands of three networks which control most of the programming and access to national audiences. However, ownership of local stations has been restricted by laws designed to protect 'the public interest,' but deregulation will lift these restrictions and bring ownership of local television stations in major-market cities under the control of a half-dozen giant corporations including the three networks. Similar patterns of concentration are also present in magazine and book publishing. Fewer than twenty companies conduct most of the business in the magazine industry, and of the 2,500 companies that publish one or more books a year, eleven account for most of the annual sales of two billion books.[73] Moreover, the largest retail outlet for books, Waldenbooks, is owned by KMart, and the second largest outlet, B. Dalton, recently tried to sell itself to Sears.[74] In sum, while there has been an enormous increase in the volume of production by the Consciousness Industry in recent years, there has also been a corresponding decline in the number of companies that control significant market shares. With that reduction, Bagdikian and others claim, there has also been a decline in the diversity of the views represented in media content. As a result, the goods available within the marketplace of ideas increasingly resemble the standardized commodities produced by an "assembly line."[75]

The transformations in information-specific sectors of the economy are dramatic indicators of the shift to information capitalism, but the current structural realignments of capitalism penetrate the entire economy. The shift from industrial to information capitalism has been characterized by four economy-wide trends since World War II: (1) concentration and monopolization; (2) centralization; (3) internationalization of production; and (4) deindustrialization of particular sectors. Information industries have been in the vanguard of these trends. They have played pivotal roles not only in internationalizing production but also internationalizing American culture.[76] They have facilitated rapid worldwide transfers of capital, and promoted feminization of the labor force, especially in the Third World.[77] J.W. Freiberg predicts these trends in global capitalism will produce the following structural changes in the organization of production in information industries: (1) further concentration and monopolization; (2) increased control by owners over content and organizational aspects of information production; (3) decreases in the use of labor and massive 'de-skilling' of the workforce as a result of automation; (4) disappearance of traditional crafts like journalism and printing and emergence of new categories of information 'specialists'; and (5) reduced effectiveness of information workers in organizing unions.[78] This pessimistic assessment defies the predictions of apologists of the information society who claim new information technologies will eliminate exploitation of labor and usher in a New Periclean Age.[79]

In my judgment, the shift to information-capitalism does not signal the end of capitalism or the advent of the post-industrial society. It marks a transition to a new stage of capitalism in which information as well as muscle and sweat generate surplus value. It may also mark the beginning of a post-Liberal society. If this transformation is successful, it will complete the project set in motion by political capitalism during the Progressive Era: the movement away from a model of governance that involves people in society as political citizens of nation-states, and towards an economistic model which involves people as consumption units in a corporate world.[80] In short, the rival corporate republics that so worried the founders of the American Republic will at last secure complete hegemony.

Neither Liberal nor Marxist critiques of censorship adequately explain, or provide recipes for resisting, the new system of market censorship that operates under information-capitalism. New models are needed. These models must be able to identify, explain, and critique the following: (1) the mechanisms whereby public knowledge is privatized; (2) the new structures of inequality produced by stratification of the global economy into information-rich and information-poor countries, regions, groups, classes, genders, or races; (3) the implications of the strategic placement of knowledge workers in information-capitalism; (4) the structural position of communications as an arena of ideological and social conflict; and (5) the epistemological foundations of the system of power-knowledge created by information-capitalism including the socially structured silences it secures.[81]

vi

Censorship and the Power-Knowledge of the World System of Political Capitalism

Market censorship has been so effectively "rationalized" in the U.S. that it resembles the dramaturgy of "an authorless theatre."[82] Very few stage directions are required to ensure that the show will go on. In contrast, the market censorship American political capitalism exports to the Third World cannot be sustained without repressive intervention. Packaged for export, political capitalism can no longer affect an appearance of neutrality. It cannot manage a convincing performance as an impersonal, immanent "rationalizing" principle. Removed from the contexts of American values, history, and ideology, political capitalism is an emperor without clothes. The American Way may be welcomed or rejected but it is not perceived as the only way. As a result, the siege mentality that silences domestic opposition to political capitalism does not translate well to an international stage. The specter of "Godless Communism" can only create "congregation through segregation" when a people share a common god, common property values, and a common tradition and mythos of persecution.

Since the early days of American independence, the U.S. has engaged in sporadic political and economic adventurism in Latin America. But such interventions were not integral to the routine functioning of the American political or economic systems. However, since World War II, American political capitalism has become a world system.

Instead of dismantling its military system as it had done at the conclusion of previous wars, after World War II the U.S. continued to maintain military bases throughout the world. It assumed responsibility for the global defenses of the "free" (non-communist) world. Under the visionary umbrella of the the Universal Rights of Man, U.S. policy and publicity celebrated bonds of global friendship. At the same time, however, U.S.-based corporations began to colonize Third World nations recently abandoned by, or liberated from, their former European colonial masters. U.S. companies took over the old trade routes and reproduced the colonial pattern of North-South dependence. Sometimes these routes were used to provide U.S. government-financed humanitarian aid to Third World nations ravaged by hunger, disease, and natural disasters. But more routinely they facilitated corporate expansion. They allowed American companies to "buy cheap and sell dear": to import raw materials from the 'periphery' (underdeveloped nations) to the 'core' (U.S. and Western Europe), and export manufactured goods from the core to the periphery. In this exchange, American-made goods became tokens, souvenirs, and publicity agents for America. As "teaching machines," they also became, de facto, agents of cultural imperialism.[83] They laid the foundations for the American Consciousness Industry to become a global industry. Thus Jeremy Tunstall's assertion that "The Media are American" describes quite literally the architecture of the World Information Order in the postwar period.[84]

In addition to facilitating rebuilding of the old colonial networks, the U.S. military also underwrote development of a new paradigm for American business operations abroad. Occupied Japan became a test case and role model for corporate development of underdevelopment in the Third World. The Japanese model appeared to offer Third World nations a shortcut to "modernization." It allowed U.S. companies to purchase Third World labor at a fraction of the amount American workers are paid. Managers of American subsidiaries abroad formed alliances with local leadership cadres who condoned this wage slavery in exchange for U.S. corporate and military protection. These leaders usually exercised censorship over local media. Because their privileges were underwritten by American political capitalism, they developed deeply entrenched interests in maintaining the status quo—a status quo that frequently involved caste-like social and economic inequalities between the elites and the people and between management and labor. As a result, political capitalism has increasingly aligned itself with reactionary governments in the Third World. So much so that some critics of U.S. foreign policy charge there is a "*structural* commitment by the United States to counter-insurgency, that is, one that inevitably follows from the pattern of interests and relationships that joins the United States to the Third World and that expresses itself in the form of a permanent war against the various manifestations of revolutionary nationalism."[85] The U.S. decision in 1984 to withdraw from UNESCO might be seen as an escalation of this permanent war.

The polarization of the world into two hostile camps after World War II facilitated corporate colonization of the Third World. The excuse of an evil empire excused the evils of cultural imperialism as regrettable but necessary steps to stop Soviet "aggression." The alibi of a nasty world quickly made it nastier. The humanistic elements in American plans for rebuilding a "war-torn world" were soon over-powered by crasser interests as hungry corporations replaced hungry children in the calculus of international defenses. And 'moderniza-tion'—once an optimistic island for American policy researchers—became an empty promise, a code-word for corporate domination of domestic politics in the Third World.

Why did this happen? How was America the liberator transformed into America the conqueror? What role did Liberalism play in the transmutation?

My answers to these questions are not pleasant. They disturb my dreams of democracy and visions of an egalitarian future. Moreover they seriously challenge the legitimacy of the tactics and strategies which currently secure the power-knowledge of Liberal societies. I offer these answers in the hope that they will also disturb, distress, and challenge the reader, so that together we may begin to engage in dialogues on freedom and control which can disturb, challenge, and interrupt the monologue of political capitalism.

My answers suggest that the levy political capitalism imposed on freedom after World War II was too high. It subjected the Third World to "the test of the marketplace." Small nations struggling to define themselves as independent, self-governing states were pitted against the interests of gigantic corporations which frequently had larger populations (more employees) and invariably had larger budgets and operating resources. Predictably, the corporations prevailed, and Progress (*cum* modernization) once more translated economic power into political power. The international triumph of political capitalism during the postwar period transformed the Third World into the foundation of the pyramid of American corporate power-knowledge. Wage-slavery in the Third World permitted American multinational corporations to realize unprecedented profits. It also permitted the American population at large, the people, to enjoy a higher standard of material well-being than ever before. Some of the new corporate profits did "filter down" to the people. In neo-Keynesian fashion, the capital imported from the Third World did fuel expansion of consumerism in the U.S. so that the American Dream of an air-conditioned home in suburbia was partially underwritten by the nightmare of the sweatshops of the Third World.

This restructuring of the world order was undertaken without publicity. It was not debated in the United Nations, although U.S. domination of the U.N. in the postwar years facilitated it. It was not openly reviewed in the U.S. Congress, although Congress passed laws which expedited it. It was never put before the people of America or Nigeria or Taiwan or Honduras or any other nation for referendum.

The withdrawal of the U.S. from UNESCO in 1984 signaled a callous indifference to the dramaturgy of debate and the rituals of multilateralism, and marked an escalation of the U.S. war against defenders of Third World political and cultural autonomy. With this move, U.S. political capitalism freed itself from the inconvenience of engaging in legitimating dialogues with those who advocate a New International Economic Order or a New International Information Order.

Nevertheless it is not useful to think of this purposive restructuring as a plot or conspiracy against the people. The men who implemented this democratic counter-revolution were no more personally unprincipled or malevolent than the men who planned and staged the first American Revolution. Both eighteenth-century and twentieth-century American revolutionaries were motivated by patriotic and personal interests. There were undoubtedly many decent men in each group: men who cared about the future, went to church regularly, loved their families, were kind to their dogs, and genuinely suffered when they saw a hungry child, whether in Boston, New York, Washington, Calcutta, Seoul, or São Paulo. However, the men who drafted the U.S. Constitution were living off of the accumulated moral capital of the Judeo-Christian tradition. The men who drafted the new world system of political capitalism were living off of the accumulated capital of Morgan, Rockefeller, Beeks, Pinkerton, Taylor, Barnum, Hearst, et al.: their "rationalized" world-view recognized no logic except the logic of profit, no principles save the principles of accounting.

Simply by acting in concert to protect their interests abroad, American corporate managers succeeded in empowering the new order. In the words of George Ball, former Under-Secretary of State in the Kennedy and Johnson administrations and partner in the international investment-banking firm Lehman Brothers: "Working through great corporations that straddle the earth men are able for the first time to utilize world resources with an efficiency dictated by the objective logic of profit." Peter Drucker has described the new world system as a "global shopping center." Cees Hamelink characterized it as a "corporate village." Richard Barnet and Ronald Muller maintain that the rise of the U.S.-dominated "global enterprise" is producing an organizational revolution as profound in its implications for modern man as the Industrial Revolution and the rise of the nation-state." They predict that 200 to 300 multinationals will soon control 80 percent of all of the productive assets in the non-communist world.[86] This organizational revolution has been secured by the communications revolution which permits instantaneous international transfers of information and capital.

American corporations and the American people rode the crest of the wave of profits produced by this revolution for almost three decades. However, in the mid-1970s global corporations increasingly became multinational corporations. Germany, France, Britain, and other developed nations began to claim larger pieces of what had become, de facto, the American Pie. The Japanese model exceeded its warranty, but it remained an effective teaching machine for both the 'haves' and the 'have-nots.' Japan's spectacular success as an independent international trading partner signaled the dawn of a new era in world capitalism. Newly developing nations would no longer be content to settle for leftovers. And the oil-rich nations, which had supplied the cheap fuel that kept the American pyramid of privilege warm, realized the wisdom of Morgan's principle of combination and became the OPEC nations. Third World delegations to the United Nations also discovered the power of combination. These developments reintroduced the wild cards into the world of big business that the architects of political capitalism had largely purged from the operations of business-as-usual in America during the Progressive Era.

As a result American domination of the world system of capitalism became increasingly fragile. The gravy days were over. American business tightened its belt. As always, the poor felt it first. Domestically, the accountants declared the Keynesian experiment a failure. International policies were also restructured to fit the dictates of more austere times. Detente and Human Rights advocacy, policies always less noble in practice than in theory, were pronounced "soft on communism."[87] These policies were replaced by a program of crackpot realism that openly identified the U.S. interest as an interest in conserving, by military force if necessary, all anti-Soviet regimes in the Third World. It did not matter if these regimes were totalitarian (*cum* authoritarian). If they were pro-American (now conflated to pro-capitalism), they passed the new litmus test. U.S. withdrawal from UNESCO used material censorship—the censorship of the high security deposit—to muffle the new voices of heterodoxy. Once more, the excuse of an evil enemy was invoked to justify the repeal of American democratic principles. In sum, it supported a policy of cutting the losses of multinationalism and preserving a healthy profit-margin. An accounting decision, not a moral decision—a decision responsive to the power-knowledge of political capitalism but wholly alien to the power-knowledge of the democratic covenants drafted by the Age of Reason.

The power-knowledge of the world system of American political capitalism is as deeply implicated in the graves at Dimbaza and the prisons in Chile as the power-knowledge of Marxist-Leninism is implicated in building the camps of the Gulag Archipelago. The primary difference is that U.S. political capitalism exports its most heinous atrocities.

Goethe once expressed the hope that America might build a more humane society because it lacked Europe's long history of brutality and repression. He regarded America as an innocent. America is no longer an innocent. Nevertheless the power-knowledge of political capitalism allows Americans to affect innocence. It keeps us from readily recognizing the tragic dimensions of America's failure of moral leadership in the postwar years. It is not just nationalism, racism, or overt and covert press censorship that obscure America's collective vision—although they contribute to it. America's blindness has deeper roots. It is a systemic defect of the U.S. democratic heritage.

It does not reflect only the moral bankruptcy of political capitalism. It also reflects the failure of the moral vision of the founding fathers: the failure of the moral imagination of the Liberalism of the Age of Reason which legitimized separation of public and private morality. The same dualism which allowed Thomas Jefferson to cook the morality books also allows contemporary men and women to separate personal morality from business morality. It encourages responsible and decent human beings to divorce their personal commitments to religious or secular ethics from their professional and political lives! This allows them to engage in "business-as-usual" without reflecting upon the ethical or moral consequences of their actions.

The Declaration of Independence and the Constitution provided the moral authority for the creation of the American nation-state. The rules of discourse which made these democratic covenants possible were at least formally democratic and egalitarian. They empowered a legislative process to create and repeal America's collective commitments. They commissioned an independent, diverse, adversarial press to monitor and censor the abuses of power-holders.

Political capitalism established its control by circumventing these rules of discourse. Therefore, according to the rules of a dialogically based democratic theory, the power-knowledge of political capitalism is neither rational nor consistent.[88] It does not require the most powerful citizens of the corporate state—private property owners—to legitimate their power.

Just as communism insulates the power of Party leaders against the test of dialogue, political capitalism insulates the power of its leaders against the demands of reflexive public criticism. The power structures of political capitalism operate outside the legislative process. In sum, like the institutional structures created by Party orthodoxies, they increasingly pose a "threat to freedom, equality, toleration—all the great values of the Enlightenment."[89]

Artful Dodges

We are not thinking frogs, nor objectifying and registering mechanisms with their innards removed: constantly, we have to give birth to our thoughts out of our pain and, like mothers endow them with all we have of blood, heart, fire, pleasure, passion, agony, conscience, fate, and catastrophe. Life—that means for us constantly transforming all that we are into light and flame—also everything that wounds us; we simply can do no other.

Nietzsche.

CHAPTER EIGHT

The Imprimatur of Power

i

Knowledge and Power

The perspective developed in these pages differs radically from conventional critiques of censorship. Its precedents are secured in the literature of social science rather than in the literature of Liberal political theory. Studies in communications, anthropology, sociology, and economics support the claim that censorship is an enduring feature of human communities. They affirm the conclusion that power and knowledge are bound together in an inextricable knot.

In contrast, Liberal political theory claims that Liberalism severed that knot. It maintains that Liberalism abolished censorship when it took away the badges of church and state censors. Liberal political theory views censorship as something that others do. It treats censorship as a reactionary practice of un-Enlightened (non-Liberal) societies.

My argument is not an argument for censorship. It is an argument for reflexivity: for the development of a self-conscious and self-critical awareness of what we do. It is an argument for consistency in theory and practice: for a consistency which could make what we say, and what we do, one.

Three schools of thought about thought provide the epistemological moorings for my position: (1) the classic tradition within the sociology of knowledge which draws upon the works of Friedrich Nietzsche, Wilhelm Dilthey, Karl Marx, Emile Durkheim, Max Scheler, Karl Mannheim, Alfred Schutz, Georg Lukacs, and others; (2) recent revisions of this classic tradition by scholars like Mary Douglas and

Michel Foucault who are committed to developing "anthropologies" or "archaeologies" of knowledge; and (3) emergent "constructivist" or "post-critical" perspectives in the philosophies of science and history which document the role human interests, interpretive processes, passions, and power play in generating and securing knowledge. In spite of their diverse disciplinary orientations, each of these positions recognizes that knowledge bears the scars of its social genesis: that time, place, kin, class, and ego leave their imprint on ideas.[1]

The recent constructivist turn in thought about thought has endowed the classic texts in the sociology of knowledge with new meanings, relevance, and urgency. As a result we are finally beginning to take the implications of these texts seriously. We are at last discovering that we cannot excuse our own voices from their discipline. The new constructivism forces us to acknowledge that we all "harbor concealed gardens and plantings."[2] It supports the conclusion that we are all motivated by interests, passions, wounds, loyalties, hopes, and ambitions. All of us, scientists as well as civilians.

In contrast to objectivist theories of knowledge which assume that knowledge, truth, and facts are "out there" to be discovered or uncovered, the new sociology or anthropology of knowledge assumes that knowledge, truth, and facts are social constructions, artifacts of communication, community, and culture. That is, it supports the claim that knowledge, truth, and facts are "in here": in language and mind, in our perceptual and interactional strategies, in our rage for order and our lust for power, etc. This assumption has profound epistemological consequences. Knowing what is "out there" is very different from knowing what is "in here." Objectivist epistemologies (which look "out there") permit the theorist/researcher a great deal of hubris. They ascribe special epistemological privileges to theorists. Objectivism separates the truth-claims of theorists from the truth-claims of civilians. It subjects the truth-claims of ordinary folk to rigorous scientific skepticism, but does not examine the problematic character of its own logic of assertion.[3] This refusal of reflexivity systematically obscures the role of hierarchical structures in the production of knowledge, and thereby protects a utopian image of the purity of theorizing.

Unlike objectivist theories of knowledge, the perspective developed in these pages provides no sanctuaries for theorizing. It regards passion, power, and institutional arrangements as *constituents of knowledge*: all forms of knowledge, including theory. It does not treat these constituents as extraneous distortions, idols, or reifications. And it does not assume that the elimination of charismatic fervor, private property,

Oedipal conflicts, or Party privileges can produce interest-free knowledge. That is, this revisionary view claims that as a process and product of human communication and community, knowledge is, *and should be*, firmly planted in the groundings of human concerns. Acceptance of this thesis burdens the theorist/researcher with new epistemological obligations. S/he can no longer deny the imprint of human passions, power, and institutional arrangements on systems of knowledge.

Nevertheless a responsible theory of power-knowledge does not just entail archaeological expeditions. It does not just involve digging around in someone else's garden and exposing the roots of their concerns. Its goal is not merely ideology-critique. Although, to be sure, the mud-raking and mud-slinging of ideological criticism have great tactical value in struggles against repressive powerholders. But a responsible theory of power-knowledge is not just critical of others. It is also open to self-criticism. It acknowledges that the "de-mystifications" produced by ideological critique are themselves inspired by ideology. That is, it recognizes that these de-mystifications are always a way of saying my way is better than your way.

My confrontation with the power-knowledge problem has led me to rethink radically the role human interests play in the production of knowledge. It has forced me to acknowledge that interests do not merely intrude upon processes of inquiry like thieves in the night. To the contrary, they make inquiry possible. They provide the groundings for and auspices of knowledge.[4] That is, my perspective on power-knowledge recognizes that we know because we need to know. We have a vested interest in knowing. Knowledge may help us to rule or survive the rule of others. It may give us aesthetic satisfaction or material rewards. It may help us to win the boy or girl of our dreams, provide us with a ticket to a rousing good time, or merely serve as a holding action against boredom. Our vocabularies of motive vary. But we *always* approach knowledge through the portals of our interests.

It is on this point that my approach to the study of the social conditioning of knowledge departs most radically from—and is unfaithful to—the classic texts. My perspective supports the conclusion that we must abandon the established traditions of Western philosophy which require us to assume that knowledge can only exist where human interests and power relations are suspended. I affirm Michel Foucault's conviction that,

> We should admit rather that power produces knowledge (and not simply by encouraging it because it serves power or by applying it because it is useful); *that power and knowledge imply one another; that there is*

> *no power relation without the correlative constitution of a field of knowl-*
> *edge, nor any knowledge that does not presuppose and constitute at the*
> *same time power relations.*[5]

Therefore my power-knowledge thesis assumes that both apologia (arguments for) and critiques (arguments against) are colored by the prevailing patterns of power. It maintains that knowledge is not produced willy-nilly through a series of independent cognitive acts which just happen to create bodies of knowledge that are useful or resistant to power. To the contrary, my perspective assumes that it is confrontation with power-knowledge—confrontation with power and the processes and struggles which challenge it—that determines the form and content of systems of knowledge. That is, it assumes that our 'from' always foreshadows our 'to.'

A reflexive theory of power-knowledge further assumes that no point in the dialectic is innocent of the *imprimatur* of power. That is, it regards every eye as a jaundiced eye. Therefore I do not view "the censored" as the fabled strangers or outsiders celebrated in Romantic myths of transcendence. The views of the censored are not more "objective" than your view or mine, they are just more dangerous. Those who attract the attention of censors are a strategic category of outlaws. They are epistemological criminals: cosmological mess-makers who dirty the discrete (sacred) presuppositions in which the prevailing order is secured. Their power (or potential for power) derives from their capacity to spoil the terms of the bargain which has made a viable version of social reality possible. Their incongruent ideas and inconvenient plans are anomalies, misfits, monsters: the stuff of which nightmares are made. They require special coding (tabooing) as "evil," "unnatural," or "irrational."[6] For the dialectic of apologia and critique—the struggle between the powerful and their opposition—entails a symbolic transformation in which the anomalies of the shadow world are exorcised by a ritualistic inversion of the cosmology of power. So that Foucault's portrayal of the condemned—"In the darkest region of the political field the condemned man represents the symmetrical, inverted figure of the king"—applies with greatest precision to movers and shakers who require only a pen or podium to disturb the peace.[7]

In sum, my power-knowledge thesis forcefully and resolutely endorses Mary Douglas's assertion that "our colonization of each other's mind is the price we pay for thought."[8] It maintains that none of us escapes the social structuring of mind. All of us—Liberal, objectivist, scientist, and civilian—are secured to the firmaments of human concerns by the knot that binds power and knowledge. Therefore, I believe the essential task of an adequate theory of knowledge is to inventory the costs of the cosmological bargains we must all make. I regard censorship as a crucial issue in any attempt to specify the constituents of what Foucault has described as the "anatomy of power."

However, my approach to the study of censorship does not view all cosmological bargains as equally desirable. Thus, for example, I distance my approach from Plato's elitist understanding of the Good Lie since his bargain cynically separates theory and practice. Indeed (with Socrates' help) I would distance my revisionary stance from all attempts to manipulate, massage, or manage people as if they were things. However, I recognize that all social compacts extract a price and regard tolls secured in words as less repellent than bonds sealed in blood. This is my bargain: my hierarchy of commitment, critical canon, and form of irony. I prefer talk to violence.

Therefore my perspective embraces the ideals of freedom of inquiry and free speech articulated by apologists of Enlightenment from Socrates, Spinoza, Bayle, and Milton to Voltaire, Diderot, Jefferson, Franklin, Marx, and Gandhi. It views both Corporate Liberalism and State Socialism's reductions of these ideals to foils for protecting monopolistic interests—whether private or state—as betrayals of the emancipatory intent of these great ideas. It attributes these betrayals to human decisions: bad decisions, decisions which are often motivated by greed. But my perspective also maintains that unresolved contradictions within the founding texts of the Liberal and Socialist Enlightenments authorize bad decisions: make them possible, logical, and for a time, compelling.

ii

The Specter of Relativism

A reflexive reading of the classic texts on the social conditioning of knowledge is impertinent because it raises the specter of relativism but offers no assurance that it can effectively exorcise it. Admitting that my view is no better than your view causes epistemological embarrassments. It permits you to reject my arguments without displaying your credentials.

It casts suspicion upon all fundamentalist claims. Therefore it cannot escape the wrath of orthodox thinkers of every ideological persuasion. Of these, philosophers will probably be especially hostile. Historically, philosophers have demonstrated a very limited tolerance for reflexivity.

Logicians schooled in the conventional texts of their disciplines will dismiss my position on the grounds that it commits a *circulus vitosus*. They will point out that thought which relativizes truth-claims thereby negates its own claim. That is, they will say that I am bound by my own knot. This is the "fallacy" that philosophers cited to mute the resonance of Karl Mannheim's sociology of knowledge. Mannheim was deeply disturbed by the implications of this charge, and his inability to counter it effectively was the decisive factor in his retreat from the radical posture of his early essays.[9]

Relativism is the philosopher's nightmare. Throughout the ages philosophers (and sorcerers) have dedicated their energies to securing the firmaments of knowledge. But relativism underscores the precarious character of all intellectual activity. Therefore it is the common enemy of philosophers who are in all other respects opposed to each other.

To escape the threat of cognitive insecurity, philosophers fabricate theories of knowledge in which some facet of nature or mind is endowed with certain authority. They conceive of epistemology as a kind of small-claims court with procedural rules which subjects the claims of empiricism, logic, mathematics, aesthetics and other subdisciplines to rigorous interrogation. But they regard examination of the nature of truth itself as beyond the court's jurisdiction.

Philosophy requires suppression of relativism. That is why apologists of relativism like Schopenhauer, Nietzsche, Wittgenstein, Foucault, and Douglas believe that their own projects represent solutions to *the problem* of philosophy and therefore mark the end of philosophy.

Dilthey, Marx, Durkheim, Scheler, and Mannheim do not assume such a radical posture.[10] Each of these authors dilutes his examination of the social origins of knowledge with a prescription for securing more stable firmaments. All retreat from relativism. Dilthey suggested that we might catch glimpses (fragments) of secure knowledge. Marx maintained that historical materialism would produce objective knowledge. Durkheim exempted scientific knowledge from cultural relativism. Scheler never surrendered his Catholic commitment to universal truth. Mannheim placed his hope for transcendent knowledge in synthesizing perspectives to be fabricated by "free-floating" (classless) intellectuals whose education would sever the knot that binds power and knowledge.

Members of our generation who take these classic texts seriously cannot retreat. The loopholes preserved in the classic texts have not survived critical scrutiny.

The context of contemporary scholarship is pervaded with relativism. Mary Douglas underscores the radical contingency of being in the modern world:

> It is part of our culture to recognize at last our cognitive precariousness. It is part of our culture to be sophisticated about fundamentalist claims to secure knowledge. It is part of our culture to be forced to take abroad the idea that other cultures are rational in the same way as ours.[11]

The logicians' complaint is no longer effective in demobilizing relativistic perspectives. The objectivist grounds which secured the philosophers' charges have been eroded by "scandalmongers" within the ranks of the philosophy of science.[12]

iii

Cosmological Mess-making Within the Philosophy of Science

Polanyi, Kuhn, Feyerabend, Toulmin, Hanson, Pepper, and others have countered the established arguments within their field with activist theories of knowledge.[13] By emphasizing the importance of existential factors (interests, collegial networks, value commitments, and aesthetic considerations) in processes of scientific discovery, they have exploded the positivistic vision of science as a hermetically sealed realm of pure cognitive activity. These cosmological mess-makers have demonstrated that scientists, like civilians, seek knowledge, make discoveries as a result of their interests, wounds, passions, and delights. Indeed P.B Medawar suggests that the processes of scientific discovery are largely rhetorical. He maintains that doing science, like doing journalism or history, involves looking for an interesting story to tell.[14]

The scandalmongers in the philosophy of science have not brought an end to philosophy. But they have reinvented its covenant. They have reduced assertions of "truth" and "fallacy" to human dimensions by relocating the resonances of these terms within history and tradition. In sum, they have returned these terms to their human contexts. They have restored the human voice to the discourse of science. Polanyi *et al.* have thereby ended the artificial isolation of apologia and critique. As a result epistemology can no longer be viewed as a small-claims court restricted to the jurisdiction of philosophers.

In contrast to established traditions in the philosophy of science and logic, the scandalmongers replace the conventional division of scholarly labor with holistic theories of knowledge. They treat epistemological work as the core of the discovery process in every discipline. Michael Polanyi maintains that this new covenant is required in our time because the "critical" path outlined by Kant and the empiricists has been so *successfully* pursued that it has undermined its own groundings:

> We have plucked from the Tree a second apple which has forever imperilled our knowledge of Good and Evil, and we must learn to know these qualities henceforth in the blinding light of our new analytical powers. Humanity has been deprived a second time of its innocence, and driven out of another garden which was, at any rate, a Fool's Paradise.[15]

iv

Relativism as Apologia for Censorship

Exile from the Fool's Paradise of objectivism poses troubling dilemmas for opponents of arbitrary forms of censorship. These freedom fighters must reject all perspectives which replace discredited notions of objectivity with *unrestrained* relativism because relativism can be as easily translated into a brief for arbitrary censorship as for humane tolerance.

Power sets the conditions of knowledge. From the point of view of Liberal ideology, Lenin was a fanatic—an authoritarian—because he said publicly what most modern heads-of-state say only in private (secret).

Why should freedom of speech and freedom of press be allowed? Why should a government which is doing what it believes to be right allow opposition by lethal weapon? Ideas are more fatal than guns. Why should a man be allowed to buy a printing press and disseminate pernicious opinions calculated to embarrass the government.[16]

Why, indeed? The relativist's plea, "Because governments can be mistaken," is too easily muffled by the hubris and might of voices in authority.

In spite of its failure to keep many of its promises to the people, the Enlightenment did advance the cause of liberty in the Western world. Liberal political theory has served as a powerful emancipatory hedge against overt forms of church and state censorship. Objectivism secured this hedge. Objectivism has been a useful weapon in the battles against censorship. Objectivism's separation of theory (knowledge) from practice (power) posited Faustian man's hope of establishing an independent (neutral) method for assessing truth claims. It was a noble ideal. An emancipatory ideal.

Today, however, the human architecture of that ideal is exposed. Faustian man's hopes have been betrayed. Liberalism has become a method of administration, and objectivism has become a cover for repression as well as a souvenir of the great wars of Enlightenment.

The question is no longer *whether* power skews knowledge, but *how*. . . . And for *whom* are the fictions by which we all must live our collective lives most useful?

A new method for resisting domination must be articulated. Otherwise, our quest for more viable and equitable groundings for knowledge cannot succeed.

V

Reluctant Slaves and Hypocrites: Censorship and Relativism Today

To the Chilean and Bantu parent whose child has assimilated an alien culture and apostasy of desire through imported electronic media produced by Western capitalism, Liberal apologetics for "the free-market-of-ideas" are not merely unconvincing, they are ludicrous. S/he experiences cultural relativism as a tragic existential reality, not merely as an interesting intellectual possibility. In this respect, epistemological naiveté is a privilege of the developed world.

But recent evidence suggests that even this insularity is being punctured. In Liberal societies public opinion polls report declines in citizens' confidence in public institutions. Moreover the failure of ideologies is not confined to capitalist countries.

We live in a period of profound skepticism. We have exposed all of the "good lies" but still crave their solace. Our Jeremiahs warn that the failure of ideological controls must inevitably lead to an expansion of harsher forms of control.[17]

At a time when opponents of arbitrary forms of censorship are most in need of effective power-knowledge for countering the worldwide expansion of censorship, we find our traditional protection against censorship has lost its credibility. Improvement in the human prospect is therefore contingent upon the articulation of credible emancipatory power-knowledge. Alvin Gouldner maintained,

> All other struggles hinge on this point. The struggle against poverty (or for equality) is a struggle based on the accounts of social reality made by official managers or movement leaders. Given their censorship of the media, there is no way to know what needs doing and what indeed has been accomplished. The new or old managers of society, it may be relied upon, will invariably tell us that they have done well, or at least the best that could be done, for the poor and underprivileged (considering the circumstances) and that they have, in any event, done better than their competitors would.[18]

vi

Exile or Emancipation

Like Polanyi, I regard our exile from the Fool's Paradise of objectivism as a liberation. The cosmological messes that have deprived us of our illusions of security and permanence contain the ciphers from which we can forge a new talisman against authoritarian censorship. The common thread which runs through our critiques of Liberalism, Objectivism, Scientism, and Socialism is hypocrisy (*hubris*). Each of these systems of power-knowledge says that it is something more than it is or something other than it is. Each posits a good lie to establish its authority. As a result, each is compelled to tell many bad lies to cover up the failures of that authority. Bad lies are easily exposed. They make us cynical.

However, if we accept responsibility for our own fate, if we look "in here" (in human interests and history) instead of "out there" (in Revelation, Nature, Materialism, etc.) for knowledge, we can use our cynicism to craft institutional structures which may more effectively control the controllers. We can recognize our cognitive insecurity and our vulnerability to good lies. We can use parables of persecution to secure a new talisman against censorship.

CHAPTER NINE

The Semantics of Censorship and Resistance

i

Writing-Between-the-Lines

Throughout history the great victories of heterodox thought have been won by equivocation: by what Leo Strauss described as "writing-between-the-lines."[1] Writing-between-the-lines requires metaphoric insurrection, allegoric disguises, hidden ciphers, cryptic symbols, ambiguity, paradox, enigma, esotericism, and illicit changes in signs. Writing-between-the-lines allows a writer to tell deadly serious jokes, to say one thing and mean another, to use praise-to-blame or blame-to-praise. It allows the devil to play devil's advocate.

Writing-between-the-lines requires reading-between-the-lines. It creates a conspiratorial bond between the writer and readers who can 'crack the code.' Writing-between-the-lines is necessary when pressures towards orthodoxy are in the ascendancy in politics, religion, public morality, art, science and the marketplace. Without reading-between-the-lines, Strauss contends, we cannot understand the texts of Anaxagoras, Protagoras, Socrates, Plato, Xenophon, Aristotle, Avicenna, Averroes, Maimonides, Grotius, Descartes, Hobbes, Spinoza, Locke, Bayle, Wolff, Montequieu, Voltaire, Rousseau, Lessing, and Kant.

Domination, repression, and the stale cake of custom constrict the range of univocal discourse. They force emancipatory ideas between-the-lines. But serious litterateurs seldom accept this exile with mute resignation. They frequently seize the opportunity to plumb the paleosymbolic depths of equivocal expressions.[2] It is within this subterranean netherworld that the community-founding powers of language can be rediscovered or invented. It is here that the "no-longer" and the "not-yet" are uncovered.

Those who recognize that an inseparable knot binds power and knowledge cannot dismiss Aesopean language as irrational or distorted. They realize it is also frequently the ragged cutting edge of emancipatory communication, for even in the most permissive times the artful evocations and contra-factuality of Aesopean mischief have a freer range than the language of theory. As Herbert Marcuse noted:

> Art breaks open a dimension inaccessible to other experience, a dimension in which human beings, nature, and things no longer stand under the law of the established reality principle. Subjects and objects encounter the appearance of the autonomy which is denied them in their society. The encounter with the truth of art happens in the estranging language and images which make perceptible, visible, and audible that which is no longer or not yet, perceived, said, and heard in everyday life.[3]

Thus, for example, some of the most challenging ideas about gender and society produced by the feminist movement have been born of the language of counterfactuality: in the utopian and anti-utopian fictions of writers like Joanna Russ, Ursula LeGuin, Marge Piercy, and Margaret Atwood. Fiction permits a protagonist like Russ's "Female-Man" to come to life and defy readers' taken-for-granted assumptions about gender, social order, and rationality.[4] The language of theory does not permit this kind of insurrection: subject to the established reality principle (in this case patriarchy), theory must code Russ's character as a clown, a misfit, or an aberration.

Art is not in any fundamental sense more pure or less political than the language of theory, it just seeks wisdom and plays politics by a different set of rules. The Aesopean art of writing-between-the-lines did not end with Kant. In Moscow and Harvard Square, Kabul and Santiago, Peking and Padua, Greenham Commons and Seneca Falls, opponents of political hegemony, scientific orthodoxies, bureaucratic conformity, religious intolerance, cultural imperialism, and oppressive gender politics keep the tradition alive.

ii

Litterateurs as "Ideological Saboteurs"

Andrei Sinyavsky (Abram Tertz), who did hard time for literary crimes against the Soviet state, characterized litterateurs as "ideological saboteurs."[5] This description is apt and incisive. Ideology pretends to speak with the authority of univocal discourse even though its symbolic content is always incompletely concealed. Ideologues claim (or simulate) a monopoly of explanatory powers by asserting that their position articulates a single vocabulary of truth. Thus, for example, the president or party minister's account of "the state of the union" is prefaced by prayers or pageants of patriotism, and it is always taken seriously.

In contrast, litterateurs ask not to be taken seriously. They dissimulate. They maintain that they are only playing: just telling stories. Their dissembling counter-claim allows litterateurs to retain the metaphoric resilience, the equivocal powers, necessary to subvert or transcend the absolutism of the linear discourse of ideology. In this respect, then, the romantic's assertion that poetry is more dangerous than philosophy is not merely wishful thinking.

Nevertheless writing-between-the-lines is not enough. It is a patois or slave-song. Prisoners see freedom through bars. Equivocation, like criticism, makes sense as prelude. Forced back upon its own resources by sustained external censorship, it becomes increasingly hermetic. At best, it produces esoteric communication that can be decoded by an intellectual or conspiratorial vanguard, i.e. Diderot's *Encyclopédie* may have caused a revolution but it had a very exclusive readership before the event. Nevertheless the Encyclopédie Wars generated an extraordinary bond of solidarity and loyalty among the small band of readers who could penetrate the code and appreciate the parody. Political satire and cabaret humor continue to generate a similar sense of solidarity and release at the clandestine edges of official culture in the Soviet bloc nations. However at its worst, equivocation is transmuted into a voice without an echo. If the cat-and-mouse game goes on too long, the cat usually gets the mouse. Polish novelist Tadeusz Konwicki cogently describes the corrosive effect that prolonged confinement between-the-lines has on the literary imagination:

> Initially it may be positive because it forces an author to find subtle
> forms of expression to evade the censor's ban. But these forms soon

become conventions, the secret language becomes public, and the censor will ban it too. So new, more subtle forms must be devised. And so it goes, on and on, the literature becomes increasingly more obscure, eventually losing all traces of life.[6]

A disenfranchised *intelligenz* in a Soviet bloc nation may save his soul and vent his frustration by spending years in the library of the Academy of Science writing Aesopean footnotes to minor texts, but his fire will not ignite unless the notes are read, understood, and translated into the rhetoric of resistance.

iii

Irony

Irony is the purest form of equivocal discourse. It is a deliberate form of cosmological mess-making in which at least one party to the exchange deliberately engages word-mischief to a subversive end. Georg Lukacs describes it as "the highest freedom that one can attain in a world without God."[7] Irony is a favorite conceit of the satirist, rabble-rouser, visionary, and clown. In its pursuit the cosmological explorer or jokster meticulously scours the edges of our everyday assumptions and paradigmatic presumptions in search of the cracked cornices from which irony can be crafted. Irony involves an element of deliberate pretense. It plays with the rules, the 'of course' assumptions, that we normally take seriously (and for granted). Irony's mischief is calculated to puncture our complacency. This is why the eighteenth-century ironist Friedrich Schlegel warned, "Irony is no joking matter."[8]

Kenneth Burke also takes irony very seriously. He regards it as one of the master tropes through which human beings can discover and describe truth. Burke views irony as synonymous with dialectics and antonymic to relativism. For where ideology is constructed in the midst of the battle, taking the part (the issue at hand) as the whole, irony proceeds from a higher plane. Its analytic angle is frankly hierarchical.[9] From a distance that is often possible only in pretense (play), it forces a union between a pair of mutually exclusive but internally consistent perspectives. The outcome of this shotgun marriage may be absurd or insightful. Or both. But whatever its result, the competing perspectives are stripped of some of their innocence and power. The absolutism of each claim temporarily dissolves.

Irony has been defined as a method "to censure with counterfeited praise and praise under pretense of blame."[10] The classic formula for constructing literary irony derives from Attic drama and is relatively simple. In the comedic form, a contest (*agon*) takes place between two types of characters, the *alazon* or Impostor and the *eiron*. The Impostor enters the scene full of pretension, but is finally routed by the Ironical Man, who proves not to be the fool he originally seemed to be. In tragedy the part of the *alazon* is taken by *hubris*; but where the defeat of the Impostor is comic, the defeat of the Hero attempting to defy his destiny is tragic. The contest between the *eiron* and *alazon* is, of course, directly analogous to the contest between the litterateur and the censor.

Where irony crafts synthetic statements by integrating the apparently irreconcilable terms of competing perspectives into a new and more satisfying pattern, it is perceived as constructive, creative, community-founding. It is heralded as a synthetic statement, seminal idea, or paradigmatic breakthrough. But where the ironizing of experience fails to produce a satisfactory resolution, does no more than underline "reality disjunctures," it is condemned as destructive, nihilistic, antisocial.[11]

Irony's destructive probes are not indiscriminate, however. There is nothing haphazard or erratic about ironic forms. The ironist is a logical insurrectionist, not a logical illiterate. Indeed ironic assertion requires far more linguistic craftsmanship and precision than the propositional language of univocal discourse. Ironic messages require "double reading." As Allan Rodway puts it, "Irony is not merely a matter of seeing a 'true' meaning beneath a 'false,' but of seeing a double exposure (in both senses of the word) on one plate."[12] Thus, for example, an ironic reading of the democratic urge recognizes that equality is a noble ideal, one of the fundamental Rights of Man. But it also recognizes that this noble ideal is secured by envy "for envy undercuts the superiority by which we set ourselves apart."[13]

There could be no irony without the univocal pretenses (*hubris*) of established systems of power-knowledge. The ironic probe seizes upon the gaps—the anomalies or contradictions—in established explanatory systems. The puzzles it poses are paradoxes, not chimeras. For contra-dictions only become visible in the refracted afterglow of the assertion of a powerful network of dictions. Inequality is only offensive to those who believe in equality.

iv

A Theory of Double-Meaning

The ideological sabotage achieved by irony displays the cunning affects of language. Moreover it shows that these effects are not fortuitous: that it is possible to map the logic of their apparent illogic, to fathom the logos beneath their mythos. Students of irony like Edward Lear, Lewis Carroll, and Sigmund Freud demonstrated that there is some sense in all nonsense. But students of power-knowledge soon discover that all sense includes some nonsense. They realize that ambiguity, misinterpretation, and error are common, even essential ingredients of communication. As Wilhelm von Humboldt put it, "All understanding is simultaneously a noncomprehension; all agreement in ideas and emotions is at the same time a divergence."[14]

Therefore those who want to understand the testaments of epistemological criminals must first understand that all discourse (including theoretical discourse) requires a double-reading because language itself has a dual nature. *It is both univocal and equivocal.* It is a process and product of culture. It not only refers to, it refers back. It draws upon (infers, evokes, and embraces) the 'symbols'— the historical testaments, traditions, desires, and mythos—that make up the collective memory and future hopes of a people. This subversive view of language explicitly defies the statutes enforced by the epistemological policemen of logical formalism. It affirms Paul Ricoeur's assertion that, "language itself is from the outset and for the most part distorted: it means something other than what it says, it has a double meaning, it is equivocal."[15] This revisionary understanding of language maintains that all discourse involves interpretation— requires deciphering. In sum, it aggressively affirms George Steiner's widely quoted dictum, "every act of communication is an act of translation."[16]

In contrast to conventional canons of logic, a theory of double-meaning treats equivocal forms like allegory, analogy, metaphor, and metonymy as valuable interpretive strategies. A theory of double-meaning does not share Aristotle's contempt for rhetoric. It does not regard the art of persuasion as a secondary art: as merely the politics of the sales talk. It embraces a theory of knowledge which assumes that the imprimatur of power leaves an indelible mark on all knowledge. Consequently it acknowledges the critical importance of rhetoric as a way of knowing: a means of creating community and securing truth-claims. A theory of double-meaning challenges the traditional logician's assumption that equivocal language is a barrier to or hazard of communication. To the contrary, it assumes that the equivocal nature of language is essential to communication: that it not only makes communication necessary, it makes it possible. It suggests that humankind is quite literally "saved by wonder." As Ricoeur puts it, "Enigma does not block understanding, but provokes it; there is something to unfold, to 'dis-implicate' in symbols." Therefore, Ricoeur contends, "That which arouses understanding is precisely the double meaning, the intending of the second meaning through the first. . . . it is the very excess of meaning in comparison to the literal expression that puts interpretation in motion."[17] In conversation, it is precisely because one party thinks the other's viewpoint is askew—needs correction or further elaboration—that an utterance becomes necessary. As Wilhelm Dilthey pointed out, "Interpretation would be impossible if the life-expressions were totally alien. It would be unnecessary if there were nothing strange about them."[18]

Equivocation empowers alternative interpretations. It makes dialogue possible. It leaves us free to consent or dissent. It permits the other to select, correct, amend, or invent meanings from our messages. Equivocation lets each of us gild our own lily without engaging in solipsism.

Pretense is our deliverance. We conquer the alienation of our cosmic loneliness by pretending that discourse can fully resolve our differences. We idealize the possibility of fully achieving intersubjectivity. We pretend we can achieve epiphany by discovering the "I" in "Thou." We each say "I love you" and pretend we have said the same thing even though I am not you and you are not me.

A theory of double-meaning spoils our illusions. It maintains that,

> . . . it is impossible for us ever to get a perfect likeness mutually. There is, to use Gadamer's phrase always "the infinity of the unsaid" . . . Reality lies in our corruption of each other's gestalts on both self and world . . . [19]

The theory of double-meaning asserts that communication is necessary because language is equivocal, and possible because we 'pretend' it is univocal.

V

The Censor's Warrant

Censorship tries to enforce an artificial separation of the dual functions of language. Theorists 'pretend' language is essentially univocal.
Poets 'pretend' it is essentially equivocal. Formal rules of censorship
are encoded in the language of legal theory. When censorial strictures
attempt to contain the language of the poet, primitive or romantic,
the ironic basis of literary censorship is exposed. Univocal discourse—
the singular voice theoretic discourse tries, without complete success,
to affect—is far more amenable to censorship than equivocal language. Theoretical discourse is bound to empirical reality: to the
world of sensually verifiable 'facts.' Its aesthetic range is extremely
narrow. It can encode what Lukacs described as "illustrating literature," but it cannot capture the emancipatory potential of the "not-
yet" (*nochnicht*) and the "no-longer" (*nichtmehr*).[20] The "not-yet"
and the "no-longer" do not merely illustrate reality, they try to master
it. They violate the existing reality principle. Therefore they can only
break through the official denials and excommunications of the language of theory by following circuitous routes: by assuming equivocal
voices and speaking in the language of possibility, contra-factuality,
and transcendence.

Thus, for example, the language of theory has no difficulty in
framing an interdiction forbidding criticism of an autocratic ruler
on the grounds of national security. But it cannot rationally articulate a prohibition against publishing a love poem in which an
unfaithful lover (the autocratic ruler) betrays the loyalty and innocence of a faithful virgin (the people). The Countess Rostopchina case, one of the most imfamous incidents of literary
sabotage in Czarist Russia, demonstrates the paradox. Rostopchina wrote a love ballad, "The Forced Marriage," which required reading-between-the-lines. In the poem, Rostopchina
recounted the complaints of a husband that his wife does not love
him and is unfaithful to him because he took her by force. The
censors assumed Rostopchina was describing her own relations
with her estranged husband. Titillated by her apparent indiscre-
tion, the censors passed the poem. However, careful readers immediately deciphered Rostopchina's subversive intent, and the

poem in which the husband actually represented Russia and the wife symbolized Poland was memorized by every learned Russian.[21]

Viewed from a perspective which appreciates the powers of equiv-ocation, the censor who seeks subversion in sonnets, cookbooks, or mathematical symbolism is conscientious, astute, even insightful—not simply paranoid. The erstwhile censor and specialist in the her-meneutics of cookbooks is responding rationally to the inadequacy of his/her theoretical warrant by improvising compensatory counter-measures. Our censor provides pragmatic affirmation of the primary tenet of the theory of double-meaning: that it is impossible to ever completely purge language of equivocation. Thus, for example, the Soviet censorial bureaucracy *Glavit* proscribes irony and Aesopean language.[22] But no bureaucratic manual—no grammar of administra-tive rationality—can ever fully articulate procedures for identifying it. Indeed, history shows that when administrators have come closest to precisely articulating such procedures, as they did in the Soviet Union under Stalin (Zhdanovism), they themselves have found it necessary periodically to relax the controls in order to avoid totally sapping literature of its vitality and therefore its administrative usefulness.

vi

Communication as Conspiracy

The history of censorship and the theory of double-meaning dem-onstrate that communication is possible only because language is both equivocal and univocal. These dual affects work together to create semantic and syntactic coherence. They are allies: co-conspirators in the communicative process.

Univocal discourse seems to slide along the surface of language—conveying the communicator's autonomous intent—but it only 'makes sense,' 'sounds right,' because it carries with it a hidden cache of equivocal souvenirs which allows speakers and listeners to establish essential connections with their own existential experiences and res-ervoirs of knowledge. A well-known example: in a major wartime radio address Franklin Roosevelt tells his audience that they have nothing to fear but "fear itself," and hundreds of millions of grown-up children throughout the world (who have much to fear) remember their fears of the dark and daddy's reassuring presence. They may listen to the American's President's arguments, critically weigh the evidence he presents, assess their own priorities, and steel themselves for the sacrifices of a long war effort (or steal their neighbor's ration books). But those who had daddys, who exorcised the goblins of night, hear more than univocal discourse. They hear more than Roosevelt says, and perhaps sleep a little sounder.

Without the extra baggage that equivocation brings to communication—without the support of analogous reasoning and metaphoric slippage—ego cannot be bridged. And speakers and listeners cannot tap the collective memory, vocabulary of motive, or apostasy of desire of their generation and culture.

The univocal and equivocal affects of language cannot be separated and isolated by censors or logicians without disrupting or aborting communication. Indeed even machine language is constructed upon a hidden scaffolding of metaphoric equivocation.[23] And, conversely, texts constructed entirely of equivocal imagery (if such texts could be constructed) would be no more than unintelligible word-salads. Too much equivocation leaves the listener/audience behind, e.g. hermetic poetry, some experimental film, and absurdist dramas.

Philosophies which fail to appreciate the complexity of the double nature of language cannot illuminate the dialectic of freedom and control or provide adequate theories of rationality. Such philosophies are easily recruited, drafted, or distorted to service the monologues of control.

CHAPTER TEN

Dialogue and Democracy

i

Making History

My narrative deals harshly with hypocrites: godless inquisitors, democratic pretenders, and ruthless utopians. But it celebrates the triumphs of the spiritual children of Socrates: the triumphs of those cosmological mess-makers who have managed to build cognitive nests within the paradoxes created by the inflated claims of dominant systems of power-knowledge. But these celebrations usually mix revelry with regret.

Thus, I celebrate the triumphs of the freedom-fighters of the eighteenth and nineteenth centuries who secured significant margins of autonomy for literary, scientific, and commercial pursuits; but I consider these margins too narrow and too packed with conditional clauses to permit further advances. I reject Liberalism's claim that it abolished censorship when it confiscated the badges of church and state censors. I contend that in Liberal societies Enlightenment merely transferred the offices of the Censor from a civic to a private trust. And that therefore the discontinuity that separates pre- and post-Enlightenment censorships is largely semantic.

Nevertheless I do not think that it is better to be unenlightened than Enlightened. I acknowledge that it is usually better to be conscripted by texts—better to be enrolled by persuasion, contractual obligations, and manipulation—than enslaved by force and violence (though I recognize as well the role texts—the Bible, orders of inquisition, encyclicals, encyclopedias, declarations, manifestoes, constitutions, contracts, trade agreements, etc.—play in securing force and violence).

I maintain that even under the best of circumstances, Liberal societies do not keep the promises upon which Enlightened philosophies and symbols of legitimation were secured. These promises were utopian. They were based upon flawed understandings of the nature of human perception, language, community, and power-knowledge.

The unkept promises of the Enlightenment require apologists of Liberalism to cover up. Their cover-ups secure the groundings for subterranean censorship in Liberal societies. Hypocrisy becomes an integral feature of mature Liberalism. As a result, subterranean censorship not only reproduces itself, it also inhibits political critique and thereby constricts the autonomy of citizens of Liberal states.

The parables of persecution presented in these pages demonstrate that every social compact extracts a toll in human suffering, and that under all social structures—aristocratic, ecclesiastic, capitalist, or socialist—those who lack privileged access to power-knowledge routinely pay the highest tolls. These parables indicate that censorship is a strategy used by the powerful to deny the powerless access to power-knowledge. They suggest that today a form of meta-censorship permits censors to operate under assumed names. And that therefore a Panopticon rather than an inquisitorial model of censorship is more relevant to an examination of our situation, whether that situation involves censorship in capitalist or socialist contexts.

My narrative does not surrender itself to relativism. Rather it recognizes that the cosmological bargains that make social order possible vary in severity: that some impose harsher terms than others. These terms can be inventoried, calculated, compared, and tabulated. Thus, for example, numbers of citizens incarcerated, impoverished, or undernourished might serve as very crude measures of the generosity or callousness of an affluent society. I argue tht censorship is the key index for all such calculations: the cutting edge for all efforts to secure emancipatory ideas.

While I offer no briefs for censors, I can offer no sure recipes for eliminating them. Rather I am forced to acknowledge that every social compact is embedded in a hierarchy of value, and that the coherence and integrity of such hierarchies can only be preserved by enforcing prohibitions against challenges to their most sacred prescripts.

ii

Backing into a More Egalitarian Future

If there is a lesson to be learned from the eclipse of the first Enlightenment, it is that true enlightenment cannot be secured by vanguards. It cannot be imposed from above.

The people are not necessarily virtuous or wise. But democracy is nevertheless the work of the people. Democratic communities are secured in their talk: in the dialogues of citizens. Socrates, of course, knew this all along. The Mechanicks tried to explain it to the Publicans. If they'd had a chance, the Peasants might have explained it to the Commissars. But vanguards have historically been better talkers than listeners.

The talk of vanguards—the monologues of Professionals and Party leaders—created and sustains the power-knowledge of Panopticonism. This (esoteric) talk promotes institutional ideologies which systematically deny the legitimacy of the voices of the people. It provides the technical and managerial expertise which is used by those in power to deny citizen participation in political debates by fostering the impression that many public issues are inherently too complex for lay people to comprehend or debate competently. The talk of vanguards creates socially structured silences which encourage the people passively to accept elitism. This monologic discourse violates the terms of classic social contract theories of democratic state power. In short, it tells the people that they lack the communicative competence necessary to make rational decisions in a complex world, and that they should therefore leave the "social contracting" to the professionals.[1]

The world is indeed complex. The New England town meeting—the American paradigm for dialogically based democracy—is obsolete. We live in an age of "secondary orality." In our time scripts and wires come between ideas and expression. Events only happen if they are verified by camera or text. Technical quality (professional craftsmanship) has become an essential constituent of the epistemology of verification.[2]

New information technologies reproduce and entrench old structures of power and privilege. Dinosaurs do not nuture doves. Barring nuclear disaster, it is therefore unlikely that centalized systems for the control of capital, images, and people will be dismantled. The global shopping center and the corporate village are not science fictions. They are paradigms of the power-knowledge and pedagogy of the world system of information-capitalism. Not even socialist monetary or cultural systems can fully escape their imprimatur.

The gravediggers of Panopticonism will not be Luddites intent upon smashing wires and cutting cords. Complex industrial societies cannot function without technology, expertise, and professionalism. They cannot operate without systems of control.

Does this mean that democracy is obsolete? That the excuse of an evil world is now the only excuse? That critics should use their shovels to dig bombshelters instead of graves for Panopticonism?

I think not! Both Party leaders and Political capitalists are the legitimate heirs of the egalitarian revolutions of the nineteenth century. Both are saddled with inconvenient ideologies: theories that mock their daily practices. Both have too much power and too little domestic opposition. Yet there is no convincing evidence that either capitalist or socialist elites have *entirely* abandoned their theoretical commitments. Indeed, it appears that some of their most violent repressions are direct functions of their messianic commitments to the reified abstractions of their respective systems of power-knowledge. The end justifies the means not only because it entrenches personal privilege but also because it satisfies troubled consciences.

Today both party regulars and political capitalists are on the defensive. Both are experiencing crises of face. Gulags and ghettoes are symptoms as well as violations. The U.S. and U.S.S.R. are now compelled to secure their systems of dominance by maintaining enormous international military machines. Holding the world hostage to military power undermines both nations' capacities to meet domestic needs and remain economically solvent. Both party regulars and political capitalists might welcome a way out.

Indeed, preventing nuclear war may require them to find one! They may, at last, be forced to examine the terms of the cosmological bargain that secures the nuclear age. Martin Luther King underlined the bottom line of that bargain when he asserted:

> We no longer have a choice between violence and nonviolence. The choice is either nonviolence or nonexistence.

Therefore, for both ideological and pragmatic reasons, it *might* be in the interests of leaders on both sides of the great ideological divide to help facilitate the unfinished work of the Enlightenment *if* the risks are not too high. That is, if the risks are less than the current risks, which are indeed very high!

The proposals outlined below may appeal to party leaders and political capitalists for five reasons.

First, implementation does not require any incumbent to surrender his or her office. It does, however, require all office-holders to submit to egalitarian structures of legitimation.

Second, these proposals recognize the necessity of control systems in complex industrial societies. They are not anarchistic. They do not propose to eliminate managers or their lieutenants.

Third, transition to the new system of enlightened power-knowledge would be non-violent. Violence violates the founding premises of dialogically based democratic theory. The end (dialogic enlightenment) never justifies *that* means! In this respect, the power-knowledge of the new enlightenment is a spiritual child of the great traditions of non-violence articulated by the Quakers, Tolstoy, Gandhi, and Martin Luther King. Contra Marx, it recognizes the necessity of performing "menial service for freedom" and regards *needles, not clubs* as appropriate tools for that service.

Fourth, these proposals reunite theory and practice by enforcing rules of consistency. They rectify the failure of the first Enlightenment by endorsing the repressed tenet of Socrates' teachings: "I have been always the same in all my actions, public as well as private . . . " Realizing the *telos* of consistency would be extremely embarrassing for political capitalists and Party leaders. They would have to come out of their closets, wipe the egg off of their faces, and confront past hypocrisies. But ultimately the principle of consistency would liberate them from troubled consciences. The morality books would no longer need to be cooked. But they would have to be revised. Our generation would have to rediscover, and reinvent philosophy. As Jurgen Habermas has pointed out, the West would have to articulate new ethical principles and moral premises to fill the void left by the decline of the resonance of Judeo-Christian morality. Moreover, our critique cannot just discredit instrumental rationality, it must replace it with a new, dialogically based system of power-knowledge. This enlightened power-knowledge and the moral philosophy which secures it must resolve "the contradiction between the rational claim that cognition is universal and the culture-elitist restriction of access to philosophizing to a few."[3] In short, it must recognize that the people are capable of managing their own affairs without the paternalism of princes or the patronage of professionals.

Fifth, the founding premises of these proposals advance the egalitarian movements envisioned by Diderot, Jefferson, Marx, and Gandhi. They complete the emancipatory projects of the first Enlightenment. In sum, these ideas are extentions of the theory, but not the practice, of political capitalists and party leaders.

Nevertheless my reading of history provides little basis for optimism. I do not think that the arguments of the advocates of a new enlightenment will persuade Panopticons to leave their towers, and join the people in dialogues toward more democratic covenants. If Panopticons join in these dialogues at all, they will do so only because they have exhausted all other alternatives. Political capitalists and party leaders will only jump on the train when it becomes clear that it will pull out of the station without them.

This may not happen. Unless capitalism or socialism undergoes severe structural crises—political, economic, or military breakdowns—the technology of Panopticonism may continue to inhibit, deflect, and defuse resistance. The people may leave the social contracting to the professionals. The long historical movement toward creation of more egalitarian social orders, which took hold in the Western world in the sixteenth century, may at last be contained. Socrates' children may finally be denied.

iii

Empowering Critical Discourse

What can champions of the songs of *Eirons* do to facilitate a new enlightenment?

If they live in the developed world, they cannot take to the mountains and form armies of liberation. Citizen-armies may sometimes prevail in struggles against military juntas and armies of occupation in satallite nations. They may liberate the people from domestic tyrants, colonial exploiters, or imperialistic adventurers. But these victories do not bring an end to the recurrent cycle of violence and domination. They do not deliver the people to dialogically based democracies. In the developed world, guerrilla armies cannot succeed. Under the conditions of modern warfare, David cannot slay

Goliath. And, even if he could, it would be at the risk of empowering
new technologies of terror.

It is, of course, patently absurd to suggest that a song or a poem
can disarm the Soviet or capitalist military-industrial or information
complexes. Words against warheads!

However, we live in a time of limited options. The alternative—
sit back, enjoy our Fritos and football and wait for the bomb—is
even more absurd.

In an absurd world, an absurd alternative may be the only alternative. In the developed world, Mount Olympus may be the only
place we can develop forces for resistance. Armies of liberation may
not be able to liberate us. But perhaps we can liberate ourselves by
becoming "caption-writers" in service of the lost promises of
Enlightenment.

iv

Reflexive Power-Talk

The first step toward a new enlightenment is to expose the technology
of Panopticon control to the light of day by empowering cultures of
critical discourse. In so far as possible, these cultures of critical discourse must render the technology of Panopticon control "legible"
and "visible."[4] Ideological critique can be of use here. Its mud-rakings
can expose the backstage operations of political capitalists and Party
leaders, and thereby render invisible governments visible. This is an
essential preliminary move since we have to be able to identify the
chain of command before we can devise effective strategies for making
and keeping it responsive to the will of the people.

The second step toward a new enlightenment requires the people
to reclaim their own voices. This is, of course, easier said than done!
The return of the repressed always involves a long and hazardous
journey. But we know that cultures of critical discourse cannot take
root when the people's knowledge of power is secured only by the
monologues—public relations, advertisements, and party lines—of
the powerful. The pedagogy of the oppressed must begin somewhere.

I suggest we *consider—talk about, not ratify*—the principles and propositions put forth by Bruce Ackerman in *Social Justice in the Liberal State* (1980). Ackerman proposes that we begin to think about politics as a way of talking about power instead of a way of securing natural rights or entering into social contracts. I have my own reservations about Ackerman's project. An essential element is missing from his recipe.[5] Ackerman provides us with excellent suggestions for programming the software of the Information Age, but no instructions for gaining access to its hardware. That is, he does not tell us how to secure the material foundations for reflexive power-talk. He does not tell us who will sponsor a new enlightenment. Until this question is resolved, Ackerman's recipe for reflexive (self-critical) power-talk can only articulate rules for talking about power. It cannot become power-knowledge.

The recipe is incomplete. But Ackerman's monologue invites completion through dialogue. It offers readers a set of rules for conducting that dialogue. It does not prescribe the outcome of the dialogue. It leaves the reader/talker free to propose his or her own answers to the question of resource distribution and/or redistribution. It recognizes that *that part of the recipe must be written by the dialogues of the people.*

In spite of its idealism, Ackerman's recipe for reflexive power-talk offers a compelling articulation of some of the constituents of a dialogically based democratic society. The following is a loose revisionist summary, interpretation, and elaboration of the recipe:

Rule One: Rationality is the first principle of enlightened power-talk. All power-holders would be obliged to respond to questions regarding the legitimacy of their power with good reasons. They could not simply suppress the questioner. No form of power, neither state nor capital, would be exempt from legitimating dialogues. In short, Rule One secures power in the logic of the best argument.

I would add a corollary to Rule One: ends as well as means must be open to legitimating dialogues. Power-holders would not be permitted to invoke canons of instrumental rationality to silence questioning of goals. The concept of Rationality covered by Rule One would be considerably broader than what is conventionally envisioned by Rationalists, Empiricists, and Utilitarians. It would embrace coherence as well as correspondence theories of truth. Moreover it would encourage questioning of its own groundings. That is, criteria for identifying 'good reasons' and 'the best argument' would remain open to questioning and subject to amendment. So that, epistemological work would become part of the discovery process in reflexive power-talks just as it has become part of the discovery process in science.[6]

Rule Two: Consistency is the second principle of enlightened power-talk. Power-holders must be consistent in justifying their claims to power. The reasons given to justify power on one occasion cannot be inconsistent with the reasons given on another occasion. Moreover power-holders cannot claim special epistemological privileges. They cannot claim to have an inside track on virtue, moral authority, or intellectual insight.

In short, Rule Two emulates Socrates. It insists on consistency and denies all claims to epistemological privilege. It therefore challenges the legitimacy of two central structures of current capitalist and socialist power-knowledge: (1) the state secret and (2) the authority of professionals.

Secrecy regarding troop movements, the location of supply ships, etc., may be necessary in wartime, but institutionalization of rule by state secret (intelligence agencies) undermines the principles of democracy.

Industrial societies require experts, scientists, technologists, and managers. Citizens require the advice and counsel of these professionals. However, democratic decision-making operates on the principle of 'one-man one-vote.' So that when it comes to making decisions on public issues, the good reasons of the plumber deserve the same hearing as the good reasons of the professor.[7]

Rule Three: Reflexivity (or neutrality) is the third principle of enlightened power-talk. Reflexive power talk is egalitarian. Power-holders cannot assert that their conceptions of the good or plans for the future are intrinsically superior to those of their fellow citizens. Positions must be secured by strong arguments, not merely by strong arms or strong credentials. In short, Rule Three requires all power-holders to put their cards on the table and play the game fairly.

According to Ackerman, the essential task is to "deny *any* fundamental power structure the priceless advantage of invisibility—to define a world where *all* power is distributed so that each person might defend his share in a conversation that begins (but does not end) with the move: 'because I'm at least as good as you are'." Under these rules, pulling rank, citing credentials instead of reasons, using technical data to obfuscate, and invoking procedural rules to mute or deflect justificatory dialogues are, by definition, illegitimate, repressive communications, violations of democratically grounded free speech. As Ackerman puts it, "A sustained silence or a stream of self-contradictory noises are decisive signs that something very wrong is going on."[8]

This recipe for reflexivity provides us with a simple set of ground rules for empowering free speech. In the tradition of Socratic dialogues, it does not impose any views on us. It simply offers us a set of procedural rules for ensuring that each of us can express his/her own views. The recipe does not prescribe the content of those views. It does not rig the rules in favor of any position. It provides no guarantees that you or I will like the outcomes of the community-founding dialogues the rules empower. The recipe for reflexivity merely presents a set of rules for conducting legitimating discourses which are free of internal and external constraints. These rules facilitate what Jurgen Habermas has described as "the ideal speech situation" and thereby maximize the chances that the best (most rational) arguments will prevail.[9]

In theory, democratic covenants already incorporate many of these ideas, but they are seldom realized in practice. However, this does not mean they cannot be realized. Indeed these rules are formalizations of the informal rules that empower vital friendship networks, loving families, enriching collegial relationships, and rewarding pedagogical bonds. They are rules for reconstructing society from the ground up. They allow us to take the business of nation-building into our own hands. We do not need to "Wait for the Revolution." We can begin to empower reflexive power-talk in our homes, neighborhoods, and schools. In part, this is what the feminist critique of instrumental rationality is already doing. It is what some elements in the movement for industrial democracy seek to do. It is what secures three of the "four pillars" (social responsibility, grass-roots democracy, and nonviolence) in the platform of West Germany's Green Party. In sum, these rules affirm Gandhi's dictum, "There is no way to peace; peace is the way."

Reflexive power-talk empowers us to create cultures of resistance. It allows us to make history. Thus, for example, those of us who are teachers can surrender our monologues (our "narration sickness") and begin to introduce the principles of reflexivity into the pedagogic process. And those of us who are students can begin instructing our instructors in the requisites of democratic discourses. Paulo Friere's "education for critical consciousness" can serve as an exemplar for our mentoring.[10] All of us, students, teachers, street-sweepers, mechanicks, journalists, and waitresses can begin to apply our critical consciousness to the analysis of the products of the Consciousness Industry. We can expose the power-knowledge that lies behind the corporate monologues and attempt to engage the agenda-setters in power-talk. Further, we can render "news" obsolete by developing dialogically based "information literacy."[11] These are small steps in a long revolution but, as a wise man noted long ago, a journey of a thousand miles must begin with a single step.

V

More Words Against Warheads

The small steps empowered by these cultural strategies are necessary steps. Enlightenment is an essential move in any effort to build a just society from the bottom up. But enlightenment is not enough. The slave may know she is a slave but that knowledge does not set her free. Without a plan for action, critical consciousness produces bitter fruits—frustration, cynicism, pessimism, nihilism, and despair.

The work of a new democratic enlightenment must include illumination of the measures needed to build a new society. Otherwise it will expose the totalitarian structures secured by information-capitalism but provide no means of resisting, rewiring, or dismantling them. In short, without concrete political and economic strategies for realizing the *telos* of a new enlightenment, reflexive power-talk is just talk.

Because my study of the history of censorship convinces me that vanguardism betrays the democratic dreams of the people by reproducing the relations of domination they seek to escape, my proposal for reflexive power-talk leaves definition of the *telos* of a new democratic enlightenment to the people. As a result, it must also leave definition of the political and economic means for achieving that *telos* to them.

However, my historical study of betrayals by vanguards does suggest some ideas that the people might want to consider, analyze, and critique in their talk about political and economic strategies for developing alternative systems of power-knowledge.

First, it is necessary to recognize the centrality of mass media to the control systems of information-capitalism. Mass media should not be thought of as independent or ancillary to the agenda of information-capitalism. The Fourth Estate was a useful fiction of Liberalism. However, information-capitalism's deregulation, privatization, and commodification of information is rendering Liberal concepts of "fairness" and "the public interest" obsolete. As a result, more than ever before mass media is acting as "the cultural arm" of established powers. Under information-capitalism the television station, press conference, and software design units are replacing the factory gate as sites for ideological warfare. Information-capitalism is firmly in control of these sources of cultural production. Therefore, any movement which seeks to challenge the totalitarian structures of information-capitalism needs to develop systematic communication strategies.

Second, it is necessary to recognize that new information technologies (including both producer information products like design and software, and consumer information commodities such as videos, personal computers, etc.) enter the marketplace "already constituted as expressions of capital and its needs."[12] They are not wired to facilitate democratic agendas. As a result, democratic activists must develop communication strategies which consciously seek to counter the totalitarian programming hardwired into these technologies. In sum, they not only require democratic commitments, they also need an adequate theory of mass communication as well as technological expertise and production skills. What is at stake in the new ideological warfare is nothing less than the power to define reality.

Third, it is not enough for opponents of information-capitalism to produce alternative constructions of reality. They must also produce epistemologies which legitimate these constructions, for, as we have seen, established powers establish the rules of evidence that will prevail within their provinces. And within the provinces in which Panopticonism prevails, these rules are frequently secured by secrecy.

Fourth, in addition to producing alternative interpretations of reality, opponents of information-capitalism must also create innovative networks of communication for distributing their messages. Thus, for example, video co-ops may become the electronic culture's equivalent of the medieval print shop.

Fifth, lessons can be learned from the history of recent democratic social movements. Veterans of failed movements frequently attribute their defeat to "the media": to mass media's abilities to co-opt, trivialize, reframe, undermine, and distort movement agendas.[13] The war wounds of these veterans can suggest some defensive strategies that democratic activists could adopt. In *Movements and Messages: Media and Radical Politics in Quebec* (1983), Marc Raboy identifies some of the lessons learned the hard way by democratic forces in Quebec and elsewhere. Raboy concludes that democratic communicative strategies should: (a) create feelings of solidarity, feelings of belonging to a common culture; (b) challenge mainstream media by offering audiences alternative interpretations of reality; (c) embody democratic principles in their own organizational structures; (d) be independent of both business interests and the state; and (e) have links with popular, political and union movements without being organically tied to them.[14] However, not all opponents of information-capitalism have been crushed. Revolutionaries and terrorists are not the only activists who understand the power of the media. Lessons can also be learned from democratic movements which have successfully used the media. Greenpeace, for example, has been very effective in staging dramatic media events by providing their own film crews and producing high quality footage which appeals to large audiences.

Moreover, advocates of democratic change should not ignore the fact that the power-knowledge of information-capitalism has given birth to new categories of workers as well as new categories of outlaws. Knowledge-workers are strategically positioned in the new information order. Alvin Gouldner thought they represented a new revolutionary class.[15] To date there is little to support Gouldner's claim. Unionism is in decline among information workers. The conditions of work in most segments of the information industry do not promote development of a collective consciousness. New job titles proliferate, old print-related crafts disappear, and 'interfacing' with a video display screen supplants interaction with co-workers. Nevertheless the effects of deregulation, privatization, concentration, and internationalization of information industries as well as 'de-skilling' of the labor of knowledge workers could combine to radicalize some segments of this group. Their expertise could make them particularly dangerous opponents of information-capitalism and very useful allies in democratic movements against the totalitarian structures of information-capitalism. Moreover some political activism critical of information-capitalism's code of technical efficiency has sporadically occurred among such unlikely cadres of knowledge workers as computer scientists and engineers.[16] In some ways the position of knowledge workers today is analoguous to the position of the Mechanicks and Publicans who made the first American Revolution.

Information-capitalism's commodification of time and knowledge have transformed these once priceless entities into liquid assets. The outlaws of the information age steal them. In America, time and information pirates have become modern folk-heroes, especially among the young who regard computer hackers and the HBO Bandit as new-age Robin Hoods. However, the habitual criminals of information-capitalism usually engage in less dramatic exploits. They frequently carry brief-cases and commit their crimes at the Xerox machine or at the meetings of the IBM users' club.

Although largely unorganized, popular resistance to the privatization of knowledge indicates that the triumph of information-capitalism is not yet assured.[17] It also suggests some addenda to Raboy's list: (a) capture the public imagination by rewiring or reprogramming new technologies so that they can serve as tools of popular resistance; (b) cultivate alliances with information workers but be wary of signs of incipient vanguardism; (c) create outreach projects to bring technological expertise and equipment to groups denied access to these resources.

Sixth, contra Gouldner, Marx, and Diderot and Company, intellectuals have demonstrated that they cannot be trusted to rebuild the world to democratic specifications. Nevertheless as citizens with useful skills they may have a role to play in developing strategies for resisting information-capitalism. They cannot rebuild the world, but they can rebuild their theories about the world. As we have seen, neither Liberalism nor Marxism can provide theories which adequately explain an economy in which information produces surplus value. As a result, neither of these world-views can provide satisfactory tools for resisting the censorship of information-capitalism. However, the baby should not be thrown out with the bathwater. Lessons can be learned from our ancestors, but citing prescient passages from *Areopagitica* or *Grudrisse* is no substitute for developing media-critical theories which directly address the problems posed by information-capitalism. In my judgment, media-critical theories should: (a) reject mechanical models which see media contents as simple 'reflections' or 'superstructures' of corporate or state control systems; (b) recognize that the double nature of communication requires dialectical models; (c) acknowledge that the message sent is not always the message received; (d) examine the class functions of mass media; (e) analyze the new international system of social stratification created by information-capitalism; (f) consider the stategic positioning of knowledge-workers in the new order; (g) expose the

power-knowledge wired into the circuitry of new information technologies; (h) develop rigorous models for criticizing media which are
as accessible to civilians as they are to specialists so that all citizens
can engage in what Umberto Eco has described as "semiotic guerrilla
warfare;" (i) articulate epistemological groundings for cultures of
critical discourse; and (j) police vanguardism in theory and society
by keeping theory and theorists responsive to the rules of reflexive
power-talk.[18] This proposal does not fully outline the work of a new
media-critical theory; it only marks some preliminary openings for
dialogue. In sum, it permits intellectuals to offer words against warheads, but it does not permit their words to carry the weight of
warheads in reflexive power-talks.

vi

Conclusion

The rules of reflexive power-talk do not preclude the development
of hierarchies or the organization of chains of command. But these
rules do make all offices, public and private, contingent. They insist
upon conformity to the essential premise of just power outlined by
Dag Hammarskjold: "Only he deserves power who everyday justifies
it."[19]

Institutionalization of this 'permanent revolution' in power-talk
would not create a heaven on earth. Mistakes would still be made.
In our struggles to discover the Good, Sisyphus would remain our
brother. We would not be able to sever the bond that unites power
and knowledge. But reflexive power-talk might allow us to recover
the defense against the censorship that entrenchment of Panopticonism destroyed.

Forging such a defense would be a major triumph for the people.
But it would only be a defensive measure. All victories against the
forces of darkness are partial victories. Richard Sennett makes this
eminently clear in presenting his case against Bakunin's quest for
heaven on earth—Bakunin's quest for "a society which is reborn, in a
qualitative purification." Contra Bakunin, Sennett maintains:

> Domination is a necessary disease the social organism suffers. It is built
> into the chain of command. The chain of command is an architecture

of power which inherently does injury to the needs and desires of some at the will of others. There is no way to cure this disease; we can only fight against it. There can be partial, important victories; it is possible to structure the chain of command so that controls are not omnipotent and universal. It is possible to prevent the alchemy of absolute power into images of strength which are clear, simple, and unshakeable. It is possible for the subordinates to see themselves as more than hopeless victims. Authority can become a process, a making, breaking, a re-making of meanings. It can be visible and legible.[20]

Even if the rules of reflexive power-talk governed our power-talk, human societies would continue to measure progress from scaffold to scaffold. But partial victories are still victories: affirmations and vindications of the songs of the *Eirons*. They permit the people to reclaim their own words, songs, and laughter—at least for a while.

Notes

Chapter One

1. The term "power-knowlege" is adopted with reservations because in the conventional academic mind it has become almost synonymous with the perspective of Michel Foucault. The concept of power-knowledge developed here owes a large debt to Foucault, but it owes much larger debts to Nietzsche and the long established tradition of the sociology of knowledge which draws not only on Nietzsche's insights but also on the work of Marx, Dilthey, Weber, Durkheim, Mannheim, Lukacs, Scheler, G. H. Mead, and others. To be sure, Foucault's studies have been very useful in stimulating current dialogues about knowledge and power. Moreover the ambition of Foucault's project and his prolific execution of that ambition merits enormous respect. Nevertheless I believe that his originality has been greatly overestimated. In developing his archaeology of knowledge, his linguistic philosophy, and his negation of humanism, Foucault simply followed Nietzsche's lead. Others followed that lead long before Foucault and shared the concern over the power and knowledge nexus—the Nietzschean legacy on the genealogy of knowledge as well as the Marxian conception of the social embeddedness of consciousness are clearly present in ways that anticipate Foucault in Weber, Lukacs, and Mannheim's reflections on the relationship of power and knowledge. Foucault's work, however, had the advantage of arriving on the intellectual scene in the wake of positivism's collapse. Where Mannheim's early works in the sociology of knowledge were caustically rejected by his contemporaries, kindred ideas put forth by Foucault were much more readily accepted. Indeed Foucault's ideas are currently regarded as intellectually chic in many circles, particularly in America where lack of familiarity with the classic traditions of Continental social theory is the norm (except among Marxian scholars). In my judgment, most attempts of American literary critics to incorporate the ideas of Foucault and Structuralists and post-Structuralists like Barthes, Derrida, and others tend to degenerate into empty exercises in formalism because they lack grounding in social theories which could provide them with viable concepts of social structure. Foucault bore some responsibility for the myopia of some of his enthusiasts. He skillfully managed his claim to originality by consistently denying all attempts either to contextualize his work or note points of convergence with contemporaries working within similar theoretical frames (e.g. Raymond Williams, Mary Douglas, and others). For further discussion of Mannheim's difficulties, see Kurt H. Wolff, "The Sociology of Knowledge and

Sociological Theory," in *Symposium on Sociological Theory*. Edited by Llewellyn
Z. Gross (New York: Harper and Row, 1959). For other discussions of Foucault's
debts to Nietzsche, see Ronald Hayman, *Nietzsche: A Critical Life* (New York: Penguin,
1980) and Jurgen Habermas's critical essay on Foucault cited later in this note. Mark
Poster offers an ambitious and sympathetic assessment of Foucault's debts and
contributions to Western Marxism in Foucault, *Marxism and History* (Cambridge:
Polity Press, 1985).

My own perspective on power-knowledge shares some ground with Foucault's and
other students of Nietzsche. But it departs radically from them in other respects. I do
not embrace the Nietzsche-Foucault rejection of humanism: this view conflates the *is*
of the historical participant and the *ought* of the analyst, and thereby leaves an opening
for re-entry of the omniscient positivistic observer. On this point, see Jurgen Habermas,
"The Genealogical Writings of History: On Some Aprorias in Foucault's Theory of
Power," *Canadian Journal of Political and Social Theory/Revue Canadienne de Théorie
Politique et Sociale* X, 1–2 (1986): 1–9. Contra Nietzsche-Foucault, but like Habermas,
I believe advancement of emancipatory causes can be served by revitalization of the
humanistic hermeneutic. My debts to Habermas are therefore larger than my debts
to Foucault. I regard Habermas's reflections on the conditions which can empower
emancipatory dialogues as a powerful alternative to Nietzsche-Foucault's anti-human-
ism. My own argument casts Socrates' humanism, his denial of the public-private
schism, in a crucial role in developing democratically based dialogues. My debts to
Habermas are evident in Chapter Ten. Elsewhere I record the limits of my affirmations
of Habermas's perspective. See my "Power and Knowledge: Toward a New Critical
Synthesis," in *Ferment in the Field, Journal of Communication* 33,3 (Summer 1983):
342–54.

In sum, the concept of power-knowledge developed here involves a synthesis of
ideas drawn from Nietzsche, Marx, Lukacs, Mannheim, Foucault, Williams, Douglas,
Gadamer, and others as well as from my own sociological observations and reflections
on history.

2. Jonathan Miller also uses the concepts of constituent and regulative censorship.
See his essay, *Censorship and the Limits of Permission* (London: Oxford University
Press, 1962).

3. The concept of reflexive power-talk evolved out of my reading and synthesis of
the ideas of Bruce A. Ackerman and Ben Agger on "neutral dialogue." See Ackerman,
Social Justice in the Liberal State (New Haven: Yale University Press, 1980) and Agger,
"A Critical Theory of Dialogue," *Humanities in Society* 4,1 (Winter 1981): 191–208.
I am indebted to Llewellyn Z. Gross for calling these ideas to my attention in a personal
dialogue.

4. Critics on the left and right agree that such an impoverishment took place but
they do not agree on the causes of or solution to this impoverishment. See, for example,
Max Horkheimer and Theodor W. Adorno, *Dialectic of Enlightenment* (New York:
Herder and Herder, 1972) and T. S. Eliot, *Notes Toward the Definition of Culture*
(New York: Harcourt, Brace, 1949). Discursive language became the only acceptable
language for asserting truth claims in post-Enlightenment cultures. Transcendent forms
(poetry, fiction, counter-factuality) which allow rejection of the empirical given-ness
of the world lost their force. Yet these are subversive forms which have had the
metaphoric resilience necessary to convey hidden meanings (via Aesopean language,
allegories, cautionary tales, etc.) even under the most stringent censorial regimes. For
effective critiques of the restrictive frames of instrumental language, see, in addition

to the works of Adorno and Horkheimer, George Steiner, *After Babel: Aspects Of Language and Translation* (New York: Oxford University Press, 1975) and Herbert Marcuse, *The Aesthetic Dimension* (Boston: Beacon, 1978). The use of non-discursive language in confounding censors is extensively discussed by Leo Strauss in *Persecution and the Art of Writing* (Glencoe: Free Press, 1952) and by Aleksandr Nikitenko, *The Diary of a Russian Censor* (Amherst: University of Massachusetts Press, 1975). My narrative explores this theme in detail in Chapter Nine.

5. Leo Strauss explores a closely related theme in *Persecution and the Art Of Writing*. Strauss argues that conventional approaches to the sociology of knowledge lack adequate historical basis. He maintains that the phenomena of persecution is an essential, but neglected, key to understanding Occidental intellectual history. Similarly, the assumption that accounts of persecution can, indeed *must*, be translated into anti-authoritarian power-knowledge is, of course, expressed in the most compelling terms in the passionate convictions of those survivors of the Nazi Holocaust who contend that they are obliged to *bear witness* "so that it can never happen again."

6. I do not intend to co-opt the traditions of non-Western peoples here. They object (I think correctly) to our usurpation of their experience—to our attempts to remold it into conceptual categories shaped by Western experience. I treat Socrates as a citizen of the world: spokesperson for no cause except the cause of intellectual integrity. I use Socrates as an exemplar of resistance against censorship: against imposition of alien opinions by force or fraud. I recognize that within other cultural traditions other exemplars are more salient. For example, Gandhi can also be described as a citizen of the world. His resistance has served as an exemplar for civil rights activists throughout the world. I also recognize the problematic nature of terms like first, second, third, and fourth world which are ethnocentric or at least technocentric. Again, my justification is rhetorical: the terms have wide currency in the vocabulary of Liberals.

7. Hugh Donaghue, "Transborder Data Flows: New Management Tool." Paper presented at conference on World Communications: Decisions for the Eighties, The Annenberg School of Communications, Philadelphia, May 12–14, 1980. Interviews with business leaders in the film *The Controlling Interest* echo this argument repeatedly and in almost precisely the same words.

Chapter Two

1. My definition of censorship is an extension of the *OED* definition. I approach the analysis of censorship from a sociological perspective. Consequently my definition of the term is much broader than definitions which have currency in Liberal free-speech theory. Where free-speech theory is concerned with the formal logic of legal protections of speech rights, I am concerned with analyzing the socio-logics which actually operate in organizing and sustaining real human communities and communications. My definition of the term encompasses all socially structured proscriptions or prescriptions which inhibit or prohibit dissemination of ideas, information, images, and other messages through a society's channels of communication whether these obstructions are secured by political, economic, religious, or other systems of authority. It includes both overt and covert proscriptions and prescriptions.

As a result of this sociological focus, my analyses of censorships in Liberal societies seek to raise consciousness about the form of censorship the Liberal model fails to address, specifically material or market censorship. Where free-speech theory is concerned about Skokie Nazis, Lyndon La Rouche, and other causes brought to the attention of the American Civil Liberties Union and the courts, I am more interested in the socially structured silences of political capitalism which almost never receive sustained public attention but nevertheless render some ideas and their authors unpublishable. Although the priorities of the ACLU are not my priorities, I do not dispute the legitimacy of Liberal concerns. While I think debates about the kinds of conundrums in free-speech theory which put Skokie Nazis in the headlines often deflect public attention away from more common and pervasive forms of censorship operating in American society, I nevertheless believe these debates should continue. I believe that Liberal free-speech theory has a significant role to play in preserving civil liberties in America. I do not seek to repeal these liberties but to extend or amend them to include all the people. To this end, I have cut a far wider theoretical path than do researchers working within the paradigms of Liberal free-speech theory.

2. Dallas W. Smythe, *Dependency Road: Communications, Capitalism, Consciousness, and Canada* (Norwood, N.J.: Ablex, 1981), 235.

3. There are, of course, the exceptions which Liberals are always eager to celebrate as *proofs* of press freedom. The hegemonic effect noted by Marxists is not complete. For a perceptive discussion of dialectical counter-currents in capitalist mass media, from a socialist perspective, see Hans Magnus Enzensberger, *The Consciousness Industry* (New York: Seabury, 1974).

4. From the perspective of a theory of power-knowledge which recognizes the ubiquity of constituent censorship in the formation and maintenance of human communities, repression of Marxist-Leninism (especially Stalinism) within Liberal societies is analoguous to suppression of the early Christians by the Romans. Both Marxist-Leninism and Christianity are monolithic thought systems which are incompatible with the heterodox assumptions of classic nineteenth-century Liberalism and the polytheistic assumptions of Roman paganism.

5. Baudelaire quoted by Elemire Zolla in *The Eclipse of the Intellectual* (New York: Funk and Wagnalls, 1968), 22. For an examination of the politics of the romantic protest, see Alvin W. Gouldner, "Romanticism and Classicism: Deep Structures in Social Science," in *For Sociology* (New York: Basic Books, 1973). Nevertheless Baudelaire's protest against the domination of matter does anticipate to some extent later critiques of the reification of thought and desire by Lukacs and members of the Frankfurt School.

6. In *Clarel*, Melville laments the plight of humankind in industrial society:

Debased into equality:
In glut of all material arts
A civic barbarism may be:
Man disenobled—brutalized
By popular science—Atheized
Into a smatterer—

For discussion and exemplification of the mass culture / high culture debate, see relevant entries in *Mass Culture: The Popular Arts in America*, edited by Bernard Rosenberg and David M. White (Glencoe: Free Press, 1957); and *Culture for the Millions*, edited by Norman Jacobs (Princeton, N.J.: Van Nostrand, 1961). See also Herbert Gans's neo-Liberal defense of pluralism, *Popular Culture and High Culture* (New York: Basic Books, 1974). In contrast to these Liberal critical traditions, 'Critical' theorists have embraced terms like "the culture industry" (Adorno) and "the consciousness industry" (Enzensberger) to focus attention on the social contexts of mass production in the cultural area. Although there are also elitist elements in 'Critical' theory, the focus on the social organization of production avoids the blaming-the-victim convention of much corporate-funded communications' "effects" research.

7. Bakhtin maintains that, "It can be said, with some restrictions to be sure, that medieval man in a way led *two Lives*: one *official*, monolithically serious and somber; beholden to strict hierarchical order; filled with fear, dogmatism, devotion, and piety; the other, of *carnival* and the *public place*, free; full of ambivalent laughter, sacrileges, profanations of all things sacred, disparagement and unseemly behavior, familiar contact with everybody and everything." Mikhail Bakhtin, quoted by Tzvetan Todorov in *Mikhail Bakhtin: The Dialogical Principle*. Translated by Wlad Godzich (Minneapolis: University of Minnesota Press, 1984), 78.

Synthetic production of popular culture permits the controllers of culture selectively to mirror and cultivate ideas. It takes some of the ideas and values that circulate among the people, ascribes legitimacy to these ideas and values, then projects them back to the people as their culture. Laughter and cynicism are permitted to go as far as is required to maintain the credibility of the controllers, but they never seriously challenge the system of control. The dog barks but it does not bite.

8. David W. Ewing, *Freedom Inside the Organization: Bringing Civil Liberties to the Workplace* (New York: E. P. Dutton, 1977), 3. Presidential directives enacted during the first term of the Reagan Administration subsequently expanded and tightened controls over publications by government employees and former employees. Ewing analyzes formal rights of employees. A large body of sociological research examines both formal and informal constraints on worker autonomy. See, for example, the following standard works in organizational sociology: Alvin Gouldner, *Patterns of Industrial Bureaucracy* (New York: Free Press, 1954); C. Wright Mills, *White Collar* (New York: Oxford University Press, 1951); and Charles Perrow, *Organizational Analysis: A Sociological View* (Monterey: Brooks-Cole, 1970). Also see Harry Braverman's *Labor and Monopoly Capital: The Degradation of Work in the Twentieth Century* (New York: Monthly Review Press, 1974) and Michael Burawoy's *Manufacturing Consent: Changes in the Labor Process under Monopoly Capitalism* (Chicago: University of Chicago Press, 1979). These researches indicate that organizational freedom, like income, is distributed hierarchically, with workers in professional and managerial positions generally exercising greater control over the work process than workers who are paid an hourly wage. Marx, of course, presented the classic analysis of the alienation of labor, and members of the nineteenth-century labor movements in Europe and America saw their revolt as a revolt against "wage slavery." Contra Marx, Emile Durkheim and his followers saw professionalism as the answer to the alienation of industrial societies. They believed that the autonomy of the professions could serve as anchors for a pluralism which would restrain the excesses of capitalism. See Durkeim's *The Division of Labor in Society* (Glencoe: Free Press, 1947). Recent empirical studies suggest that the 'managerial revolution' is now extending its reach into the professions and reducing or eliminating the autonomy of professionals in such fields as health care and higher education. For an excellent analysis of the corporate restructuring of health care, see Paul Starr, *The Social Transformation of American Medicine* (New York: Basic Books, 1982). For discussion of the managerial revolution

in higher education, see Jake Ryan and Charles Sackrey's analytic essays in their jointly authored *Strangers in Paradise: Academics from the Working Class* (Boston: South End Press, 1984).

9. Thorstein Veblen, *The Higher Learning in America* (New York: B. W. Huebsch, 1918).

10. Freud, quoted by Eric Rhode in "The Outline of a Couch," *Times Literary Supplement* (London), Nov. 24, 1978, p. 1355.

11. Eli M. Oboler, *The Fear of the Word: Censorship and Sex* (Metuchen, N.J.: Scarecrow Press, 1974), 60–62.

12. E. P. Thompson, "Time, Work-Discipline, and Industrial Capitalism," *Past and Present* 38 (Dec. 1967), 59–97. Thompson's ideas are provocatively applied to American social history by Stuart Ewen in *Captains of Consciousness* (New York: McGraw-Hill, 1976).

13. Richard Sennett, "Our Hearts Belong to Daddy," *New York Review of Books* XXVII (May 1, 1980), 32.

14. See John Cheever, *Falconer* (New York: Knopf, 1977); and Michel Foucault, *Discipline and Punish: The Birth of the Prison* (New York: Pantheon, 1977).

15. George Gerbner, "Television: The New State Religion?," *Et Cetera* (June 1977), 147.

16. Herbert I Schiller, *Who Knows: Information in the Age of the Fortune 500* (Norwood, N.J.: Ablex, 1981).

17. Georg Lukacs, *History and Class Consciousness* (Cambridge, Mass.: MIT Press, 1971).

Chapter Three

1. George Steiner, *After Babel: Aspects of Language and Translation* (New York: Oxford University Press, 1975), 29. See also J. G. A. Pocock, *Politics Language and Time: Essays on Political Thought and History* (New York: Atheneum, 1971), 14.

2. Ibid.

3. Hans-Georg Gadamer, *Philosophic Hermeneutics* (Berkeley: University of California Press, 1976), 9. Heidegger underscores the primacy of futurity in his doctrine of the productivity of the hermeneutic circle. See Martin Heidegger, *Being and Time* (New York: Harper and Row, 1962). Gadamer contends, "It is not so much judgments as it is our prejudices that constitute our being."

4. In my view, Gadamer's "prejudice," Ricoeur's "enigma," Kuhn's "anomalies," and Polanyi's description of the role of "sub-lingual gestalts" as anchors of personal knowledge are largely consonant. Gadamer describes his attempt to rehabilitate the concept of "prejudice" as follows: " . . . the historicity of our existence entails that prejudices in the literal sense of the word, constitute the initial directedness of our whole ability to experience. Prejudices are biases of our openness to the world." Gadamer, *Philosophic Hermeneutics*, 9. See also Paul Ricoeur, *Freud and Philosophy* (New Haven: Yale University Press, 1970); Thomas S. Kuhn, *The Structure of Scientific Revolutions* (Chicago: University of Chicago Press, 1970); Michael Polanyi, *Personal Knowledge* (Chicago: University of Chicago Press, 1958).

5. Hans Magnus Enzensberger, *Der kurze Sommer der Anarchie*, excerpted and

translated by Ingrid Egger in her review of Enzensberger's *Mausoleum*, *Telos* 34 (1977–78): 205.

6. Michel Foucault, *Discipline and Punish: The Birth of the Prison* (New York: Pantheon, 1977).

7. Thus, for example, the classic accounts of the struggle for free speech and free thought are stories of epochal thinkers, kings, popes, and inquisitors. Ordinary people seldom make the archives. See, for example, J. B. Bury, *A History of Freedom of Thought* (London: Oxford University Press, 1913); Edward Gibbon, *The Decline and Fall of The Roman Empire* (New York: Modern Library, 1932; orig. 1776); and Henry Lea, *A History of the Inquisition of Spain* (New York: Macmillan, 1906) and *A History of the Inquisition of the Middle Ages* (New York: Harper and Bros., 1888).

8. Statistics on genocide are always problematic. The figures cited here are taken from the following sources. Figures on the U.S.S.R. and Germany are based on data reported by Leo Kuper in *Genocide: Its Political Use in the Twentieth Century* (New Haven: Yale University Press, 1982) and Irving L. Horowitz, *Taking Lives: Genocide and State Power* (New Brunswick, N.J.: Transaction Books, 1982). Statistics on China were supplied by the Chinese State Statistical Bureau to the Associated Press in 1984. U.S. experts had previously estimated the toll at between 27 and 37 million. See "Millions Starved After Mao's 'Great Leap' " by Jeff Bradley. *Buffalo News*, Sept. 30, 1984.

9. Elie Wiesel and others argue that this witness is trivialized when it is used to prove arguments and support ideological positions. He reports that, "At first the testimony of survivors inspired awe and humility. But popularization and exploitation soon followed." The camps lost their evocative power. "The Holocaust became a literary 'free for all' . . . Novelists made free use of it in their work, scholars used it to prove their theories." Wiesel is quoted by Christopher Lasch in an insightful series of reflections on the desensitizing effects discussion of the Holocaust has had on language. See "The Discourse on Mass Death: 'Lessons' of the Holocaust," in *The Minimal Self: Psychic Survival in Troubled Times* (New York: W. W. Norton, 1984), 100–129. Wiesel quoted on p. 112. George Steiner has explored the dehumanization of language and literature after Auschwitz in many of his writings. See, for example, *Language and Silence* (New York: Atheneum, 1976).

10. Hannah Arendt, *Eichmann in Jerusalem: A Report on the Banality of Evil* (New York: Penguin, 1977).

11. Max Horkheimer and Theodor W. Adorno, *Dialectic of Enlightenment* (New York: Herder and Herder, 1972), regard fascism as an extension of capitalism. Ralph Miliband contends there is no necessary relationship between the two systems of power-knowledge. See Miliband, *The State in Capitalist Society: An Analysis of the Western System of Power* (New York: Basic Books, 1969).

12. E. R. Dodds, *The Greeks and the Irrational* (Berkeley: University of California, 1968).

13. See Paul F. Grendler, *The Roman Inquisition and the Venetian Press, 1540–1605* (Princeton: Princeton University Press, 1977); and Elizabeth L. Eisenstein, *The Printing Press as an Agent of Change: Communications and Cultural Transformations in Early Modern Europe*, Vol. I (Cambridge: Cambridge University Press, 1979).

14. Eisenstein, *The Printing Press as an Agent of Change*, I: 199–200.

15. Ibid., 23. Within the vocabulary of stratification theory, this group would be described as a 'stratum' rather than a class.

16. Bury, *A History of Freedom of Thought*, 20.

17. Leo Strauss, *Persecution and the Art of Writing* (Glencoe: Free Press, 1952).

18. Protagoras, quoted by Bury, *A History of Freedom of Thought*, 28.

19. Werner Jaeger, *Paideia: The Ideals of Greek Culture*, Vol. II (New York: Oxford University Press, 1943), 373, n. 1.

20. For precedents in 'using Socrates,' see Alan F. Blum, *Socrates: The Original and Its Images* (London: Routledge and Kegan Paul, 1978) and Hannah Arendt, *The Life of the Mind* (New York: Harcourt Brace Jovanovich, 1978).

21. Socrates, quoted from *Apology* by Bury, *A History of Freedom of Thought*, 33–34.

22. Socrates in Plato's *Apology* in *The Dialogues of Plato*, Vol. 1 (New York: Charles Scribner's Sons, 1901), 330–31.

23. Emile Durkheim, *The Elementary Forms of the Religious Life* (Glencoe: Free Press, 1947), 300.

24. V. Gordon Childe, *Man Makes Himself* (New York: New American Library, 1951).

25. Max Weber, "The Chinese Literati," in *From Max Weber*, edited by H. H. Gerth and C. Wright Mills (New York: Oxford University Press Book, 1946). See also Yu-t'ang Lin, *A History of Press and Public Opinion in China* (Chicago: University of Chicago Press, 1936).

26. Plutarch, quoted by Eli Oboler in *The Fear of the Word: Censorship and Sex* (Metuchen, N.J.: Scarecrow Press, 1974), 32.

27. Tacitus, quoted by George Haven Putnum in "History of Censorship," in *Selected Articles on Censorship of Speech and the Press*. Edited by Lamar T. Beman (New York: H. W. Wilson Company, 1930), 18.

28. Tacitus, quoted by Edward Gibbon in *The Decline and Fall of the Roman Empire*. Abridgment by D. M. Low (New York: Harcourt, Brace, 1960; orig. 1776), 202.

29. Tacitus, quoted by Gibbon, *The Decline and Fall . . .*, 202.

30. Ibid., 204.

31. Ibid., 227.

32. Ibid., 229.

33. Ibid., 193.

34. Ibid.

35. Ibid., 238. Grotius' report is cited by Gibbon.

36. Ibid., 193.

37. James, excerpted by George Putnam in *The Censorship of the Church of Rome and Its Influence upon the Production and Distribution of Literature*, Vol. I (New York: Benjamin Blom, 1967; orig. 1906), 13.

38. Gibbon, *The Decline and Fall . . .*, 143.

39. Putnam, *The Censorship of the Church of Rome . . .*, 1.

40. Joseph McCabe, *The History and Meaning of the Catholic Index of Forbidden Books* (Girard, Kansas: Haldeman-Julius Company, 1931), 14.

41. For an account of Gnosticism, see Elaine Pagels, *The Gnostic Gospels* (New York: Random House, 1979).

42. Putnam, *The Censorship of the Church of Rome . . .*, 9–10.

43. Redmond Burke, *What Is the Index?* (Milwaukee: Bruce, 1952).

44. Sylvius, quoted by Lea, *A History of the Inquisition . . .*, III: 645–46.

45. See reports, ibid.

46. The dates given cannot be regarded as authoritative. Putnam, Lea, and Burke

often conflict. Attempts to achieve independent documentation via Langer's *An En-cyclopedia of World History* (Boston: Houghton Mifflin, 1940) only compound the confusion. Since Putnam is recognized as the authoritative source on the *Index* (of sources available in English) his dates are relied on in most cases.

47. Hilger, excerpted by Putnam, *The Censorship of the Church of Rome* . . . , 245.

48. H. R. Trevor-Roper, *The European Witch-Craze of the Sixteenth and Seventeenth Centuries* (New York: Harper and Row, 1969), 91. Eisenstein persuasively establishes the connection between the introduction of print and the dissemination of the witch-craze. Eisenstein, *The Printing Press as an Agent of Change* . . . ,I.

49. Richard Kieckhefer, *European Witch Trials* (Berkeley: University of California Press, 1976).

50. Alan C. Kors and Edward Peters, Introduction to *Witchcraft in Europe 1100–1700: A Documentary History* (Philadelphia: University of Pennsylvania Press, 1972), 6.

51. Trevor-Roper, *The European Witch-Craze* . . . , and Kieckhefer, *European Witch Trials*, both stress the harmony between Aristotelian world-views and belief in diabolical forces.

52. Kieckhefer, *European Witch Trials*, 79.

53. On Aquinas, see Charles E. Hopkins, *The Share of Thomas Aquinas in the Growth of the Witchcraft Delusion* (Philadelphia: University of Pennsylvania Press, 1940). For discussion of the Royal Society, Baconian science, and diabolicalism, see Evelyn Fox Keller, *Reflections on Gender and Science* (New Haven: Yale University Press, 1985).

54. Rossell Hope Robbins, quoted from *Encyclopaedia of Witchcraft and Demonology* (1959) by Kieckhefer in *European Witch Trials*, 2.

55. Kieckhefer, *European Witch Trials*.

56. Heinrich Kramer and Jacob Sprenger, *Malleus Maleficarum* (1484), in *Witchcraft in Europe 1100–1700*, 117.

57. Kramer and Sprenger, *Malleus Maleficarum*.

58. Ibid. See also Kieckhefer, *European Witch Trials*.

59. Luther quoted by Kors and Peters, *Witchcraft in Europe 1100–1700*, 195, from *The Table Talk of Martin Luther* (1821), edited by William Hazlitt (New York: E. P. Dutton, 1930).

60. Kors and Peters, Introduction to *Witchcraft in Europe 1100–1700*. Robin Morgan, *Going Too Far* (New York: Random House, 1977). Without more precise documentation, I assume Morgan may have gone too far in projecting this estimate.

61. Burke, *What Is the Index?*, 5.

62. Henry Lea, *A History of the Inquisition of Spain*, Vol. I (New York: Macmillan, 1906), 86.

63. Heresbach, quoted by Putnam, *The Censorship of the Church of Rome*, II: 336.

Chapter Four

1. The *pecia* system was devised in an attempt to resolve a chronic problem of medieval education, textbook shortages. The *pecia* system was an attempt to apply the principles of piece-work to manuscript production. It involved contracting out parts of manuscripts to be copied by lay copyists in their homes under university supervision.

Corruption of texts through the idiosyncrasies of hand-copying had been a persistent problem throughout the manuscript period. The creative side of this corruption has been widely chronicled. And romanticized! Undoubtedly there were fortuitous corruptions. Corruption could produce genius: the collectively authored texts of the ancients, of Chaucer, and even the Folio Shakespeare. But more often it produced error and obscurity. In *The Origin of Printing in Europe* (Chicago: University of Chicago Press, 1940), Peirce Butler points out that scholars are frequently misled by the beautifully illuminated manuscripts preserved in the treasures of monasteries, libraries, and museums of Europe. These manuscripts were preserved precisely because they were treasures, rarities of their own time as well as ours. Similarly Curt Buhler's account, *The Fifteenth Century Book, the Scribes, the Printers, the Decorators* (Philadelphia: University of Pennsylvania Press, 1960) indicates that the "sloppy, clumsy, inelegant, hastily and carelessly written manuscript" was far more common.

The *pecia* system did make books more plentiful in the twelfth century. But the imperative of material profit rather than patient atonement for sin was decidedly skewed in favor of inelegance, haste, and error. So that piece-work which would later have some applications in mechanical production of texts, proved unsatisfactory during the manuscript era. *Pecia* was abandoned in favor of the quality-controlled secular *scriptorem* a century before the invention of print.

Any generalization about production in the manuscript period requires qualification since in the pre-print era, there were no standard procedures. See Elizabeth Eisenstein, *The Printing Press as an Agent of Change: Communications and Cultural Transformations in Early Modern Europe*, Vol. I (Cambridge: Cambridge University Press, 1979); Curt Buhler, *The Fifteenth Century Book, . . .* ; Peirce Butler, *The Origin of Printing in Modern Europe*.

2. Bacon also included gunpowder in the trinity of discoveries that changed the world.

3. Will Durant used the term "typographical revolution" to describe the change from script to type in *The Story of Civilization*, Vol. VI (New York: Simon and Schuster, 1957).

4. McLuhan and Mumford have appreciated the significance of the print revolution and have attempted to capture essential features of it. But, in my judgment, Elizabeth Eisenstein's magnus opus accomplishes this elusive task. My discussion of print is little more than a footnote to her work. See Marshall McLuhan, *The Gutenberg Galaxy: The Making of Typographical Man* (Toronto: University of Toronto Press, 1962); Lewis Mumford, *Technics and Civilization* (New York: Harcourt, Brace and World, 1963); and Eisenstein, *The Printing Press as an Agent of Change*. Eisenstein presents convincing arguments contra Burckhardt which indicate that the press was indeed an influential factor in the Renaissance; see also Jacob Burckhardt, *The Civilization of the Renassance in Italy* (New York: New American Library, 1961).

5. Michael Clapham, quoted by Eisenstein in *The Printing Press as an Agent of Change . . .*, 45, from "Printing" in *A History of Technology*, Vol. II: *From the Renaissance to the Industrial Revolution*. Edited by Charles Singer, E. J. Holmyard, A. R. Hall, and Trevor Williams (Oxford: Oxford University Press, 1957).

6. Fabri, quoted by George Putnam in *The Censorship of the Church of Rome and Its Influence upon the Production and Distribution of Literature*, Vol. II (New York: Benjamin Blom, 1967; original 1906), p. 278 from Historia Suevorum.

7. Eisenstein, *The Printing Press as an Agent of Change*.

8. Ibid.

9. Benjamin Franklin, *Apology for Printers* (New York: Privately Printed, 1967; orig. *The Pennsylvania Gazette*, June 10, 1730).

10. Putnam, *The Censorship of the Church of Rome*, I: 279.

11. Eisenstein, *The Printing Press as an Agent of Change...*, 145.

12. Francis Yates, *The Rosicrucian Enlightenment* (London: Routledge and Kegan Paul, 1972). Eisenstein warns against attributing too much influence to secret societies in the preservation of letters because in point of fact the entire life of the mind was underground in Catholic Europe after 1560.

13. Paul Grendler, *The Roman Inquisition and the Venetian Press, 1540–1605* (Princeton: Princeton University Press, 1977).

14. Lea, quoted from letter to Putnam (1898) by Putnam, in *The Censorship of the Church of Rome...*, II: 325.

15. Ibid.

16. Mark Pattison, quoted by Putnam, ibid., 285, from *Casaubon*.

17. The Condemnation and Recantation of Galileo in *Versions of Censorship: An Anthology*, edited by John McCormick and Mairi MacInnes (Chicago: Aldine, 1962), 57, 61–62.

18. Erasmus, quoted in Eisenstein, *The Printing Press as an Agent of Change...* I: 144.

19. Newton, quoted ibid., 144.

20. Desiderius Erasmus, *The Praise of Folly* (Roslyn, N.Y.: Walter J. Black, 1942; orig., 1509), 94–95.

21. Eisenstein, *The Printing Press as an Agent of Change...* I: 139–40.

22. John Milton, "Areopagitica," in *Freedom of Expression: A Symposium... to Commemorate the Tercentenary of the Publication of Milton's Areopagitica*, edited by Harold Ould (London: Tercentenary Committee, 1944), pp. 180, 201.

23. Ibid., 181–82.

24. Milton specifically exempts Catholics from the franchise of free speech. His subsequent statements indicate that he conceives of the franchise in far narrower terms than Liberals like to assume. For exposition of Milton's thought which acknowledges its illiberal aspects, see *Freedom of Expression: A Symposium... to Commemorate the Tercentenary of the Publication of Milton's "Areopagitica,"* edited by Harold Ould (London: Tercentenary Committee, 1944); Leonard Levy, *Legacy of Suppression: Freedom of Speech and Press in Early American History* (Cambridge, Mass.: Harvard University Press, 1960).

25. Milton, "Areopagitica," 180.

26. Milton, quoted from "Of True Religion, Heresie, Schism, and Toleration" in Levy's *Legacy of Suppression...*, 87. It has been argued that the only reason Galileo was prosecuted was because he wrote in Italian instead of Latin. See Giorgio Santillana, *The Crime of Galileo* (Chicago: Phoenix Books, 1955).

27. Diderot, quoted by John Morley, *Diderot and the Encyclopaedists*, Vol. I (London: Chapman and Hall, 1878), 125, from *Essai sur la société des gens de lettres et des Grands*.

28. Diderot letter to Voltaire (Feb. 19, 1758), quoted by Morley, *Diderot and the Encyclopaedists*, I: 162–63. The identification with Socrates is reiterated in a suppressed passage of Volume XV on Socrates, "Socratique, philosophie." See Douglas H. Gordon and Norman L. Torrey, *The Censoring of Diderot's Encyclopédie and the Re-established Text* (New York: Columbia University Press, 1947), 56–57.

29. Robert Darnton, "The Encyclopedie Wars of Prerevolutionary France," *American Historical Review* 78 (1973): 1337.

30. Diderot quoted from Grimm by Morley, *Diderot and the Encyclopaedists*, I: 165–66.

31. Authors could not hold copyrights unless they were also printers. See R. F. Whale, *Copyright: Evolution, Theory and Practice* (Totowa, N.J.: Rowman and Littlefield, 1972).

32. Voltaire, quoted by Morley, *Diderot and the Encyclopaedists*, I: 162.

33. Robert Darnton, *The Business of Enlightenment: A Publishing History of the Encyclopédie 1775–1800* (Cambridge, Mass.: Harvard University Press, 1979), 10.

34. There was a resurgence of the persecutorial fever in 1766 when nineteen-year-old Chevalier de la Barre was put to death on a charge of blasphemy. He had been strongly influenced by Diderot's *Encyclopaedie* and Voltaire's *Dictionnaire Philosophique*. Thus Gordon and Torrey note, "Many voices were publically raised in favor of suppressing the real criminals, as the Encyclopedists were called." See Gordon and Torrey, *The Censoring of Diderot's Encyclopédie*, 24.

35. Morley, *Diderot and the Encyclopaedists*, I: 147.

36. Ibid., 152. Pottinger contends that after 1757, the death penalty was generally recognized as too severe a sanction for illicit book-dealers. See David Pottinger, *The French Book Trade in the Ancien Régime 1500–1791* (Cambridge, Mass.: Harvard University Press, 1958).

37. Ibid. Statistics on *ancien régime* and citation from Roquain are also from Pottinger.

38. Ibid., p. 60.

39. D'Alembert, cited by Morley, *Diderot and the Encyclopaedists*, I: 137–38, from letter to Voltaire (July 21, 1757).

40. Ibid, 138–39.

41. Or, at least this is the role they openly professed to believe *philosophes* should assume. After Napoleon's ascent to power, they were convinced *philosophes* must directly assume the reins of power. It is this conviction which attracted Destutt de Tracy to Thomas Jefferson, whom French intellectuals regarded as a true *philosophe* and statesman: an exemplar for the *ideologues* post-Revolutionary thought on the failure of the pre-Revolutionary vision. See Emmet Kennedy, *A Philosophe in the Age of Revolution* (Philadelphia: American Philosophical Society, 1978).

42. D'Alembert, quoted in Morley, *Diderot and the Encyclopaedists*, I: 161, from letter to M. Voland in which Diderot quotes D'Alembert (Oct. 11, 1759).

Chapter Five

1. A point emphasized by J. Herbert Altschull in *Agents of Power: The Roles of the News Media in Human Affairs* (New York: The Annenberg-Longman Communication Series, 1984).

2. Richard Weaver, *The Ethics of Rhetoric* (Chicago: Regnery, 1970), 232.

3. Stephen E. Toulmin, *The Uses of Argument* (Cambridge: Cambridge University Press, 1958).

4. For a more ambitious, linguistically informed, analysis of the anomalies in Marx's work, see Alvin W. Gouldner, *The Two Marxisms* (New York: Seabury, 1980).

5. Arnold Ruge, quoted by David McLellan in *Marx Before Marxism* (New York: Harper and Row, 1970), 130, from *Zwei Jahre in Paris* (1946). Marx himself described Paris in a letter to Ruge as "the old college of philosophy" and "the new capital of the new world."

6. Marx, quoted by McLellan in *Marx Before Marxism*, from "On the Jewish Question" (1844), 78, 138.

7. McLellan characterizes Marx's stance as Spinozian liberalism. See *Marx Before Marxism*, 78. In "Remarks on the Latest Prussian Censorship Instruction," Marx criticizes illusionary liberalism: "This is the kind of pseudo liberalism that is forced to make concessions and that sacrifices people to maintain the institution, the tools, and the object. The attention of a thoughtless public is thereby diverted." See "Remarks on the Latest Prussian Censorship," in *Karl Marx on Freedom of the Press and Censorship*, edited by Saul Padover (New York: McGraw-Hill, 1974), 90.

8. The argument was made in the debates on censorship in the Landtag or Provincial Diet in Düsseldorf, May to July 1841, reported by Marx in a series of articles in *Rheinische Zeitung*. See Marx, "Debates on Freedom of the Press and Publication," in *Karl Marx on Freedom of the Press and Censorship*, 33.

9. Destutt de Tracy, quoted by Karl Marx and Frederick Engels in *The German Ideology* (New York: International Publishers, 1970), 100, 118, from *Traité de la volonte* (Paris, 1826). See also Emmet Kennedy, *A Philosophe in the Age of Revolution* (Philadelphia: American Philosophical Society, 1978).

10. Marx and Engels, *The German Ideology*, 118.

11. Marx, "Remarks on the Latest Prussian Censorship Instruction," in *Karl Marx on Freedom of the Press and Censorship*, 92–93.

12. McLellan, *Marx Before Marxism*, 73.

13. Marx, "Remarks on the Latest Prussian Censorship Instruction," in *Karl Marx on Freedom of the Press and Censorship*, 93.

14. Marx quoted by Padover in "Young Marx as an Embattled Journalist and Editor," Introduction to *Karl Marx on Freedom of the Press and Censorship*, xviii. In "The Suppression of the *Leipziger Allgemeine* in Prussia," a series of six articles published in *Rheinische Zeitung* (Jan. 1843), Marx demonstrated that he was a student of equivocation. He asks, "how does the *Kolnische Zeitung* know what intention the *Leipziger Allgemeine Zeitung* had in publishing the letter? Why not the harmless intention of merely publishing a piece of news? Why not perhaps the loyal intention of bringing the letter to the judgment of public opinion? We have to tell our neighbor an anecdote. In Rome, publication of the Koran is prohibited. A wily Italian knew how to get around it. He published a refutation of the Koran, that is a book which bore on its title page *Refutation of the Koran*, but the content was simply the text of the Koran. And didn't all heretics know how to play this trick? And was not Vanini burned, although in his proclamation of atheism in his book, *Theatrum mundi*, he carefully and ostentatiously presented all counterarguments against it? Did not Voltaire himself, in his *Bible enfin expliquée* teach religious unbelief in the text and belief in the notes, and did anybody trust the purifying validity of these notes?" See "The Suppression of the *Leipziger Allgemeine* in Prussia," in *Karl Marx on Freedom of the Press and Censorship*, 63.

15. Marx, "Letter to Arnold Ruge" (Nov. 1842), 161–62 and "Debates on Freedom of the Press and Publication," in *Karl Marx on Freedom of the Press and Censorship*, 27.

16. Marx, "Debates on Freedom of the Press and Publication," in *Karl Marx on Freedom of the Press and Censorship*, 10.

17. Shlomo Avineri, "Aspects of Freedom of Writing and Expression in Hegel and Marx," *Social Theory and Practice* 4, 3 (Fall 1977): 284.

18. Karl Marx, "Debates on Freedom of the Press and Publication," in *Karl Marx on Freedom of the Press and Censorship*, 26, 34. See also Marx and Engels, *The German Ideology*, 64.

19. Marx, "Debates on Freedom of the Press and Publication," in *Karl Marx on Freedom of the Press and Censorship*, 27.

20. Marx, "The Suppression of the *Leipziger Allgemeine* in Prussia," in *Karl Marx on Freedom of the Press and Censorship*, 59.

21. Marx, "Debates on Freedom of the Press and Censorship," 31, 34, and Marx, "The Role of the Press as Critic of Government Officials," Marx's defense speech at his trial (Feb. 1849), in *Karl Marx on Freedom of the Press and Censorship*, 144.

22. Ibid.; see also Marx and Engels, *The German Ideology*, 103.

23. Karl Marx, "Debates on Freedom of the Press and Publication," in *Karl Marx on Freedom of the Press and Censorship*, 43–44; and Karl Marx and Frederick Engels, *Literature and Art: Selections from Their Writings* (New York: International Publishers, 1947).

24. Marx, "Remarks on the Latest Prussian Censorship Instruction," in *Karl Marx on Freedom of the Press and Censorship*, 98, 108.

25. Marx and Engels, *The German Ideology*, 50–51.

26. Marx, "Debates on Freedom of the Press and Publication," in *Karl Marx on Freedom of the Press and Censorship*, 27.

27. Marx, "Remarks on the Latest Prussian Censorship Instruction," in *Karl Marx on Freedom of the Press and Censorship*, 89, 92, 108.

28. Ibid. See also Marx, Letter to Arnold Ruge (Jan. 1843), in *Karl Marx on Freedom of the Press and Censorship*, 164.

29. Karl Marx, "Suppression of the *Neue Rheinische Zeitung* under Martial Law," in *On Freedom of the Press and Censorship*, 154. Emphasis in the original.

30. Herbert Marcuse presented a thorough critique of this aspect of Marx's thinking, particularly his neglect of eros. See Marcuse, *Eros and Civilization: A Philosophical Inquiry into Freud* (Boston: Beacon, 1955); *An Essay on Liberation* (Boston: Beacon, 1969); *The Aesthetic Dimension* (Boston: Beacon, 1978); and *One-Dimensional Man* (Boston: Beacon, 1964).

31. Karl Marx, *Capital*, Vol. 1 (London: Dent, 1957), 112–13. Quoted by Yves de la Haye, in *Marx and Engels on the Means of Communication* (New York: International General, 1980), 39.

32. In his "Introduction" to passages from Marx's texts which treat communications-relevant issues, Yves de la Haye maintains that the concepts and methods Marx used to analyze nineteenth-century "means of communication" can be extended to the study of twentieth-century communications systems. See *Marx and Engels on the Means of Communication*.

Chapter Six

1. Reported in Nadezhda Mandelstem's *Hope Abandoned* (New York: Atheneum, 1974).

2. Medvedev, quoted by Heller in "Stalin and the Detectives," *Survey* 22, 1–2 (1976): 160–75.

3. Stepniak (pseud.), *Russia under the Tzars* (New York: Charles Scribner's Sons, 1885), and Aleksandr Nikitenko, *The Diary of a Russian Censor* (Amherst: University of Massachusetts Press, 1975).

4. Andrei Sinyavsky (Abram Tertz), "Samizdat and the Rebirth of Literature," *Index on Censorship* 9:4 (Aug. 1980), 8.

5. Karl Marx and Frederick Engels, "Manifesto and the Communist Party," in *Basic Writings on Politics and Philosophy*, edited by Lewis S. Feuer (Garden City, N.Y.: Anchor Books, 1959), 28. For Marx and Engels state control was also a "temporary measure" because, of course, in their scenario, the state would "wither away" in the transition from socialism to communism, and presumably the means of communication, like the means of production, would be controlled by the people. No plan, beyond abolition of private property, was offerred for ensuring the democratic character of this control. Hence we confront the essential dilemma of all efforts to redistribute power, knowledge, and material assets. Redistribution, by definition, implies central control. Someone must have the authority to collect tickets, texts, or taxes. Some mechanism must therefore be found to keep the chain of command responsive to the will of the people.

6. Michael Heller, "Is There Such a Thing as Dissident Literature?," *Survey* 23, 4 (1977–78), 64.

7. Aleksandr I. Solzhenitsyn, *The Oak and the Calf: Sketches of Literary Life in the Soviet Union* (New York: Harper and Row, 1980), 2.

8. "The Policy of the Party in the Field of Artistic Literature," excerpt reprinted in Max Hayward's "Introduction" to *Literature and Revolution in Soviet Russia*, edited by Max Hayward and Leopold Labedz (London: Oxford University Press, 1963), viii.

9. Hayward, "Introduction", ibid., ix.

10. Michael Heller, "Is There Such a Thing as Dissident Literature?," 67–68.

11. G. V. Plekhanov, *Art and Society and Other Papers in Historical Materialism* (New York: Criole Editions, 1974).

12. Lunacharsky, quoted from Kogan's *Proletarakaya Literature* (1926) by Harold Swayze, in *Political Control of Literature in the USSR, 1946–1959* (Cambridge, Mass.: Harvard University Press, 1962), 10.

13. V. I. Lenin, "Party Organization and Party Literature," in *Collected Works*, Vol. 10 (Moscow: Foreign Languages Publishing House, 1961), 44–49. My interpretation of this essay also draws upon and is largely consistent with Swayze's discussion in *Political Control of Literature*.

14. V. I. Lenin, "What Is To Be Done?" (1902), in *Collected Works*, Vol. 5 (Moscow: Foreign Languages Publishing House, 1961), 354–55.

15. Lenin's views on the role of newspapers quoted from the following sources: V. I. Lenin, "The Character of Our Newspapers," in *Collected Works*, Vol. 23 (New York: International Publishers, 1945), 225; Vladimir Shcherbina, *Lenin and Problems of Literature* (Moscow: Progress Publishers, 1974), 178; William A. Hachten, *The World News Prism: Changing Media, Changing Ideologies* (Ames: Iowa State University Press, 1981), 67; and John C. Merrill, *Global Journalism: A Survey of the World's Mass Media* (New York: Longman, 1983), 102.

16. See George Gerbner, "Institutional Pressures upon Mass Communicators," *Sociological Review Monograph* 13 (Jan. 1969), 231–38; and Douglas Cater, *The Fourth Branch of Government* (New York: Vintage, 1965), 186–88.

17. André Gide, *Return from the USSR* (New York: Knopf, 1937).

18. Many explanations of Gorky's involvement have been offered. They range from charges of treason and opportunism to explanations suggesting that he was drugged and ultimately poisoned by Stalin's lieutenants. For an exploration of some of these theories, see Ermolaev's Introduction to Gorky's *Untimely Thoughts*. Reportedly Stalin coined the phrase "engineers of the soul" at a dinner party attended by Gorky in 1932. This motif occupied a prominent place in Gorky's speech before the Writers' Congress in 1934. See Maxim Gorky, "Soviet Literature," in Soviet Writers' Congress 1934, *The Debate on Socialist Realism and Modernism in the Soviet Union* (London: Lawrence and Wishart, 1977), 67.

19. Ibid., 65.

20. Engels only considered the topic briefly. His formula, "realism . . . implies, beside truth of detail, the truth in reproduction of typical characters under typical circumstances," became an essential prescriptive stricture of socio-realism. See Karl Marx and Frederick Engels, *Selected Correspondence* (Moscow: Foreign Languages Press, 1956), 478–79. For a discussion of this idea at the Writers' Congress, see A. I. Stetsky, "Under the Flag of the Soviets, Under the Flag of Socialism," in *Soviet Writers' Congress 1934*, 267.

21. Gorky, "Soviet Literature," 44.

22. Ibid., 69.

23. Quoted by Tertz from the full text of the transcript of the first Writers' Congress, in *Socialist Realism*, 148.

24. Gorky, "Soviet Literature," 64.

25. Swayze, *Political Control of Literature*, 135.

26. Karl Radek, "Contemporary World Literature and the Tasks of Proletarian Art," in *Soviet Writers' Congress 1934*, 131.

27. Karl Marx, *Economic Manuscripts of 1857–58*, Marx-Engels Archives, Vol. IV (Moscow, 1935), quoted from the Russian edition by Vladimer Shcherbina, in *Lenin and Problems of Literature* (Moscow: Progress Publishers, 1974), 99; and Karl Marx and Frederick Engels, *The German Ideology* (New York: International Publishers, 1970), 118.

28. Shcherbina, *Lenin and Problems of Literature*, 195.

29. Ibid., 170.

30. Edward J. Brown, The Year of Acquiescence," in *Literature and Revolution in Soviet Russia 1917–62*, 44–61.

31. For a detailed account of these cases, see Max Hayward, "Pilnyak and Zamyatin: Two Tragedies of the Twenties," *Survey* 36 (1961).

32. Brown, "The Year of Acquiescence," in *Literature and Revolution in Soviet Russia 1917–62*.

33. See the repudiations of Zamyatin by Anikst and Timofeyev in Gleb Struve's "The Transition from Russian to Soviet Literature," ibid., 2–3.

34. Evgeny Zamyatin, "I Am Afraid," excerpted in Heller's "Is There Such a Thing as Dissident Literature?," 66.

35. Evgeny Zamyatin, *We* (New York: Viking Press, 1972).

36. Maurice Freidberg, "Soviet Books, Censors and Readers," in *Literature and Revolution in Soviet Russia 1917–62*, 198–210.

37. Malenkov, quoted by Swayze in *Political Control of Literature in the USSR*, 81.

38. Freidberg details the statistics of Russian readers desertion of the writers of sociorealism. See his "Soviet Books, Censors and Readers," in *Literature and Revo-*

lution in Soviet Russia. Thus, ironically, Zhadanovism did not pass "the test of the marketplace!"

39. Enzensberger, *The Consciousness Industry: On Literature, Politics and the Media* (New York: Seabury, 1974).

40. This notion was introduced by O. Utis in "Generalissimo Stalin and the Art of Government, in *Foreign Affairs* XXX (1952): 197–214. It is further developed, with significant and persuasive critical reservations, by Swayze in *Political Control of Literature in the USSR.*

41. Joseph Stalin, *First Linguistic Letter,* excerpted in Swayze, *Political Control of Literature in the USSR,* 73.

42. Sinyavsky, " 'I' and "They': An Essay on Extreme Forms of Communication Under Conditions of Human Isolation." *Survey* 22, 3–4 (1976): 278–87.

43. Mayakovsky quoted by Heller, in "Is There Such a Thing as Dissident Literature?," 67.

44. Solzhenitsyn details his own efforts to "lighten" his secret manuscripts for publication without compromising them in *The Oak and the Calf.* For related discussions, see Elliot Schreiber, "The Rise and Fall of the Soviet Underground Press," *Communication Quarterly* 26, 3 (1978), 32–39; William Griffith, *Communist Esoteric Communication: Explication de Texte* (Boston: MIT Center for International Studies, 1967); and Myron Rush, "Esoteric Communication in Soviet Politics," *World Politics* 11, 4 (1959), 614–20. The politics of purgation also takes a toll in communicative inhibitions among political elites so that they too frequently resort to writing-between-the-lines in official communiqués and other publications in order to communicate with sub-elites whose support they solicit.

45. Solzhenitsyn, *The Oak and the Calf.* For an attempt to rebut Solzhenitsyn's indictment of the timidity of the editors of *Novy mir,* see Vladimir Lakshin, *Solzhenitsyn, Tvarsovsky, and Novy Mir* (Cambridge, Mass.: MIT Press, 1980).

46. Solzhenitsyn, *The Oak and the Calf,* 40.

47. Nina Khrushchev, quoted by Solzhenitsyn in *The Oak and the Calf,* 87.

48. Solzhenitsyn, *The Oak and the Calf.*

49. Rumjanov, quoted from "The Party and the Intellectuals" by Gerstenmaier, in *The Voices of the Silent* (New York: Hart, 1972).

50. Herzin, quoted by Isaiah Berlin in "Conversations with Akhmatova and Pasternak," *New York Review of Books* (Nov. 20, 1980), 33.

51. Andrei Amalrik divides dissident opinion in these three categories. Gerstenmaier, *The Voices of the Silent* (New York: Hart Publishing, 1972). Olga Matich's analysis of recent *tamizdat* suggests it is an inversion of socialist realism. Where socialist realism affirms official values, the unofficial and dissident politic of recent *tamizdat* is anti-Soviet, anti-Communist, and in most instances anti-Marxist. See Matich, "Unofficial Russian Fiction and Its Politics," in *Humanities in Society* 7, 3–4 (Summer-Fall 1984): 109–22.

52. Heller gives an excellent account of this genre in "Stalin and the Detectives," *Survey* 22, 1/2 (1976): 160–75. This mass literature is quite profitable. State publishers are not immune to marketing considerations. Thus, for instance, decisions regarding dispersal of the limited funds available for translation are made on the basis of their potential popularity in the marketplace rather than exclusively on ideological grounds. Thus *Rich Man, Poor Man* was deemed more worthy of translation than the *The Sotweed Factor.* See Leslie Fiedler, "Giving the Devil His Due," *Journal of Popular Culture* XII: 2 (Fall 1979), 197–207.

53. Mikhail S. Gorbachev, quoted in "The Resistance to Gorbachev" by Bill Keller, *New York Times*, Jan. 30, 1987, pp. A1 and A6.

54. Sinyavsky (Abram Tertz), *On Socialist Realism*.

55. Ehrenburg, quoted from his *Memoirs* by Max Hayward, in "Conflict and Change in Soviet Literature," in *Literature and Revolution in Soviet Russia 1917–62*, 234.

56. Lucien Goldmann, *The Philosophy of the Enlightenment* (Cambridge, Mass.: MIT Press, 1968), 91–92.

Chapter Seven

1. First-hand accounts are provided by Jefferson, Franklin, Madison, Adams, and others in their autobiographical writings, letters, and papers. Henry Steele Commager has written extensively and effusively about the early years of the Republic. His writings, perhaps more consistently than those of others, reflect what I refer to as the 'Liberal view.' Other essential sources within this genre are Zechariah Chafee, *Freedom of Speech in the Untited States* (1948); Alexander Meiklejohn's *Free Speech and Its Relation to Self-Government* (1948); Roscoe Pound, *The Formative Period of American Law* (1938); Clinton Rossiter, *Seedtime of the Republic* (1953); and Arthur Schlesinger, *Prelude to Independence: The Newspaper War on Britain 1764–1776* (1958). Important revisionary efforts in addition to Charles Beard's *An Economic Interpretation of the Constitution of the United States* (1913) and *Economic Origins of Jeffersonian Democracy* (1965) include Leonard Levy's *Freedom of Speech and Press in Early American History: Legacy of Suppression* (1960); Staughton Lynd, *Class Conflict, Slavery, and the Constitution* (1967); and Howard Zinn, *A People's History of the United States* (1980).

2. The term "captive history" is borrowed from Carolyn Marvin's "Space, Time, and Captive Communications History," pp. 7–19 of *Communications in Transition: Issues and Debates in Current Research*. Edited by Mary S. Mander (New York: Praeger, 1983).

2a. The term 'Consciousness Industry' was coined by Hans Magnus Enzensberger. See his collection of essays on literature, politics, and media. *The Consciousness Industry* (New York: Seabury, 1974). Adorno had used the term, 'culture industry,' and Mills 'cultural apparatus,' to describe essentially the same phenomena. Dallas W. Smythe enlarges and extends Enzensberger's usage in his definitive work, *Dependency Road: Communications, Capitalism, Consciousness and Canada* (Norwood, N.J.: Ablex, 1981). Smythe's work also effectively explodes the myth of consumer sovereignty.

3. Kenneth Burke offerred this analogy in *A Grammar of Motives* and *A Rhetoric of Motives* (Cleveland: Meridian, 1962); and Murray Edelman effectively plumbed its implications in *The Political Language* (New York: Academic Press, 1977).

4. Samuel Bowles and Herbert Gintis. *Schooling in Capitalist America: Educational Reform and the Contradictions of Economic Life* (New York: Basic Books, 1976), 54. Bowles and Gintis have also recently generalized these arguments to a systemic analysis of American society in their provocative new work, *Democracy and Capitalism, Property, Community, and the Contradictions of Modern Social Thought* (New York: Basic Books, 1986). However their analysis follows a path somewhat different from my own (a path that places much less emphasis on the role of mass media), and therefore

reaches somewhat different conclusions about prospects and policies for democratizing America.

5. Alan Wolfe. "Capitalism Unleashed: The Rise of Logo America." *The Nation* (May 26, 1984), 641.

6. Significantly, this argument was made by conservative judges and lawyers during the post-Revolutionary period as part of an effort to resist the emergent logic of capitalist economic development. See Andrew Fraser, "The Corporation as a Body Politic," *Telos* 57 (Fall 1983): 5–40.

7. Thomas Jefferson. "Conflict with Hamilton" in *The Complete Jefferson*. Edited by Saul K. Padover (New York: Duell, Sloan, and Pearce, 1943), 276.

8. It has been variously identified as the emergence of a post-industrial society (Bell), a transition from an industrial to an information society (Bell and others), the age of scarcity (Barnet and Mueller), the third wave (Toffler), etc. Naming the age has become a source of ideological contention, with segments on the left charging that the discovery of the 'information society' and apologies for it actually involve a rediscovery of capitalism and obfuscation of its monopolistic ambitions.

9. Wolfe, "Capitalism Unleashed," 640. The new market orientation is also radically altering the structure of its agent, the Consciousness Industry. Consider, for example, the impacts of the "deregulation movement" upon electronic media and the "managerial revolution" in higher education. Marilouise and Arthur Kroker characterize the present period as the era of ultracapitalism in their Preface to "The Phallocentric Mood: 'Bored but Hyper'," *Canadian Journal of Political and Social Theory/ Revue Canadienne de Theorie Politique et Sociale* IX, 1–2 (1985): 5. Elsewhere Arthur Kroker offers a provocative exploration of the role of mass media, especially television, under ultracapitalism. See Arthur Kroker, "Television and the Triumph of Culture: Three Theses," *Canadian Journal of Political and Social Theory/ Revue Canadienne de Theorie Politique et Sociale* IX, 3 (Fall 1985): 37–47.

10. For detailed documentation and analysis of recent structural alterations in American capitalism, see Thomas Byrne Edsall, *The New Politics of Inequality* (New York: W. W. Norton, 1984). Sociologists and institutional economists from the time of Veblen have been documenting the developments in the transformation which is currently coming to fruition. Even Max Weber noted the bureaucratic structure of corporations and their power. C. Wright Mills's *The Power Elite* (New York: Oxford University Press, 1959) can, in retrospect, be regarded as a landmark work which helped bring about a coalescence of sociological thinking on wealth and power. William Domhoff and others have continued to document the trends, noted by Mills, in such works as *Who Rules America?* (Englewood Cliffs, N.J.: Prentice-Hall, 1967), *The Higher Circles: The Governing Class in America* (New York: Random House, 1971), *The Bohemian Grove and Other Retreats: A Study in Ruling Class Cohesiveness* (Magnolia, Mass.: Peter Smith, 1975), *The Powers That Be* (New York: Vintage, 1979). Gabriel Kolko's work has also been a powerful catalyst in securing sociological understanding of this transformation. See, for example, his *The Triumph of Conservatism / A Reinterpretation of American History 1900–1916* (New York: Free Press, 1963). My analysis is strongly indebted to Kolko. In addition, see John Kenneth Galbraith's studies of the restructuring of power in twentieth-century American society, especially *The New Industrial State* (Boston: Houghton Mifflin, 1978): Thorstein Veblen's *The Theory of the Leisure Class* (New York: Kelley, 1899), and *From Max Weber*, edited by H. H. Gerth and C. Wright Mills (New York: Oxford University Press, 1946). This literature is so well known to sociologists interested in social stratification that citation may seem

banal. However, many communication scholars are unfamiliar with this literature—a literature which, in my judgment, is essential to understanding the material foundations of the so-called information society. As a result, studies of the social impacts of new information technologies by communations scholars are sometimes excessively idealistic and optimistic.

11. Smythe, *Dependency Road*: xii.

12. Q. D. Leavis, quoted by Richard Kostelanetz in *Literary Politics in America: The End of Intelligent Writing* (New York: Sheed and Ward, 1973), 189. The concept of demand management was developed by Baran and Sweezy in *Monopoly Capital* (New York: Monthly Review Press, 1966). It is effectively used too by Smythe, *Dependency Road*, and Stuart Ewen, *Captains of Consciousness: Advertising and the Social Roots of the Consumer Culture* (New York: McGraw-Hill, 1976).

13. Alexander Cockburn, "Can Capitalism Be Saved? A Chat with Sweezy and Magdoff," *The Nation* (June 9, 1984), 705.

14. Adam Smith, *The Wealth of Nations* (New York: Modern Library, 1937), 670. 'He' is not used in this sentence for stylistic continuity or as a result of a lapse into unintentional sexist usage. Rather it is intended to underscore the fact that patriarchy has established the priorities and determined the architecture of the power-knowledge of industrial capitalism.

15. Jefferson, "Origins of Self-Government," in *The Complete Jefferson*, 294.

16. Ibid.

17. Clinton Rossiter, *Seedtime of the Republic* (New York: Harcourt, Brace and World, 1953), 344. Howard Zinn points out that 69 percent of the signers of the Declaration of Independence had held colonial posts under British rule. He maintains that, "the reality behind the words of the Declaration of Independence . . . was that a rising class of important people needed to enlist on their side enough Americans to defeat England, without disturbing too much the relations of wealth and power that had developed over 150 years of colonial history. Zinn, *A People's History of the United States* (New York: Harper Colophon, 1980), 74–75.

18. Charles and Mary Beard, *Rise of American Civilization* (New York: Macmillan, 1927), Vol. 1, p. 85.

19. Arthur M. Schlesinger, *Prelude to Independence: The Newspaper War on Britain 1764–1776* (New York: Knopf, 1957).

20. James Parker used these terms to describe the Stamp Act.

21. Jefferson, "Aristocracy and Liberty," in *The Complete Jefferson*, 286.

22. David Ramsay, *The History of the American Revolution* (1789), quoted by Schlesinger in *Prelude to Independence*, vii.

23. Raymond Williams, *Keywords: A Vocabulary of Culture and Society* (New York: Oxford University Press, 1976), 137–39. See also Williams's discussions of the secularization and reification of this term, in *Politics and Letters: Interviews with New Left Review* (London: Verso, 1981).

24. Ben Franklin, "The Way to Wealth," in *The Autobiography and Other Writings* (New York: Bantam Books, 1982), 186–87.

25. See the following selections from *The Complete Jefferson*,: "Origins of Self-Government" (the people as the source of power); "Government by the People" (the mobs in the cities); "A Bill Concerning Slaves" (the mulatto question); "Plan for an Educational System" (educational tracking); "Censorship of Books," "Female Education," and "Letter to McKean."

26. Alfred North Whitehead, of course, identified this reifying tendency as the

fallacy of misplaced concreteness. Peter Berger and Thomas Luckmann, *The Social Construction of Reality* (Garden City, N.Y.: Doubleday, 1967), view reification, the tendency for ideas and social conventions to thicken and harden, as an inevitable tendency of the social process. Roland Barthes made a similar point in *Mythologies* (New York: Hill and Wang, 1972), where he exposes attempts to 'naturalize' statements as common sense, as universal or inevitable conclusions. Marx, of course, directly applied this idea to economic concepts and described the process as analogous to religious fetishism. He contended that, "There the products of the human brain appear as autonomous figures endowed with a life of their own, which enter into relations both with each other and with the human race." See *Capital*, Vol. I (London: Penguin, 1976), 165. Lukacs greatly expanded the Marxian concept of reification in *History and Class Consciousness* (Cambridge, Mass.: MIT Press, 1971). For an empirical analysis of the way this reifying process operates in the marketplace today, see Sut Jhally, Stephen Kline, and William Leiss, "Magic in the Marketplace: An Empirical Test for Commodity Fetishism," *Canadian Journal of Political and Social Theory/Revue Canadienne de Théorie Politique et Sociale* IX, 3 (Fall) 1985:1–23.

27. For an excellent revisionist interpretation of the early history of corporations in America, see Andrew Fraser, "The Corporation as a Body Politic," *Telos* 57 (Fall 1983): 5–40. Several of the examples used in this section are drawn from Fraser's researches. Fraser's fine exposition is marred only by a tendency to gloss the aristocratic elements in Jefferson's views.

28. Ibid.

29. Marx, of course, sees the formation of joint stock companies as the epochal moment in the transition to monopoly capitalism. See, for example, Marx and Engels, *The German Ideology*. Edited by C. J. Arthur (New York: International Publishers, 1970). David Noble describes the purposeful decisions which fabricated the structure of American capitalism, including patent controls and the creation of public utilities requiring consumers to lease services rather than buy equipment in order to assure a larger and continuous flow of profits. See Noble, *America by Design: Science, Technology, and the Rise of Corporate Capitalism* (Oxford: Oxford University Press, 1977). Smythe explores the role of trade associations in coordination of business policy and the Western Union/Associated Press alliance. See Smythe, *Dependency Road*.

30. Logan is quoted by Gabriel Kolko, in *The Triumph of Conservatism*, 13.

31. From its inception until the 1890s, Western Union provided the only nationwide electronic communication system. By 1904 more than a thousand railroad lines had been consolidated into six major lines, each affiliated with either Morgan or Rockefeller. By 1900 the decline in number and diversity of U.S. newspapers had already begun. By 1930, 80% of U.S. cities had press monopolies. Today the figure approaches 100%. On railroad consolidation, see Thomas Cochran and William Miller, *The Age of Enterprise* (New York: Macmillan, 1942). On information monopolies, see Ben H. Bagdikian, *The Media Monopoly* (Boston: Beacon, 1983).

32. These displays were, of course, catalogued in Thorstein Veblen's classic, *The Theory of the Leisure Class* (1899). Veblen, like most Marxists and conservatives of his day, also presents his arguments in the scientific jargon of Social Darwinism, albeit often ironically.

33. Adams is also quoted by Kolko, in *The Triumph of Conservatism*, 14.

34. Not even Franklin Roosevelt, whom conservatives branded as a "traitor of his class" and leftists villified as "the saviour of capitalism," failed to consult with business leaders in the articulation of "The New Deal" for the people.

35. Roosevelt, quoted by Howard Zinn in *A People's History of the United States* (New York: Harper and Row, 1980), 342–43.

36. Boston School Committee, quoted by Michael Katz in *Class, Bureaucracy, and Schools* (New York: Praeger, 1971), 40.

37. Ibid., 46. Private schools, church-controlled schools, and rural schools retained some autonomy, but they did not entirely escape the industrialization, standardization, and bureaucratization of education. After World War II, small-town and rural school districts were brought more tightly under the grip of industrialization by the central school movement.

38. Michael Schudson offers a good brief account of the transition from the political press to the penny press in America in *Discovering the News* (New York: Basic Books, 1978). Schudson regards "the bourgeois revolution" of the Jacksonian era as a democratic revolution. He sees "the moral war" declared by the six-penny papers against the penny press as a war between the declining Federalist elite and emergent middle class. He maintains that the upper classes were far more fearful of and hostile to the middle classes than to the lower-classes. No doubt there was a real conflict of sensibilities between the old elites schooled in European humanism and the pedestrian interests of the new industrialists, but there is little evidence to support the contention that the old elites were more fearful of the middle class than of the "uncivilized" lower classes. Schudson acknowledges that both the old elites and the middle classes were firmly committed to capitalism. However, he ignores the fact that in nineteenth-century America there were vigorous and closely aligned socialist and union movements which held strong appeal for many segments of the laboring classes, particularly newly arrived immigrants from Europe.

39. See Mark Lipper, "Benjamin Franklin's 'Silence Dogood' as an Eighteenth-Century 'Censor Morum,'" in *Newsletters to Newspapers: Eighteenth-Century Journalism*. Edited by Donavan H. Bond and W. Reynolds McLeod (West Virginia University: School of Journalism, 1977), 73–83.

40. Hale, quoted by Carl Degler in *At Odds: Women and Family in America from the Revolution to the Present* (Oxford: Oxford University Press, 1980), 27.

41. Helen MacGill Hughes's classic sociological study, *News and the Human Interest Story* (Chicago: University of Chicago Press, 1940), explored the ways in which the newspaper functions as an arbiter of moral authority, and contributes to the social construction of reality. Earlier Robert E. Park's pioneering studies of the press had noted the role of newspapers in promoting assimilation. See Park's *The Immigrant Press and Its Control* (New York: Harper, 1922). See also Jennifer Daryl Slack's "Media and the Americanization of Workers: The Americanization Bulletin, 1918–1919," in *The Critical Communications Review*, Vol. I: *Labor, the Working Class, and the Media*, edited by Vincent Mosco and Janet Wasko (Norwood, N.J.: Ablex, 1983), 23–44. The ethnic and class bias of the American periodical press and mass media has been widely noted. See, for example, George Gerbner, "On Content Analysis and Critical Research in Mass Communication," in *People, Society and Mass Communications*, edited by L. A. Dexter and D. M. White (New York: Free Press, 1964), 476–500; *Small Voices and Great Trumpets: Minorities and the Media*, edited by Bernard Rubin (New York: Praeger, 1980); *Window Dressing on the Set: Women and Minorities in Television* (Washington: U.S. Commission on Civil Rights, 1977). Critical discourse in the U.S. has focused primarily on ethnic bias in media. In Britain the class bias of media has received more attention. See, for example, *The Manufacture of News: Social Problems, Deviance and the Mass Media*, edited by Stanley Cohen and Jock Young

(London: Constable, 1973); Glasgow University Media Group, *Bad News* (London: Routledge and Kegan Paul, 1976); and Anthony Piepe, Sunny Crouch, Miles Emerson, *Mass Media and Cultural Relationships* (Westmead: Saxon House, 1979).

42. Frances Alice Kellor, head of the AAFLN, quoted by Park in *The Immigrant Press and Its Control*, 448. Kellor is also quoted by Stuart Ewen in *Captains of Consciousness*, 65. In this contemporary 'classic' in critical scholarship, Ewen provides a comprehensive account of the role advertising played in securing industrialism in America.

43. Beeks is also quoted by Ewen, ibid., 15.

44. Historians agree that the first formal prosecutions for pornography ("obscene libel") took place in England in the late seventeenth and early part of the eighteenth century. The first major case involved Edmund Curll's conviction in 1827 for publishing *Venus in the Cloister: or The Nun in Her Smock*. George Gordon describes this case as "paradigmatic." He maintains that *Venus* was "probably little different from the rest of the erotic material in its day, except possibly for its anti-clerical thrust." According to Gordon, erotic materials had been circulated without imprimatur in the sixteenth and seventeenth centuries. However, he points out that these documents "were expensive and apparently reserved mainly for private collections of higher churchmen and civil administrators who, in one way or another, decided which laws were to be enforced and which were not." *Venus* was different because it was popular and because this popularity led to the publication of similar volumes. The "Age of Scandal" saw such publications as dangerous because they might corrupt the morals of the general public. As Philip Yorke, the King's Attorney General, put it:

> What I insist upon is that this is an offense at common law as it tends to corrupt the morals of the King's subjects and is against the peace of the King. Peace includes good order and government, and that peace may be broken in many instances without an actual force: 1) if it be an act against the constitution of the civil government, 2) if it be against religion and 3) if against morality. I do not insist that every immoral act is indictable, such as telling a lie or the like, but if it is destructive of morality in general, if it does or may affect all the King's subjects, then it is an offense of a public nature. And upon this distinction it is that acts of fornication are not punishable in the temporal courts and bawdy houses are.

In America a similar pattern prevailed. The Patriarch of the Republic, Ben Franklin, wrote erotica in the 1740s and circulated it in limited editions to friends and peers. His best-known contributions to this genre are *Advice to a Young Man Choosing a Mistress, Polly Baker's Speech,* and *Letter to the Royal Academy of Brussels.* Franklin's writings for mass consumption were, however, of a very different order. Poor Richard was advised to follow far more pristine strictures than Polly Baker's consort *and* far more pristine strictures than Ben Franklin followed in Philadelphia, where he fathered several illegitimate children; in London, where he sought hospitality at the "Hell Fire Club"; and at the French court, where he freely pursued erotic pleasures.

Prosecutions for pornography in America began in Jefferson's day and accelerated as scarcity of printed materials abated and erotic materials became available to the lower classes. See George N. Gordon, *Erotic Communications: Studies in Sex, Sin and Censorship* (New York: Hastings House, 1980); and Felice Flanery Lewis, *Literature, Obscenity and Law* (Carbondale: Southern Illinois University Press, 1976).

Preservation of conventional morality took an interesting turn when it came to motion picture censorship in America. From the time the first 'photoplays' were introduced in America, moralists expressed concerns about their impacts on youth and on the Americanization of the immigrant working class. Films were condemned as mere "substitutes for saloons." Formal censorship of films began in 1909 under the auspicies of a non-governmental agency called the National Board of Censorship of Motion Pictures. State censorship boards soon followed. Edward De Grazia and Roger K. Newman (*Banned Films: Movies, Censors and the First Amendment* (New York: R. R. Bowker, 1982), 23) point out that from the beginning, "The escalating battle over movie freedom had overtones of class struggle and undercurrents of religious and racial antagonisms. When Canon Chase labeled his cohorts in the censorship movement 'Patriotic Gentile Americans,' he was expressing a barely disguised anti-Semitism." The Reverend Mr. Crafts went further, claiming the movement was "to rescue the motion pictures from the hands of the Devil and 500 un-Christian Jews." Self-regulation was the industry's response to a genuine threat of governmental censorship or prohibition. The Hays Office was the result. A former Postmaster General and a Presbyterian elder, Will H. Hays, became overseer of movie censorship. Curiously, the actual Motion Picture Production Code was drafted by a Catholic priest, Daniel A. Lord, and a Catholic newspaper publisher, Martin Quigley. However, information about Lord and Quigley's roles in composing the code was withheld by the Motion Pictures Producers and Distributors Association of America because they did not wish to further fan the religious wars even though the code itself reflected standard American middle-class values and mores.

45. Comstock's sponsors included J. P. Morgan, William E. Dodge Jr., Morris K. Jessup, and Robert McBurney. See Morris L. Ernst and William Seagle, *To Be Pure . . . A Study of Obscenity and the Censor* (New York: Viking, 1928).

46. Dewey is quoted by Schudson in *Discovering the News*, 141.

47. Max Horkheimer, *Eclipse of Reason* (New York: Seabury, 1974 (original 1947), 154.

48. Michael Schudson, *Advertising: The Uneasy Persuasion: Its Dubious Impact on American Society*. (New York: Basic Books, 1984).

49. Smythe, *Dependency Road*, 4.

50. This metaphor is borrowed from Arthur Kroker's "Television and the Triumph of Culture: Three Theses." While I have reservations about Kroker's "theses," I think he is correct in suggesting that television plays a much larger role in 'post-modern society' than either the positivistic reflection thesis (television as 'mirror' of society) or the Marxist reflection thesis (television as 'ideology') suggest. It is, as he puts it, much more than "a Xerox copy of culture, society and economy" (p. 38).

51. Ben Bagdikian, "The U.S. Media: Supermarket or Assembly Line?," *Journal of Communication* (Summer 1985): 97–109.

52. Writers who are also involved in producing are most prosperous and have greater control over their work. Most television writers work, like performers, on a per project basis, although some report employment directly by the networks or affiliates. A study involving a random sample of 150 television writers (with a 36% response rate) sponsored by the Writers Guild of America (West and East) in 1980 produced the following demographics. 83% were male, 98% were white, the average age was 50 with 23 years of employment as a writer. 58% reported working on a project-to-project basis. Earnings from writing ranged from starving artists who reported no income to one writer (a woman with many years experience, but not involved in producing) who reported a yearly income from her television work of one million dollars. Average earnings for

1980 were $134,000, with writers on hit shows or writers who also produce reporting earnings far in excess of the $200,000 figure. 66% of the writers were college graduates. 42% majored in journalism or English. Most (57%) described themselves as political "Liberals." 80% reported that they regularly practiced self-censorship. 68% reported that their work has been censored by others. 70% reported that they favor censorship under certain conditions (national security topped the list of conditions but child welfare, the good of society, pornography, and good taste were also invoked). Veteran writers, especially those who had been employed in television during the 1950s, expressed far more concern about the potential dangers of censorship than younger writers. Sue Curry Jansen, Writers Guild of America Study, 1980.

53. George Gerbner, "Television: The New State Religion?," ETC (June 1977), 147. For an analysis of the distribution of power in the fictional world of television and consideration of the concept of 'symbolic annihilation,' see Gerbner and Larry Gross, "Living with Television: The Violence Profile", *Journal of Communication* 26,2 (1976), 173–99.

54. The laughter at the furthest edges of American capitalism may be the only laughter that largely escapes colonization by the power-knowledge of political capitalism. This is why incisive and subversive knowledge of power sometimes takes root among the "inner enemies" at the margins. See Herbert Marcuse's *An Essay on Liberation* (Boston: Beacon, 1969), and Georg Simmel, "The Stranger" in *The Sociology of Georg Simmel* edited by Kurt H. Wolff (Glencoe: Free Press, 1964). It is also among these outsiders or resisters that critical researchers hope to discover and empower the constituents of an emancipatory media-critical theory. See *Resistance Through Rituals*, edited by Stuart Hall and Tony Jefferson (London: Hutchinson and the Centre for Contemporary Cultural Studies, 1976) and *Mass Media and Cultural Relationships* by Anthony Piepe, Sunny Crouch, and Miles Emerson (Westmead: Saxon House, 1978). See also Alan Blum, "Lower Class Negro Television Spectators: The Concept of Pseudo Jovial Skepticism," *Blue Collar World*, edited by Arthur Shostak and William Gomberg (Englewood Cliffs, N.J.: Prentice-Hall, 1964).

55. Conversation, August 1985.

56. Rose K. Goldsen, *The Show and Tell Machine* (New York: Dell, 1975), 7.

57. Gerbner, "Television: The New State Religion?."

58. Smythe, *Dependency Road*, 235.

59. Ralph Miliband, *The State in Capitalist Society: An Analysis of the Western System of Power* (New York: Basic Books, 1969), 47–48. Miliband also distinguishes between state actions at the 'behest' and on 'behalf' of corporations and suggests that most collaborations between state and capital are of the former type. So that under normal conditions, the system works automatically without conspiratorial collusion.

60. Historical amnesia has taken its toll on this point. Few Americans are aware of the fact that Marxists were active in the abolition movement. Moreover, Lincoln's platform itself may have been directly influenced by Marxists. Lincoln was championed as the son of a workingman. He actively sought the support of German-American immigrants in his 1860 election bid. A highly politicized faction of the German-American community was composed of exiles who had participated in the unsuccessful German Revolution of 1848. The following quotation from Lincoln's address at the 1859 Wisconsin State Fair reflects this influence. Lincoln asserted that labor, not capital, is the bulwark of American freedom: "the source from which human wants are mainly supplied." Contra the Mud Sill advocates who defended the primacy of capital, Lincoln maintained: "that labor is prior to, and independent of capital; that, in fact, capital

is the fruit of labor, and could never have existed if labor had not first existed; that labor can exist without capital, but that capital could never have existed without labor. Hence . . . labor is the superior . . . greatly the superior of capital." Lincoln's speech is excerpted in *History of the Labor Movement in the United States*, Vol. 1, by Philip S. Foner (New York: International Publishers, 1947), 292.

61. Daniel Bell, *The Coming of Post-Industrial Society* (New York: Basic Books, 1973).

62. The less celebratory but, in my judgment, more accurate term, 'information-capitalism,' is taken from Tessa Morris-Suzuki's "Capitalism in the Computer Age", *New Left Review* 160 (Nov./Dec. 1986): 81–91.

63. Alvin Gouldner used the term 'cultural capital' to describe the transformation of productive relations in the information age. Gouldner, *The Future of Intellectuals and the Rise of the New Class* (New York: Seabury, 1979).

64. Morris-Suzuki, "Capitalism in the Computer Age," 89.

65. See also Smythe, *Dependency Road*.

66. Morris-Suzuki, "Capitalism in the Computer Age," 85.

67. For discussions of "privatization of information", see Herbert I. Schiller, *Who Knows: Information in the Age of the Fortune 500* (Norwood, N.J.: Ablex, 1981); Anita R. Schiller and Herbert I. Schiller, "Commercializing Information," *The Nation*, Oct. 4, 1986, pp. 306–9.

68. Donna A. Demac, *Keeping America Uninformed: Government Secrecy in the 1980's* (New York: Pilgrim Press, 1984). See also Anita R. Schiller and Herbert I. Schiller, "Who Can Own What America Knows?," *The Nation*, April 17, 1982, pp. 461–64.

69. Schiller, *Who Knows.*

70. Philip Elliott, "Intellectuals, the 'Information Society' and the Disappearance of the Public Sphere," *Mass Communication Review Yearbook*, Vol. 4. Edited by Ellen Wartella, D. Charles Whitney, and Swen Windahl (Beverly Hills: Sage, 1983).

71. J. W. Freiberg, *The French Press: Class, State and Ideology* (New York: Praeger, 1981).

72. Bagdikian, "The U.S. Media: Supermarket or Assembly Line?"

73. Ibid. See also Bagdikian's *The Media Monopoly* (Boston: Beacon, 1983); and Herbert I. Schiller, "Behind the Media Merger Movement," *The Nation* (June 8, 1985), 696–98.

74. Isadore Barmash, "Dayton Plans Sale of B. Dalton Chain," *New York Times*, Oct. 1, 1986.

75. Bagdikian, "The U.S. Media: Supermarket or Assembly Line?", uses the assembly line analogy. See also Elliot, "Intellectuals, the 'Information Society' . . . "; and Marc Raboy, *Movements and Messages: Media and Radical Politics in Quebec* (Toronto: Between the Lines, 1983).

76. For an account of the important role the film industry played in internationalizing U.S. culture, see Janet Wasko, *Movies and Money: Financing the American Film Industry* (Norwood, N.J.: Ablex, 1982).

77. Richard J. Barnet and Ronald E. Muller, *Global Reach: The Power of Multinational Corporations* (New York: Simon and Schuster, 1975); Schiller, *Who Knows*; Barbara Ehrenreich and Annette Fuentes, "Life on the Global Assembly Line," in *Crisis in American Institutions* (5th ed.). Edited by Jerome H. Skolnick and Elliott Currie (Boston: Little, Brown, 1976), 373–89.

78. Freiberg, *The French Press*, 12. Freiberg applies Braverman's concept of "de-

skilling" in analyzing the impact of the new technologies of information production. See Harry Braverman, *Labor and Monopoly Capital: The Degradation of Work in the Twentieth Century* (New York: Monthly Review, 1975). Some critics on the left are more optimistic about prospects for resistance among information workers. See, for example, Donna Haraway, "A Manifesto for Cyborgs: Science, Technology, and Socialist Feminism in the 1980s," *Socialist Review* 80, 2 (March-April 1985): 65–107. For an analysis of the strategic position of knowledge-workers under information-capitalism, see Kevin Roberts and Frank Webster, *Information Technology: A Luddite Analysis* (Norwood, N.J.: Ablex, 1986).

79. See, for example, Frederick Williams, *The Communications Revolution* (Beverly Hills: Sage, 1982).

80. Elliott, "Intellectuals, the 'Information Society'." Recent data indicate that the economistic model is thriving in the global marketplace at the expense of the nation-state. See Robert E. Lipsey and Irving B. Kravis, "Sorting Out the Trade Problem: Business Holds Its Own as America Slips," *New York Times*, Jan. 18, 1987.

81. Morris-Suzuki, "Capitalism in the Computer Age"; Freiberg, *The French Press*; and Raboy, *Movements and Messages.*

82. Students of communication working under the influence of Louis Althusser frequently invoke this analogy. This analogy has also been adopted by British communication researchers building on the traditions of Hoggart and Williams.

83. Smythe uses the term teaching machine to describe the agenda-setting capacities of the products of the Consciousness Industry. See *Dependency Road.* In *Channels of Desire* (New York: McGraw-Hill, 1982), Stuart and Elizabeth Ewen demonstrate that even the packaging of U.S. exports sells the American way of life to Third World peoples.

84. Jeremy Tunstall. *The Media are American* (New York: Columbia University Press, 1977).

85. Richard Falk's Foreword to *Supplying Repression: U.S. Support for Authoritarian Regimes Abroad* (Washington: Institute for Policy Studies, 1981) by Michael T. Klare and Cynthia Arnson, p. viii. See also Klare's *War Without End* (New York: Knopf, 1972). I would like to see the U.S. withdraw support from Ferdinand Marcos as evidence against this argument. However, given the inevitability of Marcos's fall, it is difficult to see America's transfer of support to the Aquino government as much more than a concession to the inevitable. Failure to offer such support would have provided an opening for a challenge by communist forces in the Philippines. Nevertheless the U.S. government did use this episode to flex its diplomatic muscle among its reactionary allies, asserting that it would no longer tolerate the kinds of authoritarian excesses that had become routine during Marcos's rule. It remains to be seen whether this muscle-flexing was a policy statement or a public relations effort designed primarily for domestic consumption in the U.S. during a period when media coverage of Marcos's plundering of the Philippines economy was an embarrassment to the U.S. State Department.

86. Ball and Drucker, quoted by Richard J. Barnet and Ronald E. Muller in *Global Reach.* See also Barnet and Muller, "The Global Shopping Center," in *The Big Business Reader: Essays in Corporate America* (New York: Pilgrim Press, 1980), edited by Mark Green and Robert Massie, p. 281; and Cees J. Hamelink, *The Corporate Village: The Role of Transnational Corporations in International Communications* (Rome: IDOC International, 1977).

87. Klare and Arnson have documented the extent to which an increase in the

American role as exporter of repression paralleled the development of Human Rights diplomacy during the Carter Administration. See *Supplying Repression*.

88. Bruce A. Ackerman. *Social Justice in the Liberal State* (New Haven: Yale University Press, 1980), 4.

89. Lucien Goldmann. *The Philosophy of the Enlightenment* (Cambridge, Mass.: MIT Press, 1968), 91–92. See also discussion of Goldmann's critique of socialism in Chapter Five.

Chapter Eight

1. See, for example, Friedrich Nietzsche, *The Gay Science* (New York: Vintage, 1974); Karl Mannheim, *Essays on the Sociology of Knowledge* (London: Routledge and Kegan Paul, 1952), or the more accessible introduction by Gunther Remmling, *The Sociology of Karl Mannheim* (London: Routledge and Kegan Paul, 1975); Emile Durkheim, *The Elementary Forms of the Religious Life* (Glencoe: Free Press, 1947); Karl Marx and Frederick Engels, *The German Ideology* (New York: International Publishers, 1970); Wilhelm Dilthey, *Pattern and Meaning in History*, edited by H. P. Rickman (New York: Harper and Row, 1962); Georg Lukacs, *History and Class Consciousness* (Cambridge, Mass.: MIT Press, 1971); Alfred Schutz, *Collected Papers*, Vols. I-III (Boston: Kluwer, 1963, 1974, 1975). See also Mary Douglas, *Purity and Danger: An Analysis of Concepts of Pollution and Taboo* (London: Routledge and Kegan Paul, 1966); Michel Foucault, *Discipline and Punish: The Birth of the Prison* (New York: Pantheon, 1977) and *The History of Sexuality, I: An Introduction* (New York: Vintage, 1980). For major contributions to the development of constructivist perspectives within the philosophy of science, see Michael Polanyi, *Personal Knowledge* (Chicago: University of Chicago Press, 1958); Thomas S. Kuhn, *The Structure of Scientific Revolutions* (Chicago: University of Chicago Press, 1970); Stephen E. Toulmin, *The Uses of Argument* (Cambridge: Cambridge University Press, 1958); Stephen Pepper, *World Hypothesis: A Study in Evidence* (Berkeley: University of California Press, 1970); Norwood Hanson, *Patterns of Discovery: An Inquiry into the Conceptual Foundations of Science* (Cambridge: Cambridge University Press, 1965). See also Karin D. Knorr-Cetina, *The Manufacture of Knowledge: An Essay on the Constructivist and Contextual Nature of Science* (New York: Pergamon, 1981); Bruno Latour and Steve Woolgar, *Laboratory Life: The Social Construction of Scientific Facts* (Beverly Hills: Sage, 1979); Karin D. Knorr, A. Krohn, and R. Whitley (editors), *The Social Process of Scientific Discoveries* (New York: Cambridge University Press, 1981); and Richard Rorty, *Philosophy and the Mirror of Nature* (Princeton: Princeton University Press, 1979). For an explication of a constructivist or hermeneutic philosophy of history, see Hans Georg Gadamer, *Truth and Method* (New York: Seabury, 1975) and his *Philosophical Hermeneutics* (Berkeley: University of California Press, 1976).

2. Nietzsche, *The Gay Science*, 84.

3. Phenomenological perspectives, which recognize the social construction of knowledge, nevertheless sometimes also protect the omniscience of the theorist. See, for example, Peter L. Berger and Thomas Luckmann, *The Social Construction of Reality: A Treatise in the Sociology of Knowledge* (Garden City, N.Y.: Doubleday, 1967).

4. Although their disciplinary allegiances and evidential warrants differ greatly, the following authors nevertheless embrace this view at least in part: Douglas, *Purity and Danger*; Foucault, *Discipline and Punish*, *The History of Sexuality*, and *The Archaeology of Knowledge and the Discourse of Language* (New York: Harper Colophon, 1972); Polanyi, *Personal Knowledge* and *The Study of Man* (Chicago: University of Chicago Press, 1963); Gadamer, *Truth and Method* and *Philosophical Hermeneutics*.

5. Foucault, *Discipline and Punish*, 29. See also *The History of Sexuality*.

6. Anomalies pose a problem because they are residues, leftovers, failures in the classificatory system. They suggest the limits of established explanations, their points of vulnerability. See Durkheim, *The Elementary Forms of the Religious Life*, 301, and Douglas, *Implicit Meanings* (London: Routledge and Kegan Paul, 1975), xv, xiii.

7. Foucault, *Discipline and Punish*, 29.

8. Douglas, *Implicit Meanings*, xx.

9. Karl Mannheim, Letter to Kurt H. Wolff, quoted in Wolff's "The Sociology of Knowledge and Sociological Theory," in *Symposium on Sociological Theory* (New York: Harper and Row, 1959), edited by Llewellyn Z. Gross, 570–71.

10. Marx's critique of philosophy was as radical as those offered by the anti-philosophers. He, too, believed he had solved the problem of philosophy by reducing its "agitated layers of air" to the grammar of materialism. But he was unwilling to surrender his own claims to objective knowledge. He affirmed the rule of relativism (material conditioning of thought forms) in previous historical epochs, but he maintained that the method of historical materialism would produce certain knowledge. See Marx and Engels, *The German Ideology*.

11. Douglas, *Implicit Meanings*, xviii.

12. Michael Polanyi, quoted by Richard Gelwick in *The Way of Discovery: An Introduction to the Thought of Michael Polanyi* (New York: Oxford University Press, 1977), 26.

13. Polanyi, *Personal Knowledge*; Kuhn, *The Structure of Scientific Revolutions*; Paul Feyerabend, *Against Method*, Minnesota Studies in the Philosophy of Science, Vol. IV, 1971; Toulmin, *The Uses of Argument*; Pepper, *World Hypotheses*; Hanson, *Patterns of Discovery*.

14. P. B. Medawar, *The Art of the Soluble* (London: Methuen, 1967), 152. Jerome Bruner goes even further, suggesting that the act of perception itself is a dramaturgical process. See his *Actual Minds, Possible Worlds* (Cambridge, Mass.: Harvard University Press, 1986). Recent work in constructivist philosophies of science focuses on the analysis of scientific 'texts'; it recognizes that science is a communication process and that as a result an adequate theory of knowledge must be informed by rhetoric. See, for example, John O'Neill's "The Literary Production of Natural and Social Science Inquiry: Issues and Applications in the Social Organization of Science," *Canadian Journal of Sociology* 6 (1981): 105–20; Ken Morrison, "Some Properties of 'Telling Order Designs' in Dialectic Inquiry," *Philosophy of the Social Sciences* 11 (1981): 245–62; Digby C. Anderson, "Some Organizational Features of a Plausible Text," *Philosophy of the Social Sciences* 8 (1978): 113–35; Steve Woolgar, "Discovery: Logic and Sequence in a Scientific Text," in *The Social Production of Scientific Investigation*, edited by Knorr et al., 239–68; and James Clifford and George E. Marcus, *Writing Culture: The Poetics and Politics of Ethnography* (Berkeley: University of California Press, 1986).

15. Polanyi, *Personal Knowledge*, 268.

16. Speech made in Moscow, 1920.

17. See, for example, Habermas, *Legitimation Crisis* (Boston: Beacon, 1975); Alvin
Gouldner, *The Dialectic of Ideology and Technology* (New York: Seabury, 1976); and
Richard Heilbroner, *An Inquiry into the Human Prospect* (New York: W. W. Norton,
1974).

18. Gouldner, *The Dialectic of Ideology and Technology*, 127.

Chapter Nine

1. Leo Strauss, *Persecution and the Art of Writing* (Glencoe: Free Press, 1952).
M. F. Burnyeat contends Strauss himself used esotericism to establish his own elitist
system of academic power-knowledge, a system of power-knowledge which made him
"a guru of American conservatism." See "Sphinx Without a Secret: Studies in Platonic
Philosophy," *New York Review of Books* (May 30, 1985): 30–36. In citing Strauss's
insightful writings on the uses of esoterica, I do not embrace his conservative ethos
or endorse his alleged elitism.

There are some parallels and continuities between the double nature of language
and the public-private/theory-practice split. In my judgment the double nature of
language will always be a facet of the strains and tensions of interpersonal and inter-
group communications as well as an aesthetic delight. As Karl Jaspers puts it, "The
world is the manuscript of an other, inaccessible to a universal reading, which only
existence deciphers." Jaspers, quoted by Jacques Derrida in *Of Grammatology* (Baltimore: John Hopkins University Press, 1976), 16. Nevertheless when pressures to
orthodoxy in the larger society force writers to write-between-the-lines in order to
publish, something else is at work. This kind of equivocation is an artifact of oppression.
It is the antithesis of reflexive power-talk. And, in my judgment, it is secured by the
kind of hypocrisy that the public-private/theory-practice schism supports.

2. Jurgen Habermas, "Towards a Theory of Communicative Competence," *Recent
Sociology* 2, edited by Hans Dreitzel (New York: Macmillan, 1970).

3. Herbert Marcuse, *The Aesthetic Dimension* (Boston: Beacon, 1978).

4. Joanna Russ, *The Female Man* (Boston: Gregg, 1975).

5. Andrei Sinyavsky, "The Literary Process in Russia," *Kontinent* I (Garden City,
N.Y.: Anchor, 1976), 84.

6. Tadeusz Konwicki, quoted by Charles Sawyer in "Letter from Poland: Beating
the Censor," *New York Times Book Review* (Oct. 5, 1980), 40.

7. Georg Lukacs, *The Theory of the Novel* (Cambridge, Mass.: MIT Press, 1971),
93.

8. Schlegel, quoted by Wayne Booth in *A Rhetoric of Irony* (Chicago: University
of Chicago Press, 1974), 230.

9. Kenneth Burke, *A Grammar of Motives* and *A Rhetoric of Motives* (Cleveland:
Meridian, 1962).

10. Quintilian, quoted by Booth, *A Rhetoric of Irony*, 43.

11. The term 'reality disjuncture' is borrowed from Melvin Pollner's "The Very
Coinage of Your Brain: The Anatomy of Reality Disjunctures," *Philosophy of Social
Sciences* 5 (1975), 411–30.

12. Allan Rodway, "Terms for Comedy," *Renaissance and Modern Studies* VI
(1962): 113.

13. Llewellyn Gross, "Where Is Social Reality?," *Sociological Inquiry* XXXIII,1 (Winter 1963): 3–8.

14. Wilhelm von Humboldt, *Linguistic Variability and Intellectual Development* (Philadelphia: University of Pennsylvania Press, 1971), 43.

15. Paul Ricoeur, *Freud and Philosophy: An Essay on Interpretation* (New Haven: Yale University Press, 1970), 7.

16. George Steiner, *After Babel: Aspects of Language and Translation* (New York: Oxford University Press, 1975).

17. Ricoeur, *Freud and Philosophy*, 18–19.

18. Dilthey, quoted by Edmund Wright, "Sociology and the Irony Model," *Sociology: The Journal of the British Sociological Association* 12 (Sept. 1978), 523.

19. Ibid., 534–35.

20. Georg Lukacs, *Solzhenitsyn* (Cambridge, Mass.: MIT Press, 1971), 7.

21. Aleksandr Nikitenko gives a full account of this case in *The Diary of a Russian Censor* (Amherst: University of Massachusetts Press, 1975).

22. Andrei Sinyavsky, "Samizdat and the Rebirth of Literature," *Index on Censorship* 9, 4 (Aug. 1980), 8–13.

23. Sherry Turkle, *The Second Self: Computers and the Human Spirit* (New York: Simon and Schuster, 1984).

Chapter Ten

1. I am, of course, relying on Habermas's analysis of repressed communication. See *Knowledge and Human Interests* (Boston: Beacon, 1971).

2. Walter J. Ong, *Orality and Literacy* (Boston: Methuen, 1982).

3. Jurgen Habermas, "Why More Philosophy?" *Social Research* 38, 4 (1971): 648, and *Legitimation Crisis* (Boston: Beacon, 1975). Rudolf Bahro and the Green Party reach a similar conclusion from different premises. See his discussion of the "reconstruction of God" in *From Red to Green* (London: Verso, 1984), 211–39.

4. Richard Sennett, *Authority* (New York: Vintage Books, 1980), 168. Sennett's compelling analysis of authority is to some extent weakened by his use of metaphors like 'legible' and 'visible' and concepts like 'publics' which are artifacts of the age of print. In the age of microchips and microwaves, we cannot render authority fully legible or visible. Our victories will not only be partial victories, they will be relative victories.

5. Ackerman is not blind to the issue, but he effectively skirts it by presenting his argument within an idealized setting (an imaginary planet) which allows him to presuppose that the distribution of resources can be secured by reason. Ackerman endorses equality in the initial distribution of resources but his recipe contains no practical mechanism for redistributing existing concentrations of wealth. He is interested in making conversation not revolution. In addition to the question of resources, I have two additional reservations regarding Ackerman's project. First, his dialogically based democratic theory is designed to salvage the Liberal state. I contend that from its inception Liberalism has been flawed by elitism, and that this flaw permitted its co-optation by political capitalism. Therefore, I believe a new enlightenment, not a salvage operation, is required to empower a dialogically based democratic theory. Second, Ackerman's proposed rules for Neutral Dialogue are compelling; but, in my judgment,

his choice of the label Neutral Dialogue is unfortunate. The term 'neutral' has a checkered history. Its past associations with objectivism and elite pluralism make the concept of Neutral Dialogue seem like just one more way of saying my way is better than your way. Moreover, neutrality may suggest reassertion of the old Liberal claim that the knot that binds power and knowledge has been untied. These are not Ackerman's intentions. Ackerman is proposing rules that might 'neutralize' or restrain the unfair advantage that the powerful have in power-talks. In short, Ackerman is endorsing reflexive power talk. In order to avoid the connotations described above, I will use the terms, 'reflexive power-talk,' 'reflexive legitimating dialogues,' and 'reflexivity,' not Neutral Dialogue.

For a radical interpretation of Ackerman's Liberal proposal, see Ben Agger, "A Critical Theory of Dialogue," *Humanities in Society* 4,1 (Winter 1981), 191–208. Agger offers a cogent synthesis of the ideas of Ackerman and Marcuse. My own introduction to Ackerman's work was through Agger's exegesis.

6. Within the philosophy of science, as we have seen, there is already wide recognition of the need to develop an enlarged concept of rationality. See, for example, Michael Polanyi, *Personal Knowledge* (Chicago: University of Chicago Press, 1958) and Stephen Toulmin, *Uses of Argument* (Cambridge: Cambridge University Press, 1964). The new, humanistic or "Good" rationality is closer to the concept of rationality secured in classical rhetoric than to the more narrow instrumental concepts of rationality secured by the Enlightenment. For early critiques of instrumental (functional) rationality and apologies for a broader, substantive, rationality which encourages reflections on ends, not just means, see Max Weber, Karl Jaspers, and Karl Mannheim. This is a recurrent theme in Weber's work. See, for example, *From Max Weber*, edited by H. H. Gerth and C. Wright Mills (New York: Oxford University Press, 1946). Jaspers develops this theme in *Man in the Modern Age* (New York: AMS Press Reprint, 1933); and Mannheim examines it in *Ideology and Utopia* (New York: Harcourt, Brace, 1955). For comprehensive critiques of the repressive structures secured by the power-knowledge of instrumental rationality, see Max Horkheimer, *The Eclipse of Reason* (New York: Seabury, 1974) and Horkheimer and Theodor W. Adorno, *Dialectics of Enlightenment* (New York: Herder and Herder, 1972). My own appreciation of Good Rationality is deeply indebted to the dialogues with Llewellyn Z. Gross, exemplar and expositor.

These distinctions are crucial to development of a viable theory of power-knowedge. For, as we have seen, rulers determine the rules of rationality as well as the rules of the *polis*. Instrumental rationality explained and justified burning of witches. It "made sense" of this means but proscribed discussion of the end: "Thou shalt not suffer a witch to live" (Exodus 22:18). Good rationality would not only permit reflection on ends, it would acknowledge (and secure methods for inventorying) the parts human interests and values play in securing knowledge.

7. For a critique of rule by state secret, see Hans Magnus Enzensberger, *Politics and Crime* (New York: Seabury, 1974). For a critique of rule by techno-scientific elitism, see Jurgen Habermas, *Theory and Practice* (Boston: Beacon, 1968).

8. Bruce A. Ackerman. *Social Justice in the Liberal State* (New Haven: Yale University Press, 1980), 4–11.

9. Habermas, *Knowledge and Human Interests*. Habermas describes the constituents of the ideal speech situation as: all potential participants must have equal chances to initiate and perpetuate discourses; all participants must have equal opportunities to criticize, ground, or refute all statements, explanations, interpretations, and justi-

fications; and discourse must be free from the external constraints of domination, e.g. violence, threats, sanctions. If these conditions prevail, Habermas believes the preconditions for a rational order will be met. If these conditios are realized *within* the actual course of the dialogue, the resulting consensus will be based upon the power of the best argument.

10. Paulo Friere, *Pedagogy of the Oppressed* (New York: Seabury Press, 1970). Friere, of course, suggests that current educational practice is stagnating under the monologues of narration sickness. Under this practice the teacher assumes an active role and students assume passive roles. The teacher deposits information in students' heads the way businessmen deposit money in banks. Friere maintains that a passive education prepares students for a passive life. A passive education prepares students to accept oppression. He endorses an activist education secured in dialogue instead of monologue—an education for critical consciousness. Friere's ideas have been incorporated in the consciousness-raising process of many strains of Liberationist theology. For an insightful discussion of this application of Friere's work, see Dallas Smythe, "Needs Before Tools? The Illusions of Electronic Democracy," Paper presented at the International Communication Association, Honolulu, May 1985.

11. Cees Hamelink offers some practical guidelines for doing this in "An Alternative to News," *Journal of Communication* (Autumn 1976): 120–23.

12. Kevin Robins and Frank Webster, "Information Technology, Luddism, and The Working Class," in *The Critical Communications Review*, Vol. 1: *Labor, The Working Class and the Media*. Edited by Vincent Mosco and Janet Wasko (Norwood, N.J.: Ablex, 1983).

13. See, for example, Todd Gitlin, *The Whole World is Watching: Mass Media in the Making and Unmaking of the New Left* (Berkeley: University of California Press, 1980; Armand Mattelart, *Mass Media, Ideologies and the Revolutionary Movement* (Atlantic Highlands, N.J.: Humanities Press, 1980); and Marc Raboy, *Movements and Messages: Media and Radical Politics in Quebec* (Toronto: Between the Lines, 1983).

14. Raboy, *Movements and Messages*.

15. Alvin W. Gouldner, *The Future of the Intellectuals and the Rise of the New Class* (New York: Seabury, 1979).

16. Donna Haraway, "A Manifesto for Cyborgs: Science, Technology, and Socialist Feminism in the 1980s," *Socialist Review* 80, 2 (March-April 1985): 65–107.

17. There is also some organized resistance in the U.S., for example, sit-ins which protested curtailment of services by the Library of Congress, demonstrations by nonprofit groups like the Girl Scouts against new Internal Revenue Service regulations which imperil their operations, citizen protest against the colinization of content of children's television by toy manufacturers, etc.

18. Constituents of a new media critical theory have already been articulated in the work of scholars cited in these pages such as Smythe, Schiller, Gerbner, and others.

19. Dag Hammarskjold, *Markings* (New York: Knopf, 1964), 138.

20. Sennett, *Authority*, 189–90.

Bibliography

Ackerman, Bruce A. *Social Justice in the Liberal State*. New Haven: Yale University Press, 1980.

Agger, Ben. "A Critical Theory of Dialogue," *Humanities in Society* 4,1 (Winter 1981): 191–208.

Althusser, Louis. *Lenin and Philosophy and Other Essays*. New York: Monthly Review Press, 1971.

Altschull, J. Herbert. *Agents of Power: The Roles of the News Media in Human Affairs*. New York: Annenberg-Longman Communication Series, 1984.

Anderson, Digby C. "Some Organizational Features of a Plausible Text," *Philosophy of the Social Sciences* 8 (1978): 113–35.

Arendt, Hannah. *Eichmann in Jerusalem: A Report on the Banality of Evil*. New York: Penguin, 1977.

———. *The Life of the Mind*. 2 vols. New York: Harcourt Brace Jovanovich, 1978.

Avineri, Shlomo. "Aspects of Freedom of Writing and Expression in Hegel and Marx," *Social Theory and Practice* 4 (1977): 273–86.

Bachelard, Gaston. *The Poetics of Reverie: Childhood, Language and Cosmos*. Boston: Beacon, 1971.

Bagdikian, Ben. *The Media Monopoly*. Boston: Beacon, 1983.

———. "The U.S. Media: Supermarket or Assembly Line?," *Journal of Communication* (Summer 1985): 97–109.

Bahro, Rudolf. *From Red to Green*. London: Verso, 1984.

Baran, Paul, and Paul Sweezy. *Monopoly Capital*. New York: Simon and Schuster, 1974.

———. "The Global Shopping Center," in *The Big Business Reader: Essays in Corporate America*. New York: Pilgrim Press, 1980. Edited by Mark Green and Robert Massie.

Barmash, Isidore. "Dayton Plans Sale of B. Dalton Chain," *New York Times*, Oct. 1, 1986.

Barnet, Richard J., and Ronald E. Muller. *Global Reach: The Power of Multinational Corporations*. New York: Simon and Schuster, 1975.

Barthes, Roland. *Mythologies*. New York: Hill and Wang, 1972.

Bayle, Pierre. *Nouvelles de la republique des lettres*. (1687). Geneva: Slatkine Reprints, 1966.

Beard, Charles A. *An Economic Interpretation of the Constitution of the United States*. New York: Macmillan, 1913.

Beard, Charles, and Mary Beard. *Rise of American Civilization*. New York: Macmillan, 1927, Vol. 1.

Beauvoir, Simone de. *The Second Sex*. New York: Bantam Books, 1961.

Bell, Daniel. *The Coming of Post-industrial Society*. New York: Basic Books, 1973.

Benjamin, Walter. "The Author as Producer," *New Left Review* 62 (July-Aug. 1970): 83–96.

———. *Reflections*. New York: Harcourt Brace Jovanovich, 1978.

Bentham, Jeremy. "Panopticon," in *A Bentham Reader*. New York: Pegasus, 1969.

Berger, Peter L., and Thomas Luckmann. *The Social Construction of Reality: A Treatise in the Sociology of Knowledge*. Garden City, N.Y.: Doubleday, 1967.

Berlin, Isaiah. "Conversations with Akhamatova and Pasternak", *New York Review of Books*. Nov. 20, 1980: 25–33.

Blum, Alan. "Lower Class Negro Television Spectators: The Concept of Pseudo Jovial Skepticism," in *Blue Collar*. Edited by Arthur Shostak and William Gomberg. Englewood Cliffs, N.J.: Prentice-Hall, 1964.

Blum, Alan F. *Socrates: The Original and Its Images*. Chicago: University of Chicago Press, 1974.

Booth, Wayne. *A Rhetoric of Irony*. Chicago: University of Chicago Press, 1974.

Bowles, Samuel, and Herbert Gintis. *Democracy and Capitalism, Property, Community, and the Contradictions of Modern Social Thought*. New York: Basic Books, 1986.

———. *Schooling in Capitalist America: Educational Reform and the Contradictions of Economic Life*. New York: Basic Books, 1976.

Bradley, Jeff. "Millions Starved After Mao's 'Great Leap'," *Buffalo News*, Sept. 30, 1984.

Braverman, Harry. *Labor and Monopoly Capital: The Degradation of Work in the Twentieth Century*. New York: Monthly Review Press, 1974.

Brown, Edward J. "The Year of Acquiescence," in *Literature and Revolution in Soviet Russia 1917–62*. Edited by Max Hayward and Leo Labedz. London: Oxford University Press, 1963.

Bruner, Jerome S. *Actual Minds, Possible Worlds.* Cambridge, Mass.: Harvard University Press, 1986.

―――. *On Knowing: Essays for the Left Hand.* Cambridge, Mass.: Harvard University Press, 1966.

―――. "Social Psychology and Perception," in *Readings in Social Psychology*, pp. 85–94. Edited by Eleanor E. Maccoby, Theodore M. Newcomb, and Eugene I. Hartley. New York: Holt, Rinehart and Winston, 1958.

Buhler, Curt. *The Fifteenth Century Book, the Scribes, the Printers, the Decorators.* Philadelphia: University of Pennsylvania Press, 1960.

Burawoy, Michael. *Manufacturing Consent: Changes in the Labor Process Under Monopoly Capitalism.* Chicago: University of Chicago Press, 1979.

Burckhardt, Jacob. *The Civilization of the Renaissance in Italy* (1860). New York: New American Library, 1961.

Burke, Kenneth. A Grammar of Motives [1945] AND A Rhetoric of Motives [1950]. Cleveland: Meridian, 1962.

―――. "Interaction: dramatism," in *International Encyclopaedia of the Social Sciences*, Vol. 7, pp. 445–52. Edited by David L. Sills. New York: Macmillan and Free Press, 1968.

Burke, Redmond. *What is the Index?* Milwaukee: Bruce, 1952.

Burnyeat, M. F. "Sphinx Without a Secret: Studies in Platonic Philosophy," *New York Review of Books* (May 30, 1985): 30–36.

Bury, J. B. *A History of Freedom of Thought.* London: Oxford University Press, 1913.

Butler, Peirce. *The Origin of Printing in Modern Europe.* Chicago: University of Chicago Press, 1940.

Camus, Albert. *The Myth of Sisyphus.* New York: Random House, 1955.

Cater, Douglas. *The Fourth Branch of Government.* New York: Vintage, 1965.

Cheever, John. *Falconer.* New York: Knopf, 1977.

Childe, V. Gordon. *Man Makes Himself.* New York: New American Library, 1951.

Chomsky, Noam. *Reflections on Language.* New York: Pantheon, 1979.

Clifford, James, and George E. Marcus. *Writing Culture: The Poetics and Politics of Ethnography.* Berkeley: University of California Press, 1986.

Cochran, Thomas, and William Miller. *The Age of Enterprise.* New York: Macmillan, 1942.

Cockburn, Alexander. "Can Capitalism Be Saved? A Chat with Sweezy and Magdoff," *The Nation*, June 9, 1984.

Cohen, Stanley, and Jock Young (Editors). *The Manufacture of News: Social Problems, Deviance and the Mass Media.* London: Constable, 1973.

Darnton, Robert. *The Business of Enlightenment: A Publishing History of the Enlightenment 1775–1800.* Cambridge, Mass.: Harvard University Press, 1979.

——. "The Encyclopédie Wars of Revolutionary France," *American Historical Review* 78 (1973): 1331–52.

——. "The High Enlightenment and Low Life of Literature," *Past and Present* 51 (1971): 81–115.

Degler, Carl. *At Odds: Women and Family in America from the Revolution to the Present.* New York: Oxford University Press, 1980.

De Grazia, Edward, and Roger K. Newman. *Banned Films: Movies, Censors and the First Amendment.* New York: Bowker, 1982.

Demac, Donna A. *Keeping America Uninformed: Government Secrecy in the 1980's.* New York: Pilgrim Press, 1984.

Derrida, Jacques. *Of Grammatology.* Baltimore: John Hopkins University Press, 1976.

Didion, Joan. *The White Album.* New York: Simon and Schuster, 1979.

Dodds, E. P. *The Greeks and the Irrational.* Berkeley: University of California Press, 1968.

Domhoff, William. *The Bohemian Grove and Other Retreats: A Study in Ruling Class Cohesiveness.* Magnolia, Mass.: Peter Smith, 1975.

——. *The Higher Circles: The Governing Class in America.* New York: Random House, 1971.

——. *The Powers That Be.* New York: Vintage, 1979.

——. *Who Rules America?* Englewood Cliffs, N.J.: Prentice-Hall, 1967.

Donaghue, Hugh P. "Transborder Data Flows: New Management Tool." Paper presented at Conference on *World Communications: Decisions for the Eighties.* The Annenberg School of Communications. Philadelphia, May 12–14, 1980.

Douglas, Mary. *Implicit Meanings: Essays in Anthropology.* London: Routledge and Kegan Paul, 1975.

——. *Purity and Danger: An Analysis of Concepts of Pollution and Taboo.* London: Routledge and Kegan Paul, 1966.

——. *Rules and Meanings: The Anthropology of Everyday Knowledge.* A Selection of Readings. Middlesex, Eng.: Penguin Books, 1973.

Dreitzel, Hans (Editor). *Recent Sociology* 2. New York: Simon Schuster, 1957.

Durkheim, Emile. *The Division of Labor in Society.* Glencoe: Free Press, 1947.

——. *The Elementary Forms of the Religious Life.* Glencoe: Free Press, 1947.

——, with Marcel Mauss. *Primitive Classification.* Chicago: University of Chicago Press, 1963.

Edelman, Murray. *Political Language: Words That Succeed and Policies That Fail.* New York: Academic Press, 1977.

Edsall, Thomas Byrne. *The New Politics of Inequality.* New York: W. W. Norton, 1984.

Eggers, David. "Review of *Mausoleum* by Hans Magnus Enzensberger. *Telos* 34 (Winter 1977–78): 203.

Ehrenreich, Barbara, and Annette Fuentes. "Life on the Global Assembly Line," in *Crisis in American Institutions* (5th ed.). Edited by Jerome H. Skolnick and Elliott Currie. Boston: Little, Brown, 1976.

Eisenstein, Elizabeth L. *The Printing Press as an Agent of Change: Communications and Cultural Transformations in Early Modern Europe.* 2 vols. Cambridge: University Press, 1979.

Eliot, T. S. *Notes Toward the Definition of Culture.* New York: Harcourt, Brace, 1949.

Elliott, Philip. "Intellectuals, the 'Information Society' and The Disappearance of the Public Sphere," *Mass Communication Review Yearbook,* Vol. 4. Edited by Ellen Wartella, D. Charles Whitney, and Swen Windahl. Beverly Hills: Sage, 1983.

Enzensberger, Hans Magnus. *The Consciousness Industry: On Literature, Politics and the Media.* New York: Seabury, 1974.

———. *Politics and Crime.* New York: Seabury, 1974.

Erasmus, Desiderius. *The Praise of Folly* (1509). Roslyn, N.Y.: Walter J. Black, 1942.

Ernst, Morris L., and William Seagle. *To Be Pure . . . A Study of Obscenity and the Censor.* New York: Viking, 1928.

Ewen, Stuart. *Captains of Consciousness: Advertising and the Social Roots of the Consumer Culture.* New York: McGraw-Hill, 1976.

Ewing, David W. *Freedom Inside the Organization: Bringing Civil Liberties to the Workplace.* New York: E. P. Dutton, 1977.

Falk, Richard. Foreword to Michael T. Klare and Cynthia Arnson, *Supplying Repression: U.S. Support for Authoritarian Regimes Abroad.* Washington: Institute for Policy Studies, 1981.

Fiedler, Leslie. "Giving the Devil His Due," *Journal of Popular Culture XII,* 2 (Fall 1979): 197–207.

Foner, Philip S. *History of the Labor Movement in the United States,* Vol. 1. New York: International Publishers, 1947.

Foucault, Michel. *The Archaeology of Knowledge and the Discourse on Language.* New York: Harper Colophon Books, 1972.

———. *Discipline and Punish: The Birth of the Prison.* New York: Pantheon, 1977.

Franklin, Benjamin. *Apology for Printers* (1730). New York: Privately Printed, 1967.

———. "The Way to Wealth," in *The Autobiography and Other Writings.* New York: Bantam Books, 1982, pp. 186–87.

Fraser, Andrew. "The Corporation as a Body Politic," *Telos* 57 (Fall 1983): 5–40.

Freiberg, J. W. *The French Press: Class, State and Ideology.* New York: Praeger, 1981.

Friedberg, Maurice. "Literary Output: 1956–1962," in *Soviet Literature in the Sixties: An International Symposium*, pp. 150–77. Edited by Max Hayward and Edward L. Crowley. New York: Praeger, 1964.

──────. "Soviet Books, Censors and Readers," in *Literature and Revolution in Soviet Russia 1917–62*, pp. 198–210. Edited by Max Hayward and Leo Labedz. London: Oxford University Press, 1963.

Friere, Paulo. *Education for Critical Consciousness*. New York: Seabury, 1973.

──────. *Pedagogy of the Oppressed*. New York: Seabury, 1970.

Gadamer, Hans-Georg. *Philosophical Hermeneutics*. Berkeley: University of California Press, 1976.

──────. *Truth and Method*. New York: Seabury, 1975.

Galbraith, John Kenneth. *The New Industrial State*. Boston: Houghton Mifflin, 1978.

Gans, Herbert. *Popular Culture and High Culture*. New York: Basic Books, 1974.

Gelwick, Richard. *The Way of Discovery: An Introduction to the Thought of Michael Polanyi*. New York: Oxford University Press, 1977.

Genovese, Eugene. "Might and Right," A Review of *Authority* by Richard Sennett. *New York Times Book Review*. July 13, 1980.

Gerbner, George. "Institutional Pressures upon Mass Communicators," *Sociological Review Monograph* 13 (Jan. 1969): 231–38.

──────. "On Content Analysis and Critical Research in Mass Communication," in *People, Society and Mass Communications*. Edited by L. A. Dexter and D. M. White. New York: Free Press, 1964.

──────. "Television: The New State Religion?" *ETC* (June 1977): 145–50.

──────, with Larry Gross. "Living with Television: The Violence Profile", *Journal of Communication* 26,2 (1976): 173–99.

Gerstenmaier, Cornelia. *The Voices of the Silent*. New York: Hart Publishing Company, 1972.

Gerth, H. H., and C. Wright Mills (Editors). *From Max Weber*. New York: Oxford University Press, 1949.

Gide, André. *Afterthoughts on the USSR*. New York: Dial, 1938.

──────. *Return from the USSR*. New York: Knopf, 1937.

Gitlin, Todd. *The Whole World is Watching*. Berkeley: University of California Press, 1980.

Glasgow Media Group. *Bad News*. London: Routledge and Kegan Paul, 1976.

Goldmann, Lucien. *The Philosophy of the Enlightenment: The Christian Burgess and the Enlightenment*. Cambridge, Mass.: MIT Press, 1968.

Goldsen, Rose K. *The Show and Tell Machine*. New York: Dell, 1975.

Gordon, Douglas H., and Norman L. Torrey. *The Censoring of Diderot's Encyclopédie and the Re-established Text*. New York: Columbia University Press, 1947.

Gordon, George N. *Erotic Communications: Studies in Sex, Sin and Censorship*. New York: Hastings House, 1980.

Gorky, Maxim. "Soviet Literature," in *Soviet Writers' Congress 1934*, London: Lawrence and Wishart, 1977.

———. *Untimely Thoughts: Essays on Revolution, Culture and the Bolsheviks 1917–1918*. New York: Paul S. Eriksson, 1968.

Gouldner, Alvin. *The Dialectic of Ideology and Technology*. New York: Seabury Press, 1976.

———. *Patterns of Industrial Bureaucracy*. New York: Free Press, 1954.

———. *The Two Marxisms*. New York: Seabury, 1980.

———. "Romanticism and Classicism: Deep Structures in Social Science," in *For Sociology*. New York: Basic Books, 1973.

Grendler, Paul F. *The Roman Inquisition and the Venetian Press, 1540–1605*. Princeton: Princeton University Press, 1977.

Grene, Marjorie (Editor). *Knowing and Being*. Chicago: University of Chicago Press, 1969.

Griffith, William. *Communist Esoteric Communication: Explication de Texte*. Boston: MIT Center for International Studies, 1967.

Gross, Llewellyn Z. (Editor). *Symposium on Sociological Theory*. New York: Harper and Row, 1959.

———. "Where Is Social Reality?," *Sociological Inquiry* XXXIII, 1 (Winter 1963): 3–8.

Habermas, Jurgen. "The Genealogical Writings of History. Some Aprorias in Foucault's Theory of Power," *Canadian Journal of Political and Social Theory / Revue Canadienne de Théorie Politique et Sociale* X, 1–2 (1986): 1–9.

———. *Knowledge and Human Interests*. Boston: Beacon, 1971.

———. *Legitimation Crisis*. Boston: Beacon, 1975.

———. "Towards a Theory of Communicative Behavior," in *Recent Sociology 2: Patterns of Communicative Behavior*, pp. 114–48. Edited by Hans P. Dreitzel. New York: Macmillan, 1970.

———. "Why More Philosophy?" *Social Research* 38, 4 (1971).

Hachten, William A. *The World News Prism: Changing Media, Changing Ideologies*. Ames: Iowa State University Press, 1981.

Hall, Stuart, and Tony Jefferson. *Resistance Through Rituals*. London: Hutchinson and the Centre for Contemporary Cultural Studies, 1976.

Hamelink, Cees J. "An Alternative to News," *Journal of Communication* (Autumn 1976): 120–23.

———. *The Corporate Village: The Role of Transnational Corporations in International Communications*. Rome: IDOC International, 1977.

———. *Cultural Autonomy in Global Communications*. New York: Longman, 1983.

Hammarskjold, Dag. *Markings*. New York: Knopf, 1964.

Hanson, Norwood. *Patterns of Discovery*. Cambridge, Mass.: Cambridge University Press, 1965.

Haraway, Donna. "A Manifesto for Cyborgs: Science, Technology, and Socialist Feminism in the 1980's," *Socialist Review* 80, 2 (March-April 1985): 65–107.

Haye, Yves de la. Introduction to *Marx and Engels on the Means of Communication*. New York: International General, 1980.

Hayman, Ronald. *Nietzsche: A Critical Life*. New York: Penguin, 1980.

Hayward, Max. "Conflict and Change in Soviet Literature," in *Literature and Revolution in Soviet Russia 1917–62*. Edited by Max Hayward and Leo Labedz. London: Oxford University Press, 1963.

———. Introduction to *Literature and Revolution in Soviet Russia 1917–62*. Edited by Max Hayward and Leo Labedz. London: Oxford University Press, 1983.

———. "Pilnyak and Zamyatin: Two Tragedies of the Twenties," *Survey* 36 (1961): 85–91.

Hazlitt, William. *The Table Talk of Martin Luther* (1821). New York: E. P. Dutton, 1930.

Heidegger, Martin. *Being and Time*. New York: Harper and Row, 1962.

Heilbroner, Richard. *An Inquiry into the Human Prospect*. New York: W. W. Norton, 1974.

Heller, Michael. "Is There Such a Thing as Dissident Literature?," *Survey* 23,4 (1977–78): 64–85.

———. "Stalin and the Detectives," *Survey* 22, 1–2 (1976): 160–75.

Hopkins, Charles E. *The Share of Thomas Aquinas in the Growth of the Witchcraft Delusion*. Philadelphia: University of Pennsylvania Press, 1940.

Horkheimer, Max. *Eclipse of Reason* (1947). New York: Seabury, 1974.

——— and Theodor W. Adorno. *Dialectics of Enlightenment*. New York: Herder and Herder, 1972.

Horowitz, Irving L. *Taking Lives: Genocide and State Power*. New Brunswick, N.J.: Transaction Books, 1982.

Hughes, Helen MacGill. *The Human Interest Story*. Chicago: University of Chicago Press, 1940.

Humboldt, Wilhelm von. *Linguistic Variability and Intellectual Development*. Philadelphia: University of Pennsylvania Press, 1971.

Inquisitors-General. "The Condemnation and Recantation of Galileo," in *Versions of Censorship: An Anthology*. Edited by John McCormick and Mairi MacInnes. Chicago: Aldine, 1962.

Jacobs, Norman (Editor). *Culture for the Millions*. Princeton, N.J.: Van Nostrand, 1961.

Jaeger, Werner. *Paideia: The Ideals of Greek Culture*, Vol. 2. New York: Oxford University Press, 1943.

Jansen, Sue Curry. "Power and Knowledge: Toward a New Critical Synthesis," *Journal of Communication* 33,3 (Summer 1983): 342–54.

Jefferson, Thomas. *The Complete Jefferson*. Edited by Saul K. Padover. New York: Duell, Sloan, and Pearce, 1943.

Jhally, Sut, Stephen Kline, and William Leiss. "Magic in the Marketplace: An Empirical Test for Commodity Fetishism," *Canadian Journal of Political and Social Theory/Canadienne de Théorie Politique et Sociale* IX, 3 (Fall) 1985: 1–23.

Katz, Michael. *Class, Bureaucracy, and Schools*. New York: Praeger, 1971.

Kaufer, David S. "Ironic Evaluations," *Communication Monographs* 48 (1981): 25–38.

Keller, Bill. "The Resistance to Gorbachev," *New York Times*, Jan. 30, 1987.

Keller, Evelyn Fox. *Reflections on Gender and Science*. New Haven: Yale University Press, 1985.

Kennedy, Emmet. *A Philosopher in the Age of Revolution*. Philadephia: American Philosophical Society, 1978.

Kenyon, Frederic. *Books and Readers in Ancient Greece and Rome*. Oxford: Clarendon Press, 1932.

Kieckhefer, Richard. *European Witch Trials: Their Foundations in Popular and Learned Culture, 1300–1500*. Berkeley: University of California Press, 1976.

Klare, Michael T. *War Without End*. New York: Knopf, 1972.

———, with Cynthia Arnson. *Supplying Repression: U.S. Support for Authoritarian Regimes Abroad*. Washington: Institute for Policy Studies, 1981.

Knorr, Karin D., A. Krohn, and R. Whitley (Editors). *The Social Process of Scientific Discoveries*. New York: Cambridge University Press, 1981.

Knorr-Cetina, Karin D. *The Manufacture of Knowledge: An Essay on the Constructivist and Contextual Nature of Science*. New York: Pergamon, 1981.

Koestler, Arthur. *The Sleepwalkers: A History of Man's Changing Vision of the Universe*. New York: Macmillan, 1968.

Kolko, Gabriel. *The Triumph of Conservatism: A Reinterpretation of American History, 1900–1916*. New York: Free Press, 1963.

Kors, Alan C., and Edward Peters. Introduction to *Witchcraft in Europe 1100–1700: A Documentary History*. Philadelphia: University of Pennsylvania Press, 1972.

Kostelanetz, Richard. *Literary Politics in America: The End of Intelligent Writing*. New York: Sheed and Ward, 1973.

Kramer, Heinrich, and Jacob Sprenger. "Malleus Maleficarum" (1484), in *Witchcraft in Europe 1100–1700: A Documentary History*. Edited by Alan C. Kors and Edward Peters. Philadelphia: University of Pennsylvania Press, 1972.

Kroker, Arthur. "Television and the Triumph of Culture: Three Theses," *Canadian Journal of Political and Social Theory/Revue Canadienne de Théorie Politique et Sociale* IX, 3 (Fall 1985): 37–47.

———, with Marilouise Kroker. "The Phallocentric Mood: Bored but Hyper," *Canadian Journal of Political and Social Theory/Revue Canadienne de Théorie Politique et Sociale* IX, 1–2 (1985): 5.

Kuhn, Thomas S. *The Structure of Scientific Revolutions.* Chicago: University of Chicago Press, 1970.

Kuper, Leo. *Genocide: Its Political Use in the Twentieth Century.* New Haven: Yale University Press, 1982.

Labedz, Leopold. *Revisionism: Essays on the History of Marxist Ideas.* Plainview, N.Y.: Books for Libraries Press, 1974.

Lakshin, Vladimir. *Solzhenitsyn, Tvarsovsky, and Novy Mir.* Cambridge, Mass.: MIT Press, 1980.

Langer, William. *An Encyclopedia of World History.* Boston: Houghton Mifflin, 1940.

Laqueur, Walter, and Leopold Labedz (Editors). *Polycentrism: The New Factor in International Communism.* New York: Praeger, 1962.

Lasch, Christopher. *The Minimal Self.* New York: W. W. Norton, 1984.

Latour, Bruno, and R. Whitley (Editors). *Laboratory Life: The Social Construction of Scientific Facts.* Beverly Hills: Sage, 1979.

Lea, Henry. *A History of the Inquisition of Spain*, Vol. 1. New York: Macmillan, 1906.

———. *A History of the Inquisition of the Middle Ages*, 3 vols. New York: Harper and Brothers, 1888.

Lefebvre, Henri. *The Sociology of Marx.* New York: Pantheon, 1968.

Leghorn, Lisa, and Katherine Parker. *Woman's Worth.* Boston: Routledge and Kegan Paul, 1981.

Leiss, William, Stephen Kline, and Sut Jhally. *Social Communication in Advertising.* Toronto: Methuen, 1986.

Lenin, V. I. "The Character of Our Newspapers" (1918–19), in *Collected Works*, Vol. 23. New York: International Publishers, 1945.

———. *Materialism and Empirico-Criticism.* Peking: Foreign Language Press, 1972.

———. "Party Organization and Party Literature" (1905), in *Collected Works*, Vol. 10. Moscow: Foreign Language Publishing House, 1961.

———. "What Is To Be Done?" (1902), in *Collected Works*, Vol. 5. Moscow: Foreign Language Publishing House, 1961.

Levy, Leonard. *Legacy of Suppression: Freedom of Speech and Press in Early American History.* Cambridge: Harvard University Press, 1960.

Lewis, Felice Flannery. *Literature, Obscenity and Law.* Carbondale: Southern Illinois University Press, 1976.

Lipper, Mark. "Benjamin Franklin's 'Silence Dogood' as an Eighteenth Century 'Censor Morum'," pp. 73–83 in *Newsletters to Newspapers: Eighteenth-Century Journalism.* Edited by Donovan H. Bond and

W. Reynolds McLeod. West Virginia University School of Journalism, 1977.

Lipsey, Robert E., and Irving B. Kravis, "Sorting Out the Trade Problem: Business Holds Its Own as America Slips," *New York Times*, Jan. 18, 1987.

Lukacs, Georg. *History and Class Consciousness*. Cambridge, Mass.: MIT Press, 1971.

————. *Solzhenitsyn*. Cambridge, Mass.: MIT Press, 1969.

Mandelstam, Nadezhda. *Hope Abandoned*. New York: Atheneum, 1974.

Marcuse, Herbert. *The Aesthetic Dimension: Toward a Critique of Marxist Aesthetics*. Boston: Beacon, 1978.

Marvin, Carolyn. "Space, Time, and Captive Communications History," pp. 7–19 in *Communications in Transition: Issues and Debates in Current Research*. Edited by Mary S. Mander. New York: Praeger, 1983.

Marx, Karl. *On Freedom of the Press and Censorship*, Karl Marx Library, Vol. 4. Edited by Saul K. Padover. New York: McGraw-Hill Book Company, 1974.

————, with Frederick Engels. *The German Ideology*. New York: International Publishers, 1970.

————. *Literature and Art: Selections from Their Writings*. New York: International Publishers, 1974.

————. "Manifesto of the Communist Party," in *Basic Writings on Politics and Philosophy*. Edited by Lewis S. Feuer. Garden City, N.Y.: Anchor Books, 1959.

————. *Selected Correspondence*. Moscow: Foreign Press, 1956.

Matich, Olga. "Unofficial Russian Fiction and Its Politics," *Humanities in Society* 7, 3–4 (Summer-Fall 1984): 109–22.

Mattalart, Armand. *Mass Media, Ideologies and the Revolutionary Movement*. Atlantic Highlands, N.J.: Humanities Press, 1980.

McCabe, Joseph. *The History and Meaning of the Catholic Index of Forbidden Books*. Girard, Kansas: Haldeman-Julius Company, 1931.

McCormick, John, and Mairi MacInnes. *Versions and Censorship: An Anthology*. Chicago: Aldine, 1962.

McElvaine, Robert S. "Workers in Fiction: Locked Out," *New York Times Book Review*. Sept. 1, 1985.

McLellan, David. *Marx Before Marxism*. New York: Harper and Row, 1970.

McLuhan, Marshall. *The Gutenberg Galaxy: The Making of Typographical Man*. Toronto: University of Toronto Press, 1962.

Mead, George Herbert. *Mind, Self and Society*. Chicago: University of Chicago Press, 1934.

Medawar, P. B. *The Art of the Soluble*. London: Methuen, 1967.

Merrill, John C. *Global Journalism: A Survey of the World's Mass Media*. New York: Longman, 1983.

Miliband, Ralph. *The State in Capitalist Society: An Analysis of the Western System of Power.* New York: Basic Books, 1969.

Miller, George. *Psychology of Communication: Seven Essays.* New York: Basic Books, 1967.

Miller, James. "Information Input Overload and Psychopathology," *American Journal of Psychiatry* 116 (Feb. 1960): 695–704.

Miller, Jonathan. *Censorship and the Limits of Permission.* London: Oxford University Press, 1962.

Mills, C. Wright. *The Power Elite.* New York: Oxford University Press, 1956.

––––––. *White Collar.* New York: Oxford University Press, 1951.

Morgan, Robin. *Going Too Far.* New York: Random House, 1977.

Morley, John. *Diderot and the Encyclopaedists,* Vol. 1. London: Chapman and Hall, 1898.

Morrison, Ken. "Some Properties of 'Telling Order Designs' in Dialectical Inquiry," *Philosophy of the Social Sciences* 11 (1981): 245–62.

Nietzsche, Friedrich. *The Gay Science.* New York: Vintage Books, 1974.

Morris-Suzuki, Tessa. "Capitalism in the Computer Age," *New Left Review* 160 (Nov./-Dec. 1986): 81–91.

Nikitenko, Aleksandr. *The Diary of a Russian Censor.* Amherst: University of Massachusetts Press, 1975.

Nobel, David. *America by Design: Science, Technology, and the Rise of Corporate Capitalism.* Oxford: Oxford University Press, 1977.

Oboler, Eli M. *The Fear of the Word: Censorship and Sex.* Metuchen, N.J.: Scarecrow Press, 1974.

O'Brien, John. *The Inquisition.* New York: Macmillan, 1973.

O'Neill, John. "The Literary Production of Natural and Social Science Inquiry: Issues and Applications in the Social Organization of Science," *Canadian Journal of Sociology* 6 (1981): 105–20.

Olsen, Tillie. *Silences.* New York: Delacorte Press, 1978.

Ong, Walter J. *Orality and Literacy.* Boston: Metheun, 1982.

Ould, Herman (Editor). *Freedom of Expression. A Symposium . . . To Commemorate the Tercentenary of the Publication of Milton's Areopagitica.* London: Tercentenary Committee, 1944.

Pagels, Elaine. *The Gnostic Gospel.* New York: Random House, 1979.

Park, Robert E. *The Immigrant Press and Its Control.* New York: Harper and Brothers, 1922.

Pepper, Stephen. *World Hypotheses.* Berkeley: University of California Press, 1970.

Perrow, Charles. *Organizational Analysis: A Sociological View.* Monterey: Brooks-Cole, 1970.

Piepe, Anthony, Sunny Crouch, and Miles Emerson. *Mass Media and Cultural Relationships.* Westmead: Saxon House, 1979.

Plekhanov, G. V. *Art and Society and Other Papers in Historical Materialism.* New York: Oriole Editions, 1974.

Pocock, J. G. *Politics, Language, and Time: Essays on Political Thought and History.* New York: Atheneum, 1971.

Polanyi, Michael. *Personal Knowledge.* Chicago: University of Chicago Press, 1958.

———. "Republic of Science: Its Political and Economic Theory", *Minerva* 1 (Aug. 1962): 64–73.

———. *The Study of Man.* Chicago: University of Chicago Press, 1963.

Pollner, Melvin. "The Very Coinage of Your Brain: The Anatomy of Reality Disjunctures," *Philosophy of Social Sciences* 5 (1975): 411–30.

Poster, Mark. *Foucault, Marxism and History.* Cambridge: Polity Press, 1985.

Pottinger, David. *The French Book Trade in the Ancien Régime 1500–1791.* Cambridge, Mass.: Harvard University Press, 1958.

Putnam, G. H. *Authors and the Public in Ancient Times* (1896). New York: Cooper Square Publishers, 1967 (1896).

———. *The Censorship of the Church of Rome and Its Influence Upon the Production and Distribution of Literature* (1906). 2 vols. New York: Benjamin, 1967.

———. "History of Censorship," in *Selected Articles on Censorship of Speech and the Press*, pp. 17–28. Edited by Lamar T. Beman. New York: H. H. Wilson, 1930.

Raboy, Marc. *Movements and Messages: Media and Radical Politics in Quebec.* Toronto: Between the Lines, 1983.

Radek, Karl. "Contemporary World Literature and the Tasks of Proletarian Art," in *Soviet Writers Congress 1934* by Maxim Gorky et al. London: Lawrence and Wishart, 1977.

Rhode, Eric. "Outline of a Couch." Review of *Bergasee 19: Sigmund Freud's Home and Offices. Vienna 1938* by Edmund Engleman, and of *Sigmund Freud: His Life in Pictures and Words* by Ernst Freud, Lucy Freud, and Ilse Grubrich-Simites, *Times Literary Supplement* (London), Nov. 24, 1978: 1355.

Ricoeur, Paul. *Freud and Philosophy: Essay on Interpretation.* New Haven: Yale University Press, 1970.

Robins, Kevin, and Frank Webster. *Information Technology: A Luddite Analysis.* Norwood, N.J.: Ablex, 1986.

———. "Information Technology, Luddism, and the Working Class," in *The Critical Communication Review*, Vol. 1: *The Working Class and the Media.* Edited by Vincent Mosco and Janet Wasko. Norwood, N.J.: Ablex, 1983.

Rodway, Alan. "Terms for Comedy," *Renaissance and Modern Studies 4* (1962): 113.

Rorty, Richard. *Philosophy and the Mirror of Nature.* Princeton: Princeton University Press, 1979.

Rosenberg, Bernard, and David M. White (Editors). *Mass Culture: The Popular Arts in America.* Glencoe: Free Press, 1957.

Rossiter, Clinton. *Seedtime of the Republic.* New York: Harcourt, Brace and World, 1953.

Rubin, Bernard. Editor. *Small Voicers and Great Trumpets: Minorities and the Media.* New York: Praeger, 1980.

Rush, Myron. "Esoteric Communication in Soviet Politics," *World Politics* 11, 4 (1959): 614–20.

Russ, Joanna. *The Female Man.* Boston: Gregg, 1975.

Ryan, Jake, and Charles Sackrey, *Strangers in Paradise: Academics from the Working Class.* Boston: South End Press, 1984.

Sartre, Jean-Paul. *Between Existentialism and Marxism.* New York: Pantheon, 1975.

Sawyer, Charles. "Letter from Poland: Beating the Censor," *New York Times Book Review*, Oct. 5, 1980.

Schiller, Anita R., and Herbert I. Schiller. "Commercializing Information," *The Nation*, Oct. 4, 1986: 306–9.

———. "Who Can Own What America Knows?", *The Nation*, April 17, 1982: 461–64.

Schiller, Herbert I. Foreword to *Cultural Autonomy in Global Communications* by Cees J. Hamelink. New York: Longman, 1983.

———. *Who Knows: Information in the Age of the Fortune 500.* Norwood, N.J.: Ablex, 1981.

Schlesinger, Arthur M. *Prelude to Independence: The Newspaper War on Britain 1764–1776.* New York: Knopf, 1957.

Schreiber, Elliot. "The Rise and Fall of the Soviet Underground Press," *Communication Quarterly* 26, 3 (1978): 32–39.

Schudson, Michael. *Discovering the News.* New York: Basic Books, 1978.

Shcherbina, Vladimir. *Lenin and Problems of Literature.* Moscow: Progress Publishers, 1974.

Seagle, William. *Cato or the Future of Censorship.* London: Kegan, Paul, Trench, Trubner, 1930.

Sennet, Richard. *Authority.* New York: Knopf, 1980.

———. "Our Hearts Belong to Daddy," *New York Review of Books*, May 1, 1980.

Simmel, Georg. "The Stranger," in *The Sociology of Georg Simmel.* Edited by Kurt H. Wolff. Glencoe: Free Press, 1964.

Sinyavsky, Andrei. " 'I' and 'They': An Essay on Extreme Forms of Communication Under Conditions of Human Isolation," *Survey* 22, 3–4 (1976): 278–87.

———. "The Literary Process in Russia," *Kontinent* I, Garden City, N.Y.: Anchor Press, 1976.

——— (Abram Tertz, pseud.). *On Socialist Realism.* New York: Random House, 1960.

————. "Samizdat and the Rebirth of Literature", *Index on Censorship* 9,4 (Aug. 1980): 8–13.

Slack, Jennifer Daryl. "Media and the Americanization of Workers: The Americanization Bulletin, 1918–1919," in *The Critical Communications Review*, Vol. 1: *Labor, The Working Class, and the Media*. Edited by Vincent Mosco and Janet Wasko. Norwood, N.J.: Ablex, 1983.

Smith, Adam. *The Wealth of Nations*. New York: Modern Library, 1937 (1776).

Smythe, Dallas W. *Dependency Road: Communications, Capitalism, Consciousness, and Canada*. Norwood, N.J.: Ablex, 1981.

————. "Needs Before Tools? The Illusions of Electronic Democracy." Paper presented at the International Communication Association, Honolulu, May 1985.

Solzhenitsyn, Aleksandr. *The Gulag Archipelago*. 3 vols. New York: Harper and Row, 1978.

————. *The Oak and the Calf: Sketches of Literary Life in the Soviet Union*. New York: Harper and Row, 1980.

Spechler, Dina. "Permitted Dissent after Stalin: Criticism and Protest in *Novy Mir*, 1955–1964," in *The Dynamics of Soviet Politics*, pp. 28–50. Edited by Paul Cocks, et al. Cambridge, Mass.: Harvard University Press, 1976.

Speier, Hans. "The Communication of Hidden Meaning," *Social Research* 44 (Autumn 1977): 471–501.

Starr, Paul. *The Social Transformation of American Medicine*. New York: Basic Books, 1982.

Steiner, George. *After Babel: Aspects of Language and Translation*. New York: Oxford University Press, 1975.

————. *Language and Silence: Essays on Language, Literature and the Inhuman*. New York: Atheneum, 1976.

Stepniak (pseud.). *Russia Under the Tzars*. New York: Charles Scribner's Sons, 1885.

Stern, J. P. "Karl Kraus and the Idea of Literature," *Encounter* 45 (Aug. 1975): 42.

Stetsky, A. I. "Under the Flag of the Soviets, Under the Flag of Socialism," in *Soviet Writers Congress 1934* by Maxim Gorky et al. London: Lawrence and Wishart, 1977.

Strauss, Leo. *Persecution and the Art of Writing*. Glencoe: Free Press, 1952.

Struve, Gleb. "The Transition from Russian to Soviet Literature," in *Literature and Revolution in Soviet Russia 1917–62*. Edited by Max Hayward and Leo Labedz. London: Oxford University Press, 1963.

Supreme Sacred Congregation of the Holy Office. "Condemnation of the Works of André Gide," in *Gide: A Collection of Critical Essays*.

Edited by David Littlejohn. Englewood Cliffs, N.J.: Prentice-Hall, 1970.

Swayze, Harold. *Political Control of Literature in the USSR, 1946–1959.* Cambridge, Mass.: Harvard University Press, 1962.

Tertz, Abram. (pseud.). See Sinyavsky, Andrei.

Thomas, Donald. *A Long Time Burning: The History of Literary Censorship in England.* New York: Praeger, 1969.

Thompson, E. P. "Time, Work-Discipline, and Industrial Capitalism," *Past and Present* 38 (Dec. 1967): 59–97.

Tocqueville, Alexis de. *Democracy in America* (1835). New York: Doubleday, 1969.

Todorov, Tzvetan. *Mikhail Bakhtin: The Dialogical Principle.* Minneapolis: University of Minnesota Press, 1984.

Toulmin, Stephen. *The Uses of Argument.* Cambridge: Cambridge University Press, 1958.

Trevor-Roper, H. R. *The European Witch-Craze of the Sixteenth and Seventeenth Centuries.* New York: Harper and Row, 1969.

Tunstall, Jeremy. *The Media Are American: Anglo-American Media in the World.* New York: Columbia University Press, 1977.

U.S. Commission on Civil Rights. *Window Dressing on the Set: Women and Minorities in Television.* Washington: U.S. Comission on Civil Rights, 1977.

Utis, O. "Generalissimo Stalin and the Art of Government," *Foreign Affairs* 30 (1952): 197–214.

Veblen, Thorstein. *The Higher Learning in America.* New York: B. W. Huebsch, 1918.

———. *The Theory of the Leisure Class.* New York: Kelley, 1899.

Wade, Ira O. *The Clandestine Organization and Diffusion of Philosophic Ideals in France from 1700–1750.* Princeton: Princeton University Press, 1938.

———. *The Intellectual Origins of the French Enlightenment.* Princeton: Princeton University Press, 1971.

Wasko, Janet. *Movies and Money: Financing the American Film Industry.* Norwood, N.J.: Ablex, 1982.

Wallerstein, Immanual. "The Future of the World-Economy," in *Processes of the World System.* Edited by Terence K. Hopkins and Wallerstein. Beverly Hills: Sage, 1980.

Weaver, Richard. *The Ethics of Rhetoric.* Chicago: Regnery, 1970.

Weber, Max. "The Chinese Literati" and "Politics as a Vocation," in *From Max Weber: Essays in Sociology.* Edited by H. H. Gerth and C. Wright Mills. New York: A Galaxy Book, 1958.

Whale, R. F. *Copyright: Evolution, Theory and Practice.* Totowa, N.J.: Rowman and Littlefield, 1972.

Williams, Frederick. *The Communications Revolution*. Beverly Hills: Sage, 1982.

Wolff, Kurt H. "The Sociology of Knowledge and Sociological Theory," in *Symposium on Sociological Theory*. Edited by Llewellyn Z. Gross. New York: Harper and Row, 1959.

Woolgar, Steve. "Discovery: Logic and Sequence in a Scientific Text," in *The Social Processes of Scientific Investigation*. Edited by Karin Knorr et al. Beverly Hills: Sage, 1979.

Zolla, Elemire. *The Eclipse of the Intellectual*. New York: Funk and Wagnalls, 1968.

Index

NAME INDEX

Ackerman, Bruce, 209–11, 220, 246, 249, 250
Acton, John, 57
Adams, Charles Francis, 152, 239
Adams, John, 236
Adorno, Theodor W., 220, 221, 223, 225, 236, 250
Aesop, 69–70
Agger, Ben, 220, 250
Agrippa, von Nettesheim, 66
Akhmatova, Anna, 123, 125, 235
Aldrich, Nelson, 155
Althusser, Louis, 245
Altschull, J. Herbert, 230
Amalrik, Andrei, 235
Anaxagoras, 36, 192
Anderson, Digby, 247
Anderson, Sherwood, 129
Aquinas, Thomas, 55, 227
Arendt, Hannah, 31, 225, 226
Arentino, Pietro, 66
Aristotle, 34, 37, 51, 55, 192, 197
Arnson, Cynthia, 245
Arthur, C. J., 239
Asmus, V., 123
Astor, William, 153
Atwood, Margaret, 193
Augustine, 34
Augustus, 40–41
Averroes, Ibn Ruoshd, 192

Avicenna, Ibn Sina, 192
Avineri, Shlomo, 91, 232

Babel, Isaac, 115
Bacon, Francis, 54, 57, 61, 228
Bacon, Robert, 154
Bagdikian, Ben, 162, 170–71, 239, 242, 244
Bahro, Rudolf, 249
Bakhtin, Mikhail, 19, 223
Bakunin, Michael, 216
Ball, George, 176, 245
Baran, Paul, 238
Barmash, Isadore, 244
Barnet, Richard, 176, 244, 245
Barnum, P.T., 160, 176
Barre, Chevalier de la, 230
Barthes, Roland, 239
Baudelaire, Charles, 18, 114
Bayle, Pierre, 37, 61, 68–70, 185, 192
Beard, Charles, 236, 238
Beard, Mary, 238
Beaumarchais, Pierre, 80
Beckett, Samuel, 23
Beeks, Gertrude, 159, 176
Belik, A., 119
Belinsky, 109
Bell, Daniel, 168, 237, 244
Beman, Lamar T., 226
Bentham, Jeremy, 22, 57

Berger, Peter, 239, 246
Bergson, Henri, 57
Berkeley, George, 57
Berkeley, Governor, 142
Berlin, Isaiah, 235
Bernstein, Eduard, 107
Berthold of Mayence, 52
Berulle, Pierre, 54
Blackstone, William, 150
Blum, Alan F., 226, 243
Boccaccio, Giovanni, 46
Boccalini, 78
Boethius, Anicus, 55
Bond, Donovan, 240
Booth, Wayne, 248
Bowles, Samuel, 135, 236
Bradley, Jeff, 225
Braverman, Harry, 223, 245
Brown, Edward J., 234
Bruner, Jerome, 247
Bruni, Leonardo, 34
Buchma, 99
Buffon, Georges, 77
Buhler, Curt, 228
Bukharin, Nikolai, 109
Burawoy, Michael, 223
Burckhardt, Jacob, 228
Burke, Kenneth, 195, 236, 248
Burke, Redmond, 50, 58, 59, 226,
    227
Burnyeat, M.F., 247
Bury, J.B., 34–36, 38, 44, 225
Butler, Peirce, 228

Calvin, John, 21, 24, 66, 160
Carnap, R., 113
Carroll, Lewis, 2, 197
Carter, Jimmy, 246
Cater, Douglas, 233
Cassius, Gaius, 42
Cato the Elder, 15, 41, 47, 55
Chafee, Zechariah, 236
Chambers, Ephraim, 76
Chase, Canon, 242
Chaucer, 228
Cheever, John, 22, 224
Chernyshevsky, 109
Childe, Gordon V., 41, 226

Chrysostom, Saint John, 55
Cicero, 55
Clapham, Michael, 62, 228
Clifford, James, 247
Cochran, Thomas, 239
Cockburn, Alexander, 238
Cohen, Stanley, 240
Columbus, Christopher, 66
Commager, Henry Steele, 236
Comstock, Anthony, 159, 242
Comte, Auguste, 57
Condillac, Etienne, 85
Confucius, 5
Constantine, 48
Copernicus, 53, 68, 70
Cornell, A.B., 153
Couch, Sunny, 241, 243
Cremutius Cordus, 42–43
Cromwell, Oliver, 73
Curll, Edmund, 241
Currie, Elliott, 244

Daniel, Yuri M., 122–25
D'Alembert, Jean, 3, 73–77, 230
Darnton, Robert, 77, 230
Darwin, Charles, 57
Debs, Eugene, 154
Defoe, Daniel, 57
Degler, Carl, 240
DeGrazia, Edward, 242
Demac, Donna, 244
Depew, Chauncey, 153
Derrida, Jacques, 219, 248
Descartes, René, 57, 67
Des Perier, 80
Dewey, John, 160, 242
Dexter, L.A., 240
D'Holbach, Paul, 80
Diderot, Denis, 3, 15, 37, 57, 71–82, 85,
    87–88, 96, 146, 185, 194, 207, 215,
    229, 230
Dilthey, Wilhelm, 181, 186, 198, 219,
    246, 249
Diocletian, 43
Dodds, E.R., 33, 225
Dodge, William E., Jr., 242
Dolet, Etienne, 80
Dollenschall, Lawrenz, 88–89

Domhoff, William, 237
Domitian, 42–43
Donaghue, Hugh, 221
Dos Passos, John, 129
Douglas, Mary, 181, 184–87, 219, 220, 246, 247
Dreiser, Theodore, 134
Drucker, Peter, 176, 245
Dumas, Alexander, 57
Durant, Will, 228
Durkheim, Emile, 41, 57, 181, 186, 219, 223, 226, 246, 247

Eco, Umberto, 216
Edelman, Murray, 236
Edgeworth, 147
Edison, Thomas, 152
Edsall, Thomas Byrne, 237
Egger, Ingrid, 225
Ehrenberg, Ilya, 130, 236
Ehrenreich, Barbara, 244
Eichmann, Adolf, 31
Eisenstein, Elizabeth, 33–34, 225, 227, 228, 229
Eliot, T.S., 220
Elliott, Philip, 244, 245
Ellison, Ralph, 17
Elsevier, Louis, 67, 70
Emerson, Miles, 241, 243
Engels, Frederick, 97, 105–6, 109, 112, 118, 165, 231, 232, 233, 234, 239, 246, 247
Enzensberger, Hans Magnus, 27, 222, 223, 224, 235, 236, 250
Erasmus, Desiderius, 57, 66, 68–70, 229
Ermolaev, E., 234
Ernst, Morris L., 242
Eunomius, 48, 58
Euripides, 37
Ewen, Elizabeth, 245
Ewen, Stuart, 224, 238, 241, 245
Ewing, David, 20, 223

Fabri, Felix, 62, 228
Fackenheim, Emil, 30
Falk, Richard, 245
Farnsworth, Philo, 161
Farrell, James T., 129

Faulche, Samuel, 78
Feuer, Lewis, 233
Feyerabend, Paul, 187, 247
Fiedler, Leslie, 235
Field, Cyrus, 153
Flagler, Henry, 153
Flaubert, Gustave, 57
Foner, Philip S., 244
Foucault, Michel, 28, 116, 166, 182–86, 219, 220, 224, 225, 246, 247
Franco, Francisco, 31
Franklin, Benjamin, 3, 63, 71–75, 93, 131, 144–45, 150, 157, 160, 185, 229, 236, 238, 240, 241
Fraser, Andrew, 237, 239
Fray Lope de Barrientos, 56
Freiberg, J.W., 244, 245
Friedberg, Maurice, 234
Friedberg, Peter von, 62
Freud, Sigmund, 20, 57, 197, 224
Friere, Paulo, 211, 251
Fuentes, Annette, 244
Fust, Johann, 62, 71

Gadamer, Hans Georg, 27, 33, 58, 220, 224, 246, 247
Galasius, 50
Galbraith, John Kenneth, 237
Galerius, G.V., 43
Galileo, 28, 53, 57, 67–68, 70, 229
Gandhi, Mohandas K., 185, 206–7, 211, 221
Gans, Herbert, 222–23
Garfield, John, 154
Gelwick, Richard, 247
Gentilis, 147
George, Stefan, 35
Gerbner, George, 163–64, 224, 233, 240, 243, 251
Gerstenmaier, Cornelia, 235
Gerth, Hans H., 226, 237, 256
Gibbon, Edward, 42–46, 57, 225, 226
Gide, André, 57, 108, 234
Ginsberg, Aleksandr, 125
Gintis, Herbert, 135, 236
Gitlin, Todd, 251
Godzich, Wlad, 223
Goethe, Johann W. von, 62, 96, 177

Gogol, Nikolai, 109
Gold, Herbert, 129
Goldmann, Lucien, 130, 236, 246
Goldsen, Rose, 164, 243
Goldsmith, Oliver, 57, 70
Gomberg, William, 243
Gorbachev, Mikhail, 127, 236
Gordon, Douglas H., 229, 230
Gordon, George, 241
Gorky, Maxim, 104, 109–11, 115, 124, 234
Gould, Jay, 152
Gouldner, Alvin, 190, 214–15, 222, 223, 230, 244, 248, 251
Gramsci, Antonio, 96
Green, Mark, 245
Gregory IX, 51
Grendler, Paul F., 225, 229
Griffith, William, 235
Grimm, Jakob, 75, 78, 230
Gross, Larry, 243
Gross, Llewellyn Z., 220, 247, 249, 250
Grotius, Hugo, 45, 54, 192, 226
Gutenberg, Johannes, 50, 60, 63–64

Habermas, Jurgen, 206, 211, 220, 248, 249, 250
Hachten, William, 233
Hale, Sarah Josepha, 157, 240
Hall, A.R., 228
Hall, Stuart, 243
Hamelink, Cees, 176, 245, 251
Hammarskjold, Dag, 216, 251
Hanna, Mark, 154
Hanson, Norwood, 187, 246, 247
Haraway, Donna, 245, 251
Harding, Warren, 159
Hardy, Thomas, 27
Hay, John, 153
Hay, Yves de la, 232
Hayman, Ronald, 220
Hays, Will, 159, 242
Hayward, Max, 104, 233, 234
Hazlitt, William, 227
Hearst, William Randolph, 160, 176
Hegel, Georg W., 85, 89, 98
Heidegger, Martin, 27, 224
Heilbroner, Richard, 248

Heine, Heinrich, 57
Heller, Michael, 101, 104, 233, 235
Helmholtz, Hermann von, 113
Helvetius, Claude, 78, 85
Heresbach, 59, 227
Hermogenes, 42–43
Herzin, Aleksandr, 18, 124, 235
Hilger, Joseph, 53
Hippolytus, 48
Hitler, Adolf, 31
Hobbes, Thomas, 57, 67, 192
Hoggart, Richard, 245
Holmyard, E.J., 228
Hopkins, Charles E., 227
Horkheimer, Max, 161, 221, 225, 242, 250
Horowitz, Irving L., 225
Hughes, Helen MacGill, 240
Hugo, Victor, 57
Humboldt, Wilhelm von, 197, 249
Hume, David, 40, 57
Huntington, C.P., 153

Innocent I, 50
Innocent VII, 51
Irenaeus of Lyons, 48
Ivinskaya, Olga, 123

Jacobs, Norman, 222
Jaeger, Werner, 37, 226
James, Thomas, 45–46, 226
Jansen, Sue Curry, 220, 243
Jaspers, Karl, 248, 250
Jefferson, Thomas, 3, 37, 92, 143, 146–48, 150, 156, 178, 185, 207, 230, 237, 238, 239
Jefferson, Tony, 243
Jeremiah, 41
Jerome, Saint, 55
Jessup, Morris K., 242
Jesus Christ, 42, 47–48, 83
Jhally, Sut, 239
John XXII, 5
John of Salisbury, 56
Johnson, Lyndon B., 176
Julius III, 52

Kant, Immanuel, 57, 85, 188, 192
Katz, Michael, 240
Kazakova, Yuri, 123
Keller, Evelyn Fox, 227
Kellor, Frances Alice, 241
Kennedy, Emmet, 230, 231
Kennedy, John F., 176
Kepler, Joseph, 53, 68, 70
Kerensky, Aleksandr, 100
Khrushchev, Nikita, 99, 120–23, 128
Khrushchev, Nina, 235
Kieckhefer, Richard, 55, 227
King, Martin Luther, 205–6
Klare, Michael T., 245
Kline, Stephen, 239
Knorr-Cetina, Karin D., 246, 247
Kolko, Gabriel, 153, 237, 239
Konwicki, Tadeusz, 194, 248
Kors, Alan C., 54, 227
Kostelanetz, Richard, 238
Kramer, Heinrich, 54, 227
Kravis, Irving B., 245
Krohn, A. 246
Kroker, Arthur, 237, 242
Kroker, Marilouise, 237
Kuhn, Thomas S., 187, 224, 246
Kuper, Leo, 225

Labedz, Leopold, 233
Labienus, 41–42
Lakshin, Vladimir, 235
Langer, Susanne K., 6
Langer, William, 227
LaRouche, Lyndon, 222
Lasch, Christopher, 225
Latour, Bruno, 246
Lea, Henry, 51, 58, 66, 225, 226, 227, 229
Leavis, Q.D., 238
Lebedev, V.S., 120
Le Breton, 74, 78
LeGuin, Ursula, 193
Leiss, William, 239
Lenin, V.I., 95–96, 99–101, 103–14, 116, 118, 123, 233
Lessing, Gotthold, 35, 192
Levy, Leonard, 229, 236
Lewis, Flannery Felice, 241
Lin, Yu-t'ang, 226

Lincoln, Abraham, 154, 166, 243–44
Lipper, Mark, 240
Lipsey, Robert E., 245
Lipsius, Justus, 54
Locke, John, 57, 77, 192
Logan, James, 151
Longo, Pietro, 66, 71
Lord, Daniel, 242
Low, D.M., 226
Luckmann, Thomas, 239, 246
Lukacs, Georg, 96, 181, 195, 199, 219, 220, 222, 224, 239, 246, 248, 249
Lunacharsky, 103, 105, 233
Luther, Martin, 53, 56, 60, 66, 227
Lynd, Staughton, 236
Lysenko, T.D., 118

Macaulay, Thomas, 75
Machiavelli, Niccolo, 7, 66
MacInnes, Mairi, 229
Madison, James, 3, 146, 155, 236
Maimonides, Moses, 192
Malenkov, Georgi, 117, 234
Malesherbes, Chrétien, 78–81
Mallarmé, Stéphane, 114
Mandelstam, Osip, 115, 122–23, 232
Mander, Mary S., 236
Mannheim, Karl, 181, 186, 219, 220, 246, 247, 250
Mao Tse-tung, 30, 127
Marcos, Ferdinand, 245
Marcus, George E., 247
Marcuse, Herbert, 193, 221, 232, 243, 248, 250
Marmontel, Jean François, 147
Marr, N.Y., 118
Marvin, Carolyn, 236
Marx, Karl, 10, 17, 57, 71, 83–101, 105–6, 110, 113, 118, 136, 165–66, 181, 185–86, 206–7, 215, 219, 220, 223, 230, 231, 232, 233, 234, 239, 246, 247
Massie, Robert, 245
Matich, Olga, 235
Mattelart, André, 251
Mayakovsky, Vladimir, 109, 114–15, 120, 235
McBurney, Robert, 242
McCabe, Joseph, 47, 50, 226

McCormick, John, 229
McKinley, William, 154
McLellan, David, 87, 231
McLeod, W. Reynolds, 240
McLuhan, Marshall, 228
Mead, George Herbert, 219
Medawar, P.B., 187, 247
Medvedev, Roy, 99, 233
Meiklejohn, Alexander, 236
Melanchthon, Philip, 53
Melville, Herman, 19
Merrill, John C., 233
Miliband, Ralph, 165, 225, 243
Miller, Arthur, 129
Miller, Jonathan, 220
Miller, William, 239
Millerand, Alexandre, 107
Mills, C. Wright, 223, 226, 236, 237, 250
Milton, John, 57, 67, 71–73, 76, 93, 131, 146, 185, 229
Mirabeau, André, 91
Montaigne, Michel, 57, 69–70, 80
Montesquieu, Charles, 57, 69–70, 192
More, Thomas, 67
Morgan, J.P., 152–53, 154, 160, 165, 176, 239, 242
Morgan, Robin, 227
Morley, John, 78–79, 229, 230
Morrison, Ken, 247
Morris-Suzuki, Tessa, 168, 244
Mosco, Vincent, 240, 251
Moses, 47
Muller, Ronald, 176, 237, 244, 245
Mumford, Lewis, 228

Napoleon, 26, 95, 230
Nekrasov, Victor, 121
Nero, 42–43
Newman, Roger K., 242
Newton, Isaac, 53, 57, 69, 77, 229
Nicholas I, Czar, 89
Nietzsche, Friedrich, 180–81, 186, 219, 220, 246, 249
Nikitenko, Aleksandr, 101, 221, 233
Noble, David, 239

Oboler, Eli, 20, 224, 226
O'Neill, Eugene, 129

O'Neill, John, 247
Ong, William J., 249
Origen, 48
Orwell, George, 116
Ould, Harold, 229

Padover, Saul, 231, 237
Pagels, Elaine, 226
Paine, Tom, 131, 144
Palmer, A. Mitchell, 166
Panckoucke, C., 74–75
Park, Robert, 240, 241
Parker, James, 238
Pascal, 54, 57, 67, 80
Pasternak, Boris, 28, 122–24, 235
Pattison, Mark, 68, 229
Paul, Saint, 47
Pepper, Stephen, 187, 246, 247
Pericles, 36
Perkins, George W., 154
Perrow, Charles, 223
Peters, Edward, 54, 227
Philadelpho, Juan of Venice, 69
Phillips, Wendell, 11
Piepe, Anthony, 241, 243
Piercy, Margaret, 193
Pilnyak, Boris, 114–15, 234
Pinkerton, Allan, 160
Plato, 34, 36–37, 49, 131, 185, 192, 226
Plekhanov, G.V., 104, 109, 233
Plutarch, 41, 226
Pocock, J.G.A., 224
Polanyi, Michael, 187–88, 190, 224, 246, 247, 250
Pollner, Melvin, 248
Pontius Pilate, 42
Porphyry, 48, 58
Poster, Mark, 220
Pottinger, David, 80, 230
Pound, Roscoe, 236
Protagoras, 36, 192, 226
Pushkin, Aleksandr, 109
Putnam, George, 47, 48, 50, 65–66, 226, 227, 228, 229
Pyne, P.R., 153

Quigley, Martin, 242

Raboy, Marc, 214–15, 244, 245, 251
Radek, Karl, 109, 234
Ramsay, David, 144, 238
Ranke, Leopold von, 57
Raynal, F., 80
Reagan, Ronald, 223
Remmling, Gunter, 246
Rhode, Eric, 224
Richter, Sviatoslav, 123
Rickman, H.P., 246
Ricoeur, Paul, 198, 224, 249
Robbins, Rossell Hope, 55, 227, 251
Roberts, Kevin, 245
Robespierre, Maximilien, 131
Rockefeller, John D., 152–53, 176, 239
Rodway, Allan, 196, 248
Roosevelt, Franklin D., 200, 239
Roosevelt, Theodore, 154, 240
Root, Elihu, 155
Roquain, 80, 230
Rorty, Richard, 246
Rosenberg, Bernard, 222
Rossiter, Clinton, 141, 236, 238
Rostopchina, Countess, 199
Rousseau, Jean Jacques, 57, 77, 80, 85, 192
Rubin, Bernard, 240
Ruge, Arnold, 89, 231
Rumjancev, A.A., 123, 235
Rush, Myron, 235
Russ, Joanna, 193, 248
Ryan, Jake, 224

Sackrey, Charles, 224
Sage, Russell, 152–53
Sakharov, Andrei, 125, 127
Sand, George, 57
Santillana, Giorgio, 229
Sartine, 78
Sartre, Jean-Paul, 57
Saumaise, 68
Sawyer, Charles, 248
Scalinger, Joseph, 54, 67–68
Scheler, Max, 186, 219
Schiller, Anita, 244
Schiller, Herbert I., 170, 224, 244, 251
Schlegel, Friedrich, 195, 248
Schlesinger, Arthur, 236, 238

Schopenhauer, Artur, 186
Schreiber, Elliot, 235
Schudson, Michael, 161, 240, 242
Schutz, Alfred, 181, 246
Schwab, Charles, 153
Seagle, William, 242
Seneca, 55
Sennett, Richard, 22, 216, 224, 249, 251
Sextus V, 52
Shakespeare, William, 228
Shaw, George B., 3
Shcherbina, Vladimir, 113, 233, 234
Shelepin, Aleksandr, 122
Shostak, Arthur, 243
Simmel, Georg, 243
Singer, Charles, 228
Sinyavsky, Andrei (Adam Tertz), 101, 119, 122, 124, 125, 128, 194, 233, 234, 235, 236, 248, 249
Skolnick, Jerome H., 244
Slack, Jennifer Daryl, 240
Smith, Adam, 71, 100, 238
Smythe, Dallas, 138, 164, 222, 236, 237, 238, 239, 242, 243, 244, 251
Socrates, 11, 34, 36–40, 55, 70, 74, 185, 192, 202, 210, 226, 229
Solzhenitsyn, Aleksandr, 18, 102, 119–23, 233, 235
Spencer, Herbert, 57
Spinoza, Baruch, 57, 185, 192
Sprenger, Jacob, 54, 227
Stalin, Joseph, 95, 99–100, 104–5, 110, 112, 115, 117–19, 139, 166, 200, 233, 234, 235
Starr, Paul, 223
Steinbeck, John, 129
Steiner, George, 26, 197, 221, 224, 225, 249
Stendhal, 57
Stepniak (pseud.), 101, 233
Sterne, Thomas, 57
Stetsky, A.I., 234
Stillman, James, 155
Strauss, Leo, 35, 221, 225, 226, 248
Struve, Gleb, 234
Swayze, Harold, 233, 234, 235
Sweezy, Paul, 238

Swift, Jonathan, 69
Sylvius, Aeneas, 50–51, 226

Tacitus, 40, 42–43, 226
Taine, Hippolyte, 57
Taney, Roger, 149
Taylor, Frederick, 176
Terence, 55
Tertz, Adam, *see* Sinyavsky, Andrei
Thatcher, Margaret, 170
Thecla, 48
Thompson, E.P., 21, 224
Tiberius, 41–42
Timofeyev, 234
Tocqueville, Alexis de, 146, 167
Todorow, Tzvetan, 233
Toffler, Alvin, 237
Torry, Norman L., 229, 230
Toulmin, Stephen, 187, 230, 246, 247, 250
Tracy, Destutt de, 86–87, 96, 230
Trevor-Roper, H.R., 54, 227
Trithemius, Johannes, 62
Trotsky, Leon, 105
Truman, Harry S., 166
Tunstall, Jeremy, 245
Turkle, Sherry, 249
Tvardovsky, Aleksandr, 124, 235

Utis, O., 235
Urban VIII, Pope, 68

Veblen, Thorstein, 20, 224, 237, 239
Verjinto, 43
Vollmar, 107
Voltaire, François, 3, 57, 66, 69–71, 77, 80, 85, 88, 146, 185, 229, 230

Warhol, Andy, 16
Wartella, Ellen, 244

Washington, George, 150
Wasko, Janet, 240, 244, 251
Weaver, Richard, 84, 230
Weber, Max, 44, 219, 226, 237, 250
Webster, Frank, 245, 251
Wesley, John, 56
Whale, R.F., 230
White, David M., 222, 240
Whitehead, Alfred North, 238
Whitley, R., 246
Whitman, Walt, 155
Whitney, D. Charles, 244
Wiesel, Elie, 225
Wiethaus, Censor, 89
Williams, Frederick, 245
Williams, Raymond, 219, 220, 238, 245
Williams, Trevor, 238
Windahl, Sven, 244
Wittgenstein, Ludwig, 186
Wolfe, Alan, 237
Wolff, Kurt H., 220–21, 243, 247
Woolgar, Steve, 246, 247
Wright, Richard, 17
Wycliffe, John, 60

Xenophon, 192

Yates, Frances, 229
Yevtushenko, Yevgen, 123
Yorke, Philip, 241
Young, Jock, 240

Zamyatin, Yevgeni, 114–16, 234
Zenger, Peter, 142
Zhdanov, André, 109, 117, 139
Zinn, Howard, 236, 238, 240
Zolla, Elemire, 222
Zwingli, Huldreich, 53

SUBJECT INDEX

Age of Reason, 4, 56, 131, 146, 177
Areopagites, 71–73, 76, 143, 146

Blackmarkets, 60, 65–71, 128
Book burning, 20, 36, 40, 47–48, 51, 53,

59, 79–80; Ephesian motives, 47–48

Censorship, definitions of, 14–17, 20–25, 221–22

Calvinism, 21–22, 24, 53, 145
Capitalism: American, 31–32, 129, 131–78; corporate-state, 15–17; fascism and, 31; freedom and, 63–64; information-capitalism, 167–72, 212–16; institutions, 178; manifest destiny of, 151–53; political, 153–54, 161–67, 177–78, 237, 239; realism, 161; world system of, 171–78
Census and censorship, 14–15, 41
Constitutive censorship, 6–8, 24–25, 35, 41, 50, 181–82, 216–17, 220, 222; cosmological bargains, 184–85, 203, 205
Copyrights, as extensions of censorship, 75–76, 167
Cosmopolitanism, 70–71
Consciousness industry, 76, 134, 137–38, 140, 155–72, 223, 236, 245; television and, 162–65, 242
Critical discourse, 207–8, 216, 220–21; exposing Panoptics, 24–25; Liberal critical traditions, 18–19, 24, 136–38, 189, 220–21; reflexive power-talk, 6, 8–10, 208–17, 220, 249–50

Domitian strategy, 42, 51, 65, 128
Double-meaning, theory of, 196–201, 248

Elites, 9, 28, 59, 61, 71–73, 91–92, 134, 165, 243; *see also* Intellectuals; Pluralism
Encyclopedists, 73–83, 194; Encyclopédie Wars, 76–83; French censorship of, 79–91; uses of aesopean language, 78, 81–82
England, 26, 71–73, 81, 93
Enlightenment, 3–12, 14–18, 19, 22–24, 73–83, 202–3; American, 141–48; French, 76–88; Enlightened discourse, 4, 24, 178; failure of, 135–36; freedom and, 15, 18, 69, 136–37, 222; Marx and, 85–87, 96; new democratic, 212–17; property rights, 86–87
Ephesian motives, 47–48
Epistemology, 26–29, 181–91; Bacon and diabolicalism, 55, 227; cosmological mess-making, 84, 184, 187–88,

194–95; consistency, 181, 206, 210; constructivism, 182, 187–88, 247; epistemological criminals, 28; gaps, silences, and omissions, 29, 132–35, 140; philosophy of science and, 182, 187–88, 247, 250; rationality and, 181, 184–87, 209–10, 250; of this study, 24–29; theory of double-meaning and, 196–201, 248; validation, 27–28; verification, 27–28
Esoteric texts, 35, 204
Exoteric texts, 35, 59

Feudalism, 19
France, 48, 68, 73–83, 85, 90–91, 95, 102–3
Free-market-of-ideas, 80, 134, 137–40, 160, 167–72

Gaps, *see* Epistemology; Socially structured silences
Genocide, 30, 225; Holocaust, 31, 221, 225
Germany, 29–32, 66–67, 85–93, 129, 243
Greece, 29, 32–40; concepts of freedom, 35, 59; Greeklore and Christian cosmology, 53, 59, 70–71; humanism, 34–40; philosophy and censorship, 36; suppression of women, 36

History, 26–29, 33, 202–3; history as critique, 33–34, 37, 83; history as text, 26–29, 33–34

Ideology, 29, 183, 194, 237; the Good Lie (Plato), 4, 10, 37, 59, 185, 190–91
Information-capitalism, 167–72
Inquisition, 50–59; Spanish, 67, 79
Intellectuals, 71–73; high-culture, 18, 222–23; intellectual censorship, 88; intellectual vanguards, 9, 59, 61, 73, 100–102, 186, 204, 206, 212–17, 238; knowledge workers, 214, 244–45; as outlaws, 67–71, 131, 194–95, 215–16; rule of experts, 9, 204, 206, 210
Irony, 45, 67–71, 87, 192–201; equivocation, 193, 197–201, 248; *see also* Language, aesopean

Japan, 173, 176

Knowledge, *see* Power-knowledge; Sociology of knowledge

Liberalism, 3–12, 14–18, 19, 22–24, 38–40, 167, 185, 222, 236; critical traditions of, 18–20, 24, 136–37, 220–21; Marx and, 85–87; political theory, 181; progress and, 18, 189, 237; public/private schism, 38–40, 147–48, 178, 190–91
Literary underground: before Reformation, 60–71; in France, 73–82; in USSR, 119–27, 229; the republic of letters, 69–71
Language, 3–4, 225; aesopean, 69–70, 81–82, 192–201, 220, 231, 248; democratic discourse, 5–6; Leninist linguistics, 108, 112–14; Marx critique of idealistic concepts of, 87, 112, 247; Stalin's correction of Leninist linguistics, 118–19; of theory, 192–93, 197–99, 220; the power to name, 5–7, 237

Market censorship, 10–11, 16–17, 19, 76, 93, 138–39, 164, 237–38; commodification of thought, 93, 97, 134, 167–72, 239; and the Domitian strategy, 42; and organization of markets, 148–49, 161, 237; and press freedom, 86–87, 145–48; self-censorship by publishers, 80; and Third World, 174
Markets, 148–49; *see also* Black markets; Market censorship
Marxian theory: advocacy of censorship, 97, 233; concept of freedom, 75, 92, 231; constitutive censorship of, 94–98, 233; contradictions in, 85, 87, 97–98, 233; critique of *philosophes*, 85–87; opposition to censorship, 91–95, 97; rhetoric of, 84–85, 87–88, 95–96, 231; role of press, 92, 94–95, 106–8, 188–89; Young Hegelians, 88–90
Mass culture, 18–20, 160–67, 223
Mass production, 19; production of culture, 19–20, 168–72
Media-critical theory, 215–16
Minority views, 17, 157–58, 240–41, 243, 247; exiles, 17; red-baiting, 17, 166, 172

Nazism, 29–32; cartoon history of, 30–31; hangman's justice and, 29; power-knowledge of, 31

Objectivity, 10, 24, 182, 184, 187–90
Omissions, 29–32; *see also* Epistemology
Orality, 49–50; secondary, 204, 249

Panoptics, 22, 78, 80, 82, 161, 203–5, 207–8, 216; authorless theatre, 172; electronic panopticon, 22–23, 162–65, 242; censors without stamps, 15–17, 24–25, 80
Persecution, 11, 28, 35–36, 217, 230; of Christians, 42–45; by Christians, 42, 45–59; of Protestants, 45; of witches, 53–57
Pluralism, 15, 155; plurality of elites, 165, 167, 243
Poland, 127–28
Political capitalism, 153–54, 161–67, 177–78, 237, 239
Pornography, 46, 57, 241–42
Positivism, 35
Power-knowledge, 6–7, 10, 19, 31, 34, 181–91, 219–20, 250–51; emancipatory, 190, 199, 204–17, 249–51; knowledge and human interests, 6, 182–85, 188; knowledge and prejudice, 27, 58, 224; and relativism, 27
Print, 50, 62–65, 228, 249; and social change, 33–34, 49–55, 62–71, 76–77, 144, 228; and standardization of language and logic, 63–64; vested interests of printers, 34, 70, 75–76, 144–45
Prior censorship, 16, 20, 56, 80, 128; *see also* Constitutive censorship
Propaganda, 34
Protestantism, 44–46, 50–73, 227; and clandestine book trade, 45–46, 65–66

Reflexivity, 5, 27, 29, 181–82, 184, 210–12, 232; reflexive power-talk, 6, 8–10, 208–17, 220, 249–50
Reformation, 44–46, 50–73